BREAKING OUT OF
BEGINNER'S SPANISH

BREAKING OUT OF BEGINNER'S SPANISH

JOSEPH J. KEENAN

UNIVERSITY OF TEXAS PRESS
AUSTIN

Requests for permission to reproduce material from this work should be sent to Permissions, University of Texas Press, Box 7819, Austin, TX 78713-7819.

∞The paper used in this publication meets the minimum requirements of American National Standard for Information Sciences—Permanence of Paper for Printed Library Materials, ANSI Z39.48-1984.

LIBRARY OF CONGRESS CATALOGING-IN-PUBLICATION DATA

Keenan, Joseph J. (Joseph John), date
    Breaking out of beginner's Spanish / by Joseph J. Keenan. — 1st ed.
    p.   cm.
    ISBN 0-292-74321-1 (alk. paper). — ISBN 0-292-74322-X (alk. paper)
    1. Spanish language—Conversation and phrase books—English. I. Title.
PC4121.K38   1994
468.2'421—dc20   94-4316

Todo se lo debo a mi manager,
Flavia,
y con todo mi amor

CONTENTS

FOREWORD AND
FOREWARNING

This book is not a phrasebook and not a textbook, though it can be used with either. It is more like a guidebook—not to the Spanish-speaking countries but to the Spanish spoken in those places. It shows you the dark alleyways, the bright meeting-places, the bohemian nooks, and the pulsing thoroughfares of the language. And it shows you more than a few shortcuts, guiding you toward the Spanish you want to learn. Like a guidebook, this book's goal is to help you get around, whether you're in the boardroom or the barrio.

It is a helpful book, like a boy scout helping an elderly person across the street, and it is an irreverent book, like an impish schoolchild making faces at the teacher. It is a serious book and it is a funny book. It will tell you how to be polite to a grandmother and how to shock a gangster. It preaches Spanish with a smile, a strut, and maybe just a bit of an attitude. This book wants you to speak better Spanish, and it will stop at nothing, or almost nothing, to accomplish it.

Of course, no book can teach you how to speak Spanish. Only by *practicando*—and especially *platicando*—can you learn that. So why read it? Because, as you will soon see, this book makes learning Spanish more fun. And if learning Spanish isn't going to be fun, why bother?

ACKNOWLEDGMENTS

The idea for this book was born several years ago in the hectic world of weekly journalism in Mexico City. In those busy days, Walter Gaddis and Alan Robinson were central to polishing the idea and molding the style and teaching technique that eventually came to be used in this book. My thanks to them and to my other colleagues at the late, lamented *Mexico Journal*, among them Cindy Anders, Leon Lazaroff, Talli Nauman, John Ross, Jim Weddell, and Mike Zellner. *Gracias* also to Pete Hamill for his encouragement throughout and to Rodin Mendoza for his superb taste in music.

Many people revised parts or all of this text or made invaluable suggestions, additions, and corrections. Special thanks go to Ted Bardacke; Bob Ciaffa; C. Bruce Fitch of Brenau University and Academy in Gainesville, Georgia; William F. Harrison of Northern Illinois University; Carol A. Klee at the University of Minnesota; Dr. Marcia Rosenbusch of Iowa State University; and Nancy Rhodes of the Center for Applied Linguistics in Washington, D.C.

Mil gracias go to my sister, Fran Keenan, whose long chats on the subject and contacts at the National Clearinghouse on Literacy Education in Washington, D.C., were extremely useful; and to Dr. Uzi Selzer, a *todólogo* whose title could clearly have been earned in the field of his choosing.

Naturally, the good folks at the University of Texas Press were indispensable to making this book a reality. Their faith in the project and hard work in the editing process were crucial to keeping reader comprehension high and my errors to a minimum. Some of my errors no doubt slipped by, and for the record I should state that they are in fact mine. *Ni modo.*

Finally, the one person whose contribution to the book must be measured in gigatons instead of kilos is my wife, Flavia. It's a cliche to say that without her this book would have been impossible, but I'm going to say it anyhow: without her, this book would have been impossible. A better combination of knowledge and patience is hard even to imagine. A zillion thanks also to little Flavia—the inimitable "Nena"—who serves as a constant and humbling reminder that learning a language is child's play.

BREAKING OUT OF
BEGINNER'S SPANISH

Con mi caballo hablo en alemán, con las damas de la Corte italiano, para los asuntos de hombres en francés, pero para hablar con Dios el español. —attributed to Charles V (1500–1558)

The United States now has the fourth-largest number of Spanish native speakers in the world, with 17.3 million speakers. — *CAL/NCLE Notes* *(a publication of the National Clearinghouse on Literacy Education)*

'English Only' Is History —headline, *Miami Herald*, May 19, 1993

INTRODUCTION

You're on a bus, heading south. You've crossed the U.S. border and entered Latin America. English is behind you; a continent of Spanish lies ahead. Your pocket-size Spanish-English dictionary sits on your lap within easy reach. For practice, you look up the Spanish words for everything you see or think of: "bush," "barbed wire," "roadrunner," "driver." You made yourself understood at the ticket counter and double-checked the bus's destination with a matronly passenger, but you had some trouble telling the driver you wanted to keep your bag with you instead of sticking it in the vehicle's luggage compartment. You've held a brief conversation with the young man next to you, who asked your name, your travel plans, and (you think) your favorite major-league team. You sit back and close your eyes. Already you're a little tired. How many weeks or months of speaking like a small, semi-literate child can I stand? you wonder.

You are at the beginning of more than a bus journey. You are on your way to speaking and understanding a foreign language, a foreign culture, and a foreign people. For most of the world's inhabitants, bilingualism and even trilingualism is nothing out of the ordinary. But for most native English speakers, one language is the norm. Breaking out of that mold will take work. But, as you are about to discover, it is satisfying work, and its fruits—with a little practice—will last you a lifetime.

People's reasons for learning Spanish are as varied as the approaches they take to it. You may be studying it for use in business, school, travel, or the family. Unfortunately, there's no magic formula or secret recipe to speed your way toward fluency. But there are a few pointers that can help. Some fall under the heading of common sense; others are more like folk wisdom. Keep them in mind as your voyage progresses.

INHIBITIONS

The greatest enemy of learning a language, especially as an adult, is a person's inhibitions. These vary with the individual, of course. Some people seem to have been born without any, while others are so afraid of making a mistake that they never give themselves the chance to. Methods of overcoming these inhibitions also vary with the individual. Most people lose their fear of sounding silly after a few weeks of speaking a foreign language; others lose all inhibitions entirely after a few *cervezas* under the stars on the town plaza. One rule applies universally: to learn a language you'll have to conquer your inhibitions eventually, so the sooner you get started, the better.

One way to get started is to remember that however silly you might sound using your incorrect Spanish, you'll sound a lot worse trying to speak English to someone who speaks none. Then again, you could simply choose to clam up altogether. After all, as they say, better to keep quiet and be thought a fool than to open your mouth and remove all doubt (or, as it might be expressed in Spanish, *en boca cerrada no entran moscas*—"flies don't enter a closed mouth"). If this is your strategy, you'll neither improve your Spanish nor become acquainted with the new world—the Spanish-speaking one—that for whatever reason you are making an effort to get to know. In fact, you're probably better off staying home.

So relax. You'll definitely make mistakes. But you won't be the first one to make them.

HOW WE LEARN

Learning psychologists have covered this theme close to the point of exhaustion (or beyond it, perhaps), but a few observations might prove useful. One maxim says that you can chart your language-learning progress by three landmarks: speaking and understanding the basics, then learning the language well enough to use it and understand it on the phone, and finally being able to understand the jokes. Another common belief holds that language learning tends to be a quantum experience. That is, you will progress by small leaps and bounds, followed by long, frustrating plateaus. The plateaus, furthermore, always seem to hit when you think you should be progressing the most—after an intensive course, for example. At times it will seem that your brain is too busy absorbing new information to be bothered with relaying it to your mouth. Fear not! The information is oozing in and assuring itself a place, and one day it will suddenly be available and act as if it had been there all along. So stick with it. The day will come.

LEARNING TRICKS

Are there shortcuts for getting around the long months, even years, that are needed to reach a level of virtual fluency? In a word, no. But there are some specific teaching tools that can help. One surefire (and entertaining) way to boost comprehension and get a better "feel" for Spanish is by listening intently to songs in Spanish and writing out the lyrics as well as you can. The catchier the song, the better. A friend once learned an important usage of the subjunctive after prolonged, late-night exposure to Rubén Blades's song "Pedro Navaja," about a street tough who keeps *las manos siempre en los bolsillos de su gabán, pa' que no sepan en cuál de ellos lleva el puñal* ("his hands at all times in the pockets of his coat, so they don't know in which of them he's carrying the knife"). Try singing along with radio songs and jotting down the refrains. Learn to equate dance halls with lecture halls. Even if you don't learn much more Spanish, you'll have a lot more fun!

Another shortcut, applicable of course only in certain cases, is to turn your mind to a foreign-language romance. Just as a song can stick in your head for hours at a time, so can Mr. or Ms. Right. Arrange a date with a Spanish-speaking object-of-your-affections, and you'll be amazed how your brain works overtime, for hours and days ahead, thinking up cute and clever things to say at the appointed hour. It's really just an advanced mnemonic device, but a far more pleasant one than, say, word association.

In general—and you'll hear this repeatedly from your teachers and coaches, formal or otherwise—try to speak to as many people in Spanish as possible. While that sounds easy, the sad fact is that it's often awkward to speak to your fellow citizens in a foreign language, and from there it's a short jump to seeking out your *paisanos* wherever you happen to be and speaking with them in English almost exclusively.

The intellectual energy that goes into starting a conversation in a foreign language can be quite daunting, especially in the early stages. Still, it's worth the effort. Concentrate at first on short "conversations" (or extended greetings) and gradually lengthen them as you find people whom you feel comfortable speaking with (and are able to get away from when your vocabulary expires). When the temptation to chat with a fellow English speaker becomes too great, give in to it—but try to steer the conversation toward anecdotes about the language you are both probably trying to learn.

A useful "trick" to improve your pronunciation, which is handled in more detail in the next chapter, is to practice tongue-twisting words and phrases when you're off by yourself—in the shower, walking down the street, waiting for a bus, or on walks in the woods. Words like *problema* and *refrigerador* may require lengthy repetition before they agree to come out sounding more or less like they're supposed to. If in the process some people overhear you and look at you funny, don't worry. In most of the Spanish-speaking world, gringos are presumed to be a little daft almost by definition.

Finally, don't hesitate to ask others to speak slowly. No one expects you to understand rapid-fire Spanish in your first few months of learning it, yet many people speak that way out of habit and need to be reminded that you're comprehending at about one-fifth the rate they're speaking. A simple *Más despacio, por favor* (or *¿Puede hablar un poco más despacio, por favor?*) will do wonders for your ability to understand and respond.

SLANG AND CURSING

Most language books tell you not to use either slang or "four-letter words" in Spanish. The reasoning is somewhat foolish: by using them in a way that will no doubt be incorrect at first, you are likely to make a fool of yourself. This is true, of course, but if you were worried about that, you would never have left the cozy confines of your native tongue in the first place. Certainly it should be no deterrent to trying your hand at this most lively and emotive aspect of Spanish.

In any case, most students ignore the advice and try to incorporate some slang phrases and even obscenities into their Spanish. They do so for many of the same reasons they do so in English: (a) a little invective can come in handy at times, if only to let off steam as you travel through fascinating but sometimes frustrating new cultures; (b) all your friends—in this case, your new Spanish-speaking acquaintances—are doing it; (c) talking tough can be fun; (d) talking like a schoolmarm all the time can relay an inaccurate image of one's personality; and (e) it can also get insufferably boring.

What the language books should tell you is to slip in a little slang, try out the occasional dirty word (if that's your inclination), and make a go of it. In this book, at the risk perhaps of offending some readers, I've tried to address the issues of using slang and cursing, pointing out what to watch for and when not to use certain expressions (usually far more relevant than when to use them). As with the language itself, there are definite traps to be avoided. The only difference is that in the world of *groserías*, the penalty for falling into a trap can be considerably more painful, up to and including lengthy hospital stays. That would seem to be reason enough to include a little advice on the subject.

REGIONAL DIFFERENCES

Wherever you go in the Spanish-speaking world, you will run into speech idiosyncrasies that show up in dialect, word choice, slang, and intonation. A Mexican in Chicago won't necessarily speak the same as one in Guadalajara or Veracruz, and none of them will speak the same as a Guatemalan or a Spaniard or an Argentine. No book can cover all of these variations, and every book contains a built-in bias toward one form or another. This book's bias is toward the Spanish of the Americas, although an effort has been made to call attention to expressions that are regional or that vary significantly from one place to the next. Added emphasis is assigned Mexican Spanish, since that is the Spanish most North Americans will hear—be it on vacation or in their own countries. Aside from a handful of words that are common in one place and considered risqué in another, most regional differences are more a matter of style than substance. In general, you'll be understood regardless. And as an obvious foreigner wherever you go, you'll almost always be humored—or forgiven, in the case of risqué words—for your word choice.

HOW I CAME TO KNOW THE TERRITORY

I chose the anecdote that begins this section for a very simple reason: it was my introduction, give or take a few details, to the Spanish-speaking world. When I said you were going to wonder how many weeks or months of speaking like a small, semiliterate child you could stand, I did so because that is exactly what I wondered on my first brusque introduction to the Spanish-speaking world.

Which leads to a confession of sorts. I was not born speaking Spanish, nor did I learn it in those absorptive first years of childhood. I learned it in a way that is at once the hard way and the easy way: talking to people, struggling to listen to their answers, and grasping constantly for understanding. It took me ten years to reach a level that I am still reluctant to call "fluency"—though friends, family, and col-leagues who speak little or no Spanish are easily wowed by my prow-ess. Even kind-hearted native-speakers will tell me I have "no accent" or ask what Spanish-speaking country my "slight" accent hails from. But deep down I know better. I still make little mistakes—even fre-quently when tired or in a hurry—and my accent still seems to have good and bad days. I'm fluent enough for most purposes, but I know there's a next level, and I'm striving to get there.

This book is unusual because it was not written by a native speaker, much less a world-class expert on Spanish. Books that are written by these people are useful—indeed indispensable—because they shed light on the nuances of Spanish that foreigners only rarely manage to grasp. In fact, I used many of these books in preparing this one.

Instead, this book was written by someone whose Spanish was once halting and clumsy and, before that, simply nonexistent. I like to think that's what makes this book special and useful. I know about the frustrations of getting started in Spanish because I've been there. Many of the mistakes I warn against in this book are ones I'm familiar with because I made them. Many of the "trickster" words, discussed in Chapter 3, tricked me. The advice I give on how to learn a language, how to avoid pitfalls, and how to pronounce certain tongue twisters is something that worked for me. It may not work for everyone, but then again it may work for you. All I know is that if I wanted a guide through a minefield, I'd be inclined to choose someone who has made the trip before and not necessarily the person who drew the map. If this someone can also make the trip more fun and less frightening, then time's a-wasting! ¡Vámonos!

TEN WAYS TO AVOID BEING TAKEN FOR A GRINGO

1

A gringo, in much of the Spanish-speaking world, is a person who comes from abroad, speaks another language, and wears loud shorts. In certain countries, such as Mexico, it refers specifically to U.S. citizens, but even there the distinction is hazy. A Canadian or German who acts like a gringo will be referred to as a gringo, birth certificates be damned. Act like a gringo and you will be called one; don't act like one and you may be called one anyway. The word is descriptive first—of a style, a cultural stance, a way of life—and derogatory only later, if at all.

So how to avoid being taken for a gringo? The truth is, if you were born outside the Spanish-speaking world, there is probably nothing you can do to hide the fact. You will never fully blend in nor should you necessarily want to. But as you travel or mingle among Spanish-speakers, you may wish to smooth over the most obvious differences that set you apart. We all want to be outstanding; standing out is another matter altogether.

Since you're making an effort to speak and understand Spanish, you've already distinguished yourself from the stereotypical gringo, that mythical beast of Latin American lore who wears obtrusive shirts, smacks gum, and tends to misplace his or her wallet. But even if you're not one of *them*, you can still heed a few simple precautions that will help put you in tune with the local culture, be it in Patagonia or East Los Angeles. Dress codes and behavior are beyond the scope of this book, but some general pointers may keep others from pointing at you.

PRONUNCIATION

Spanish pronunciation should be the easiest thing in the world to master. Unlike English, where a letter can change its sound seemingly at will, Spanish letters have—with very few exceptions—the exact same sound word after word. To compare, think of the three different sounds of the letter *a* in the English pronunciation of the name Abraham; in Spanish the letter *a* in Abrahám has but a single sound, repeated three times. Still, you'll need to practice to convince your tongue to make the correct sound, to get your teeth to close or open on cue, and to master the inflections. At first it will be a struggle, but there is no reason why anyone can't learn to pronounce Spanish properly after enough use. Here are some tips on how to proceed:

1. Spanish teachers always tell their students to practice repeating the vowel sounds: *a, e, i, o, u.* Listen to these wise men and women and practice, practice, practice. If it's more fun, follow your litany with the phrase schoolchildren learn south of the border: *El burro sabe más que tú* ("The burro knows more than you"). Move your mouth as you repeat the vowels. Pretend someone fifty yards away is trying to read your lips. Clip the vowel sounds short, as you might imagine a Japanese colonel in a late-night, World War II movie would do. *A, E, I, O, U, A, E, I, O, U . . . .*

2. Next come the sounds for the letters *r* and *rr.* The double one trills, and so does the single one at the start of a word. Thus *carro* and *rancho* have essentially the same *r* sound. Your tongue won't want to trill at first; it will make a scene about being made out of concrete and will refuse to emit such a ridiculous sound. But you're not going to let your tongue push you around, are you? Trill away! Pretend you're Charo on "The Tonight Show": "R-r-r-really, Johnny, r-r-r-romance for me is r-r-r-relaxing on a r-r-r-rug, listening to r-r-r-rock and r-r-r-roll." If you've studied any French, this sound may be harder for you to get used to at first. But if you try at all, you will learn it. Many gringos do and, as far as anyone can tell, we're all born with the same kind of tongue.

3. The *d* between vowels or at the end of a word sounds more like the *th* in *thus* than an English *d. Nada* is thus pronounced "na-tha," or close to it. So light is the mid-vowel *d* that sometimes, in colloquial spoken Spanish, it's almost left out altogether; you may even see *nada* represented as *na'a* or *na'* in written dialogue. You shouldn't take it that far, but do get the hang of the soft Spanish *d* by learning a few words well: *nada, limonada, edad, comida, ciudad, cansado.* All regular past participles follow the same rule: *hablado, conocido, bebido,* and so on. The *d* at the beginning of a word in Spanish is also a tad softer than its English counterpart, perhaps more like a *dth* than a solid *d*. Shout the name David in English and you can almost feel yourself spit; shouting it in Spanish is a much less moist affair.

4. The Spanish letters *c, z, j,* and *ll* vary in pronunciation from country to country. Don't let this bother you. Either adopt the sound used in your country of choice or seek a middle ground. For most purposes, you're safe pronouncing both the *c* and *z* as an English *s*, the *j* as an *h*, and the *ll* as the *y* of "yes." (Remember, of course, that the hard *c* in Spanish, as in *ca-, co-,* and *cu-,* sounds like a *k*.) Other noteworthy regional differences include the use of *vos* instead of *tú* and the use of *vosotros* instead of *ustedes. Vos* is used in much of Central and South America and requires learning yet more verb endings (*tú quieres* = *vos querés*). Still, if you are spending time in those countries, you will probably want to use it. The same goes for *vosotros*, which is used in Spain for the second-person plural and which you will no doubt learn if you're picking up your Spanish there.

5. Other regional differences are best left alone. In many countries, for instance, there is a tendency to "swallow" the *s* sound at the end of a syllable, especially before consonants: *estoy aquí* becomes *e'toy aquí.* (It reaches such extremes that there's even a joke about the Cuban child who asks his mother how to form plurals. "Easy, *chico,*" she says, "just add an *s: el coco, lo coco.*") There's really no good reason to learn to speak Spanish that way, or with any other regional dialect, unless you're keen on being identified as having studied in a specific country. Imagine an Asian immigrant speaking English like a Boston cabbie, or a Uruguayan drawling like a Texan, and you'll understand why.

6. In Spanish, the letters *b* and *v* sound the same: almost (but not quite) like the English *b*. Like its *d* sound, Spanish's *b/v* sound is a shade softer, especially between vowels. Thus *ave* is not pronounced either "ah-bay" or "ah-vay" but "ah-bvay." Say "ah-bay" fast, without giving your lips time to spit out a hard *b* sound, and you'll get the idea.

THE WRONG WORD SYNDROME

There are dozens of cases in Spanish where you will be tempted to use a word that is patently wrong. Mostly this is a result of misleading English cognates—words that look or sound the same in English and in Spanish but harbor different meanings. Sometimes the meaning will be close in Spanish, and the lazy language learner is content to use the cognate. But you aren't like that, are you? You want to speak Spanish well and not be responsible for polluting it with English usages. Swell. For people like you, Chapter 3 in this book is dedicated to these "tricksters," and Appendix B covers more subtle nuances. Don't worry about learning them all at once. Just try to remember which words are tricky and then try to avoid stepping in them as you go along.

"YO-ISMO"

In English, a sentence is incomplete without a noun or pronoun for a subject. In Spanish, the subject of the sentence is often conveyed by the verb and is optional. Often, in fact, it is left out altogether, unless the speaker wants to emphasize the subject of the statement. This quaint little grammatical fact affects you, the language learner, in one important case: the first person. Since you are used to including pronouns, you will tend to preface all of your first-person comments with *yo*. But to a Spanish ear, this sounds like you are constantly calling attention to yourself: "*I* want this" and "*I* think that." This affliction, dubbed "*yo-ismo*," can in extreme cases make people think you're a pretty snotty individual, when you and I know that's not true. But why take chances? Try to say *quiero* instead of *yo quiero*, *creo* instead of *yo creo*, and so on. Later, when you've broken the habit, you can go back to inserting the occasional *yo* to emphasize a truly personal opinion: *El quiere casarse pero yo no quiero* ("He wants to get married but *I* don't").

THE STUMBLES

The stumbles are what you get when you're asked a simple question and your tongue runs off and hides behind your tonsils. It is a common ailment of those who have studied some Spanish—and *know* what they want to say—but lack conversational practice. Remedying this condition requires practice, of course, but also a careful study of interjections, pert comebacks, snappy answers, and sentence starters. These useful words and phrases will get you through almost every situation requiring sudden tongue work, but they are often neglected in textbooks. Lists of these gems are included in later chapters. Pick your favorites (there are usually several acceptable ones for each situation) and store them close to your tongue.

Speaking of the stumbles, you should be especially cautious of letting your English "crutch words" slip into your Spanish. It sounds awful: *Quiero . . . um . . . ir a . . . you know . . . the . . . er . . . cine, okay?* If you must, learn some Spanish crutch words and lean on them instead: *Quiero . . . este . . . ir . . . o sea . . . al cine, ¡no?* You'll still sound like a space cadet, but at least a fairly fluent one.

FORMALITIES

The gringo who makes the effort to get off the beaten path and find out-of-the-way shops and cafés is almost by definition a fairly gregarious soul. But fear of the language can make this same person seem timid, uptight, or arrogant, browsing in a shop for half an hour without saying a word to anyone and leaving without so much as a good-bye. In general, you should be happy to inflict your fledgling Spanish on anyone who crosses your path. But you should be especially eager to unleash it in cases calling for common courtesy. There is probably no faster way to separate yourself from the pack of tourists and gawkers than to look someone in the eye and speak to them in their own language—even if it's only to say "hello" and "good-bye."

For starters, you should always greet people whose lives you have invaded, if only briefly. This doesn't mean you should walk down the streets of Buenos Aires saying *hola* to everyone, but it does mean you should immediately recognize the existence of shop clerks, waiters, secretaries, and guests. The formula is simple. From the time you wake up until 11:59 a.m., you say *buenos días*; from 12:00 noon until dark, you say *buenas tardes*; and from dark until bedtime, you say *buenas noches*. Say it loud, say it proud. You'll be amazed how service improves and prices drop after a pleasant greeting.

When you leave a place, remember to say *gracias* if it's a commercial establishment, *adiós* or *hasta luego* if it's not. Better yet, when leaving a shop, say *muchas gracias* or *muy amable, gracias* or even *muchas gracias muy amable*, all run together. You'll feel much more cheerful walking out of a place after a heartfelt farewell, even if the clerk did nothing more than stare at your back the whole time you were in the store.

In general, Spanish requires more spoken formalities than English (at least as it's spoken today), which is nice because it gives you a lot of opportunities to practice those key words and phrases. Skipping over the formalities, on the other hand, will tag you as a gringo from the get-go, which is what we've decided we want to avoid. For a fuller treatment of formalities and politeness in general, there's a whole must-read chapter just ahead with bounteous tips and details.

THE VOLUME

In Baltimore or Toronto or Oxford our friends and neighbors seem to speak in reasonable tones. So why is it that these same people seem to start shouting as soon as they get through Customs? This is one of the great mysteries of cultural intercourse, and I don't foresee resolving it here. But it is worth mentioning that, as a native English speaker, you are expected to shout instead of speak and that a whole continent of Latin Americans will be grateful if you manage to do otherwise. Gringos (remember them?) tend to bunch together and speak English at volumes appropriate for a rock concert. I've even seen a Mexican head of family ask the maitre d' to be seated "away from the gringos" at a restaurant. As when greeting people, speak loud and proud—but not too loud. Contrary to gringo folk wisdom, comprehension does not increase with volume. Normal speaking tones are best, and by the time you find yourself shouting, absolutely no one will admit to understanding you at all.

ADJECTIVES

One of the most frustrating things about learning a new language is not having access to that grab bag of adjectives that we rely on to express our opinions. And since adjectives are a relatively second-class part of speech (after the big shots like nouns and verbs), many beginning students of language tend to put off learning them until some later phase of their study. In practical terms this produces human beings whose whole range of descriptions goes from "very, very" on one extreme to "not very" on the other. "How was the film?" *Muy, muy, muy buena.* "How about the meal?" *No muy buena.*

You should try to break out of this rut as quickly as possible, learning alternative ways of expressing your likes and dislikes. Pay special attention to the use of prefixes and (especially) suffixes in modifying adjectives in Spanish; by learning a few suffixes and attaching them to words you already know, you can quickly multiply the coverage of your vocabulary. *Grande*, for example, can go up in size to *grandísimo* and even *grandotote* or deflate to a semisardonic *grandecito*. Also learn some words for that vast middle ground between good and bad where, sad to say, most of our experiences tend to fall. Chapter 4 will try to help you do just that in your encounters with people.

SPEED KILLS

Just as loud doesn't equal intelligible, fast definitely doesn't equal fluent. Take it easy. You wouldn't try to break speed records on a Kawasaki when you're just learning to ride, so why try with your Spanish? Spoken English has raised slurring practically to an art form, and it's considered normal to modify (i.e., mispronounce) consonants or vowels that get in our way. The usual result is a series of phrases like

"I dunno" and "Waddaya-wamee-tudo?" In spoken Spanish, each vowel and consonant retains its particular, unalterable sound, no matter how fast you're speaking. True, if you speak fast enough, people may not catch your errors. But they won't catch your drift either, and you'll end up having to repeat everything. If that's your strategy for getting extra practice, *adelante.* Just say it slowly the second time.

BODY LANGUAGE

If slurring in English is almost an art form, then downwardly mobile dressing in English-speaking (and other) countries is long overdue for a major museum exhibition. Far be it from me to tell you how to dress on vacation or when prowling the *barrio,* but do remember the Spanish *dicho: Como te ven, te tratan* ("How they see you, they treat you"). Dressing down has not yet caught on in most Latin cultures, perhaps because millions of people dress that way for reasons not related to fashion. If you stay close to the tourist bus, what you wear isn't so important—but who wants to do that? You don't have to dress to the nines to go buy a Coke, but you should at least be in the low sevens. Otherwise, your clothes will be saying things about you that your mouth never would.

What gringos often do, since we seem to be talking about them, is to convert their Sunday barbecue outfits back home into all-purpose wear for their introduction to Latin culture. What they would never wear to church they don't think twice about wearing to a Colombian cathedral or Guatemalan village church. If you intend to show the local people that you respect their culture, the best way to start is by letting your clothes speak for you. And the clothes that speak best are the ones that cover knees and shoulders—at least away from coastal cities. You don't have to care about any of this, of course, but if you do, remind yourself that sin and skin are still closely linked in many minds.

THOSE CRAZY GRINGOS

Every now and then, it won't matter how well you say something in Spanish if what you are saying is so patently absurd that it transcends language altogether. And what is judged as absurd can vary widely from place to place. I remember witnessing a frustrated tourist trying to request, in flawless Spanish, *hielo hervido* for his soft drink. Now, if you're familiar with tourists, you'll probably realize that "boiled ice" is a sort of shorthand way of saying "ice made from boiled, or purified, water." But if you're a waiter in a small-town bus-station restaurant in Latin America, you may not make that conceptual leap at all. Instead, you will try your darndest to make sense of your customer, and then will probably go back to the kitchen and heat up a couple of ice cubes. Many innocent requests like this can turn into Major Cultural Confusions if you're not careful. Asking for ice to put in a soda that is already cold is considered downright silly in many places, for instance. Asking for a "pizza with meat on it," in at least one place I've been, can lead to a pizza with a slab of steak lying on top. And so on.

This, of course, is part of the beauty of getting to know foreign cultures: learning that what you had considered a given all your life is often not a given at all. So if you find that nothing you say in Spanish seems to get your point across, consider changing tack. What you are saying, not how you are saying it, may be the culprit. Then change your order to *pollo frito* and a beer and forget about it. Just pray that they don't come in a bowl, and together.

MINDING YOUR VERBAL MANNERS

2

Being polite is something many people, especially the young, associate with visits to Grandma. In daily life, only bootlickers and dweebs make a special effort to be polite; the rest of us are as we are—take us or leave us.

Actually much of what goes for politeness is implicit in our behavior and requires no special effort. Society has carved on our minds the notion that if we don't follow certain preestablished, communal norms, it will use harsh and unfriendly epithets to describe us behind our backs. So we take it for granted that you should open the door for the elderly, avoid using expletives in public places, and refrain from cutting in front of people on the exit ramp. We don't think of it as being polite; we just do it because society says so.

Spanish-speaking society has its own set of unspoken norms that you, as an outsider, won't have had beaten into your head from birth. This means that you will have to pay attention to them and actually work at being polite. In addition, you will want to master the subtleties of verbal manners that you now unthinkingly control in English. Consider these examples. Do you say the same sweet-sounding phrases to a mean-faced bureaucrat as you do to a pleasant cashier? Of course not. Nor do you use the same words or tone with an elderly person that you use with someone more your age. Getting a feel for subtleties in Spanish requires getting a handle on the language that is used to express manners.

In Spanish, there is really no good translation for "polite." *Cortés, amable,* and *pulido* all come close but are better translated by their English cognates: "courteous," "amiable" (or "nice"), and "polished." Instead, a Spanish speaker will talk about someone's *educación*, which goes beyond a person's schooling to cover upbringing in general and manners in particular. *Es una persona educada* means that so-and-so is a person who has good manners and is polite in dealing with others. The person in question could be a grease monkey in the neighborhood lube shop or a physics professor, a kindergarten dropout or a triple Ph.D.; *educado* simply means that the person has decent manners. "Well bred," though somewhat out of favor in modern egalitarian societies, conveys the right idea.

In passing, it's worth noting that *rudo* is not the equivalent of "rude," nor is it a good opposite for *educado*. A Spanish-speaker would probably use *mal educado, sin educación,* or *de poca educación,* or would resort to *grosero*. This last word, in context, refers to a foul-mouthed individual, but in a more general sense it comes closer to "rude." *Se portó muy grosero con nosotros* = "He was very rude to us."

Being polite, of course, is more than simply uttering elegant phrases at key points in a conversation. To achieve the rank of *educado* and skirt all that is associated with *grosero*, you'll need one part proper language and one part common sense. We've already addressed the rudiments of good manners in our brief review of greetings and good-byes (see Chapter 1). The phrases *buenos días, buenas tardes,* and *buenas noches,* in conjunction with *gracias* and *hasta luego,* will get you through 90 percent of your daily encounters. But that's about all they'll do. If your goal is to go beyond the point of just getting by, you'll want a more in-depth look at the universe of Spanish formalities.

MEETINGS AND GREETINGS

Politeness begins upon meeting a person. You meet 'em, you greet 'em. The question is, how?

The answer depends on the person you're meeting. If there's little or no chance of ever seeing the person again, you're safe and sufficient with the *buenos días . . . hasta luego* formula. If you think the person may figure in your future life, or if the meeting is the result of an introduction, you're expected to go beyond that. From a second encounter onward, except in the case of repeated encounters with employees (shop clerks, the doorman, waiters, the gardener), you should usually employ a more personal greeting than just "good day" or "good night."

Most students of Spanish have been drilled in the basic forms of greeting, but they're worth a quick review. On being introduced to a person, you have at your disposal a number of stock responses: *mucho gusto, tanto gusto,* and *encantado* (or *encantada*) in roughly descending order of frequency. For less formal introductions and situations *¿qué tal?* and *hola* work well. Save *muchísimo gusto* for someone you've been dying to meet.

Once you've been introduced to a person, you'll naturally be expected to greet this individual at all future encounters, be it on the street or at a party. How you do this reflects (a) who the person is and (b) who you are in relation to that person. Here are some of the common options, in more or less descending order of formality:

1. *¿Cómo está?* or *¿Cómo está usted?*

2. *¿Cómo le va?*

3. *¿Qué tal?*

4. *¿Cómo estamos?*

5. *¿Cómo estás?*

6. *¿Qué hay de nuevo?*

7. *¿Qué pasó?* or *¿Qué pasa?* (varies by country)

8. *¿Qué me cuentas?* or *¿Qué me dices?*

9. *¿Qué onda?* (Mexico) or *¿Quiúbole?* (mostly Mexico and the Caribbean)

10. Slangy variations of the preceding, such as *¿Qué pasotes?* or *¿Qué pasión?* (from *¿Qué pasó?*), *¿Qué hongos?* (from *¿Qué onda?*), and so on. Save these for the people whose street gang you're looking to join.

It bears noting that all these expressions—except *¿Cómo está?* and *¿Cómo está usted?*—imply some level of friendliness. Said another way, if you're not on especially friendly terms with the person, stick to the first expression listed above. It is the only appropriate form for greeting a person whose social, familial, occupational, or political position warrants your respect, and thus is the safe choice for those who aren't, strictly speaking, your buddies. *¿Cómo estamos?* has paternalistic overtones and is often used by older people to greet younger ones—even if the younger ones are thirty or forty years old. This greeting is also a safe one when you're on good terms with the person but aren't sure whether to use *tú* or *usted* (more on that bugaboo in a bit).

A common way of sprucing up any greeting is to use the person's name, title, or both. The commonest titles are *Don* and *Doña* (for older people) and professional titles like *Doctor, Contador* (accountant or C.P.A.), *Ingeniero, Profesor, Maestro* (any teacher or craftsperson and sometimes even mechanics and plumbers), and the ubiquitous *Licenciado* (virtually anybody who wears a tie). These are used far more often than their English equivalents, especially in the workplace.

As an example of how greetings work, let's take the case of Juan Doe, assistant director in charge of flange production, arriving at his office. For simplicity's sake, let's presume all of the males in his workplace are named Alberto Alvarez and all the females Teresa Ruiz. Juan parks his car on the street and walks toward the office building. In order, he meets and greets the following:

The eighty-year-old doorman:
Buenos días, Don Alberto.
The security guard:
Buenos días.
The sixty-year-old elevator operator:
¿Cómo le va, Doña Tere?
The receptionist:
Hola, Tere. ¿Cómo estás?
A same-aged colleague in the hall:
¿Qué tal, Alberto?
A younger colleague at her desk:
Buenos días, Tere. ¿Qué hay de nuevo?
A visiting branch manager:
Buenos días, Señora Ruiz. ¿Cómo le va?
A co-worker and best friend:
¿Quiúbole, Beto?
The immediate boss:
Hola, Alberto. ¿Cómo estás?
An older co-worker:
¿Qué me cuenta, Don Alberto?
An employee:
Buenos días, Alberto. ¿Cómo estamos?
The division director:
Muy buenos días, Señor Alvarez. ¿Cómo le va?
The office boy:
¿Qué pasó, Beto?
The factory owner and CEO:
Buenos días, Don Alberto. ¿Cómo está usted?
The secretary:
Buenos días, Tere. ¿Qué tal?

By now, as you might imagine, Juan is exhausted and it's time for his coffee break.

A couple of general tips on greetings are in order. First, note that when greeting so many people, you will naturally gravitate toward new ways of saying the same thing. That's because saying *buenos días* to twenty-five consecutive people can be extremely boring.

Second, use nicknames only if the person is accustomed to being called that. In other words, pay attention to whether others call a certain José "Pepe" before you call him that. Use generic nicknames— such as *viejo, compadre,* and *jovenazo*—only when you feel certain that the person won't be offended by your informality.

Third, if you're a male, avoid affectionate pet names for female friends, employees, and co-workers. In Latin America it is common to hear men calling women co-workers and employees things like *linda* and *cariño.* To most North Americans this treatment is patronizing at best and at worst borders on sexual harassment. Men in Latin America have been slow about concerning themselves with these matters, but that's no reason for you to imitate them.

Fourth, if you're a woman, stick to more formal modes of address until you're sure that your friendliness won't be taken as encouragement by the wolfish male mind. It's unfortunate that you have to consider this issue, but that doesn't make it any less real.

And fifth, greet everyone possible, especially when meeting a group of people. If you've met the people before, you are expected to take the trouble of greeting each of them individually. Not to do so can be interpreted as an offense. The same goes for saying goodbye. If you're in too much of a hurry or there are simply too many people involved, make sure you issue an all-encompassing *¡Qué tal, cómo están!* or *Hasta luego,* and make sure it's interpreted as all-encompassing.

USTED VERSUS TÚ

From the moment you greet a person, you will start to think about whether so-and-so is an *"usted* person" or a *"tú* person." Native Spanish speakers make this decision instinctively; you will have to think it through, and repeatedly. It is a concept that doesn't have an easy English equivalent, but it is usually not that hard to keep straight. Perhaps the most functional system for converting the concept into English is to use *usted* in Spanish with anyone you would address with "Mr.," "Mrs.," "Ms.," or "Miss" in English. Mr. Brown is your neighbor, so you use *usted* with him. Once you get to know him and call him "Fred," you can switch to *tú.* Your lawyer is Ms. Smith, so she's an *usted* person; if you call your lawyer "Betty," then you would also probably use *tú* with her. And so on.

This rule of thumb works even when you don't actually know the person's name. Your waiter's name is Juan Pérez, but you probably wouldn't know that. If you did, though, would you call him "Juan" or "Mr. Pérez?" That will generally depend upon his age, your age, and so on. If it would feel awkward calling a twenty-two-year-old "Mr. Pérez," go ahead and use *tú* with him. Then again, if the twenty-two-year-old happens to be an undersecretary for tax policy in the finance ministry—or a traffic cop—you would probably call him "Mr. Pérez" and thus use *usted*.

As a rule, people aren't bashful about telling you to use *tú* with them if they feel it's appropriate. Almost no one will tell you to use *usted* when you're using *tú*—it's the equivalent of putting you in your place. So when in doubt, you're far safer using *usted* and waiting until you're told to do otherwise.

The best way to choose the right form is to listen to the conversation around you. Let's say you're meeting a group of friends at a restaurant. Upon arriving, someone you don't know is sitting with your friends. You are introduced to this person as Betty (your name), and she to you as Yolanda (her name). This is your first clue: almost certainly you are expected to *tutear* (use *tú* with) this person. To play it safe, though, you can return the greeting with a noncommittal *mucho gusto* and keep your ears open. If Sam asks Yolanda, *¿Dónde estás trabajando ahora?* then you can feel safe using *tú* yourself. Likewise, if you're addressed with *usted*, you should respond with *usted*.

That said, there are a few cases in which the *tú-usted* relationship is not reciprocal—that is, when you will use *tú* with the person and he or she will use *usted* with you, or vice versa. Almost always this is the result of a considerable age difference. You might use *usted* with your friends' parents, for instance, and they will likely use *tú* with you. (This, incidentally, fits under the "Mr. and Mrs." rule.) Turn the formula around for your children's friends.

MAGIC WORDS

Besides greeting people, expressing thanks is probably the daily act that most requires a modicum of civility. *Gracias* is the obligatory comment, of course, but you can spice it up with a *muchas* before it or a *muy amable* after it or both, as noted in Chapter 1. By doing so, you'll sound both more polite and more fluent. *Muy gentil* is also used, but it sounds somewhat strained.

When being thanked, you can respond with *por nada, de nada, no hay por que,* or *no hay de que.* They're all about the same and mean "You're welcome." You will hear *para servirle* a lot from clerks and waiters, but don't use it yourself unless it is genuinely your job or duty to serve the person, or unless you're feeling especially subservient.

Another common linguistic nicety is asking permission. In Spanish, as in English, the most typical way of asking permission is essentially to excuse oneself for having the audacity to ask. Thus we ask a person's "permission" to squeeze by them in an aisle. Here are some options for communicating your humility while asking someone to move over or let you by, again in descending order of formality:

1. *Con permiso*
2. *¡Me permite!*
3. *Perdón*
4. *¡Se puede!*
5. *Comper'* (a slangy version of *con permiso*)
6. *Hágase un poco para allá, por favor*
7. *Abreme espacio* or *Abreme cancha*
8. *Hazte pa'llá*

The first five expressions are formal enough for just about any occasion. *¡Me permite!* is sometimes used ironically, as when someone is clearly blocking the way; say it very innocently for greatest effect. *¡Se puede!* is also the common way to ask to see something in a store; it presumes you will wait for an affirmative response before, say, taking a painting down off the wall or an earring out of a glass case. Unless the object you wish to see is obvious (you're pointing at it, for instance), you should use the full phrase: *¡Se puede ver!*

The last three expressions on the list convey informality or rudeness, depending on the person you are speaking to and and your tone of voice. *Hazte pa'llá*, for instance, can be used for either "Scoot over a little" (with a friend) or "Get out of the way" (with a stranger). *Abreme cancha* is very slangy.

The phrase for "Coming through!"—as when carrying a two-hundred-pound sofa down the hall—is *¡Golpe avisa! Excúsame*, incidentally, does exist as a Spanish expression, but it doesn't mean "Excuse me." Use something (anything!) else.

Here's a cultural tip. One nicety that many foreigners have trouble learning is to say *gracias* when someone sends *saludos* through them to another person: *Salúdame a tu esposa* ("My regards to your wife") is something you will hear constantly if you are married, for instance. Your English-speaking reflex will be to answer "Okay, I will," but in Spanish it is customary to thank the person for this *detalle* ("thoughtfulness" or "consideration").

As *gracias* is the universal word for "thank you," *por favor* is all you will ever need for "please." Always remember to use it when asking for something. If you're tired of it and want to flex some Spanish muscles, use instead *si es tan amable*, generally placed after your request: *Un café, si es tan amable*. It means *por favor*.

SUGAR VERSUS SACCHARINE

Spanish speakers are famous for going a bit overboard with their floridness and politeness, and it is a matter of opinion whether foreigners learning the language should leap in after them. Use your own judgment. For instance, Spanish speakers will often refer to their house as *su casa* or *tu casa*—"your house"—meaning that now that you know them, you should consider their abode to be yours. This can get pretty confusing at times: someone will be giving you directions to their home and at the end they will point to the map they've improvised and say, "And here is your house." You'll be tempted to respond, "But my house is nowhere near there!"—until you recall this subtle gesture of hospitality. It can get even more confusing when a non-native speaker, from whom such a gesture is generally not expected, tries to communicate it.

Slightly less silly-sounding in the mouths of foreigners is the statement *Está usted en su casa* when someone comes to visit. It's really nothing more than a way of saying "Make yourself at home" and shouldn't be made to sound more grandiose than that. To use it really correctly, save it for when a houseguest makes a simple request, such as "Can I use the phone?" To this you reply, with a wave of the hand, *Estás en tu casa*.

A word on homes is in order at this point. In much of the Spanish-speaking world, homes are considered private reserves, and it is not especially common to receive an invitation to visit someone's house. So first of all, don't expect to receive such an invitation. And don't be surprised if your offers of hospitality—"Hey, Pedro, how about popping by after work for a beer?"—are taken as a nice gesture instead of as a genuine invitation. Furthermore, never drop in unannounced on a friend in the Spanish-speaking world. Finally, you may be told while visiting someone's house that some object you admire *es tuya* ("it's yours," "take it"). Not only shouldn't you accept such offers, you should be careful about making them. Sooner or later a literal-minded guest might take you up on it!

Other sweet-sounding phrases that border on the sickly sweet include solemn declarations of humility (saying *su servidor* instead of "I"), exaggerated requests for cooperation (*Tenga usted la bondad de traerme un café*), and overly formal greetings (*Me es grato tener la oportunidad de conocerlo*). All sound like you're reading out of a phrasebook—and a phrasebook written for royal weddings, at that.

ASKING AND GETTING

Politeness is particularly important when asking someone for something, since otherwise you may not get it. Bicultural lore is full of anecdotes about Party A getting something in twenty minutes that took Party B three weeks to get, simply because Party A asked politely and Party B was viewed as rude. Whether you plan to use your Spanish to get government authorizations or good directions, your command of these niceties is critical.

It's easy to sound rude or clumsy when making a special or even routine request in Spanish, especially since most students of the language are taught the imperative as the sole way of asking for things. Thus many students of Spanish will tell their hostess, *Tráigame un café* ("Bring me a coffee"), thinking that's the correct, formal, and polite way to petition one. A good hostess will bring you one anyhow, but on some interior level she's thinking, "Sure, here's one in your lap, schmuck." Fortunately, it's quite easy to sound natural when asking for something, but most Spanish texts neglect to mention the most frequently used form of the imperative in daily life: the indicative. That is, most people don't say *Tráigame un café, por favor* but *¿Me trae un café, por favor?* An added advantage to this form is that you don't have to worry about those strange imperative forms and can stick to the tried-and-true indicative instead.

The *¿me trae?* + *por favor* formula is all you'll ever need for restaurants and the like. But this use of the indicative also works for most other situations and can employ a number of different verbs in addition to *traer*, especially *permitir, dar, prestar,* and *regalar. Permitir* is the most formal: *¿Me permite un cigarro?* will get a cigarette off your future father-in-law. *Prestar* and *regalar* are the least formal, and the latter implies you're going to keep what you're given: *¿Me prestas tu pluma?* means "Lend me your pen." *¿Me regalas tu pluma?* is "Can I have your pen (forever)?" In colloquial use, *pasar* is common and equates with *prestar: ¿Me pasas el cenicero?* means "Pass the ashtray over here, would ya?" Another common formal way of asking for things is equivalent to "May I" in English: *¿Puedo tomar un cigarro?* ("May I have a cigarette?").

ETC.

Phone Spanish is generally even more polite than face-to-face Spanish. Listening to it, you will hear a lot of phrases like *si es tan amable* and *si no es mucha molestia* tacked on to simple requests. Once you get the hang of it, you'll be doing the same thing. To ask for someone on the phone, you can be formal—*¿Me puede comunicar con* *el Sr. So-and-so?*—or informal—*¿Está por ahí So-and-so?*. It will depend on whom you're calling. To say "Speaking" when someone calls and asks for you, just say *Él* (or *ella*) *habla.*

Interrupting is considered bad form in any language, of course, but some foreigners seem to do it more when the conversation they are interrupting is in a foreign language—i.e., one they don't understand that well. Be aware of this, and be conspicuously polite when you do need to interrupt, directing yourself to the party whom you are momentarily cutting out of the picture. Act, in other words, as if you were cutting in on a dance. *¿Me permite un momento?* you can ask.

Certain situations call for specific graces from you. Some are verbal graces and some aren't, but all come under the heading of *buena educación.*

1. When you pass by someone who is eating, and presuming you are at least vaguely acquainted with the person, wish him or her *provecho* or *buen provecho* ("bon appetit," as we'd say in English). Don't say it to total strangers in restaurants, though.

2. North Americans like to toss things. "Here's the pencil you asked for," they'll say as they wing a fine-pointed no. 2 lead pencil by your ear. "This is no good," they'll say as they crumple a sheet of paper and lob it at the wastebasket. In the Spanish-speaking world, this behavior is considered barely short of barbaric.

3. Ditto for pointing at people.

4. Be conscious of not "giving your back" to people. Many people from non-Latin cultures do it without intending offense. But in Spanish-speaking cultures it's common to see people realize there is someone behind them listening, do a half-turn, say *perdón*, and continue speaking in a way that includes the previously excluded person.

SWEET SORROW

Departures are easily handled in Spanish by any of a number of words, but *adiós* and *hasta luego* are sufficient for almost every circumstance. *Adiós*, as you may have been taught, is generally used for more lasting farewells. *Nos vemos* is also a common colloquial send-off, equating with "See you later." *Ciao* (or *chao*) and *bye* are making rapid headway into Spanish from their respective languages.

Slightly more formal leave-taking makes use of phrases like *Que le vaya bien*, used only when the person you say it to is doing the leaving. More fancy is *Vaya con Dios*, but unless you're a nun or a priest, it comes close to the saccharine category. When taking leave of a group or passing by people on your way out, it's considered nice manners to say *Con permiso* to the people who are staying on. Usually it is used for people whom you didn't actually say hello to on your way in. Leaving the dentist's office, for instance, you say *Gracias* to the dentist and the receptionist and *Con permiso* to the people sitting in the waiting room.

For less formal departures and with the younger set, you can say things like *Cuídate* (roughly, "Take it easy") and *Pórtate bien* ("Behave yourself") to people when they are leaving. If it's nighttime and the person is presumably leaving to go home to sleep, you can say *Que descanses* ("Rest up"). As a rule, try to respond with a farewell that is different from the one used by the other person. If someone says *Hasta luego*, you say *Nos vemos*; if they say *Nos vemos*, answer *Hasta luego*.

3 TRICKSTERS

Every non-native speaker of a foreign language is afraid of making mistakes. And good thing, too. A little fear forces us to concentrate harder and causes the memory of our mistakes to linger—long enough to correct them the next time we open our mouths.

Most mistakes are grammatical and are eliminated only after long periods of trial and error. Other mistakes, though, are almost the fault of the languages themselves. Spanish and English, because of their long history of coexistence and their many common origins, contain a lot of words that are similar on the surface but are used quite differently. This makes instinctive translation at times as dangerous as a cross-eyed knife-thrower.

Fortunately things aren't quite that bad. A lot of these false cognates are so frequently tripped over by students of both languages that they can be identified in advance. In the following list of "tricksters," you'll find some of the Spanish words most commonly misused by native English speakers. Review the words and keep them in the back of your brain. You won't overcome all of your instincts overnight, but knowing your enemies—in this case, the tricksters—is the first step toward conquering them.

ACOSTAR Not "to accost," which is *acosar*. *Acostar* simply means "to lie down" and is usually used in the reflexive. *Me voy a acostar* = "I'm going to lie down" or "I'm going to bed." If by doing this you are accosting someone, you may be in the wrong bed.

ACTUAL Not "actual" but "current" or "present." *La actual administración* means "the current administration" or the one in power at the moment. To convey "actual" in the sense of "factual" or "genuine," you would resort to *verdadero, auténtico, genuino, real*, etc. "This is an actual Picasso" is expressed by *Este es un auténtico Picasso.*

ACTUALMENTE   Worth a special mention because "actually" is so common as a sentence-starter in English: "You must be starving." "Actually, I just ate." *Actualmente* won't work here, since it means "at present" or "currently." Confusing the two can lead to some strange situations. Think of someone telling you, "You and your brother are invited for lunch"—to which you want to answer, "Actually, he's my husband." If you use *Actualmente, es mi esposo*, what you are saying is "At present, he's my husband." For "actually," try the phrase *la verdad es que: La verdad es que acabo de comer.* When "actually" is used in mid-sentence for emphasis, you can use either *realmente* or some other construction altogether. For example, "He actually ate it!" can be expressed as *¡Realmente se lo comió!* or *¡Sí se lo comió!* or *¡De verdad se lo comió!*

AFECCIÓN   This doesn't mean "affection" but usually a medical condition. *Tiene una afección cardiaca* = "He (or she) has a heart condition." Use *afecto*—or better yet, *cariño*—to convey your affection.

AMERICANO   Almost more of a political issue than a semantic one. Still, the use (and misuse) of *americano* by "Americans"—i.e., U.S. citizens—should be kept in mind by anyone eager to avoid unnecessary offense. In Spanish and Spanish-speaking countries an *americano* is simply a person from "the Americas," including South and Central as well as North America. Thus if you tell a Chilean that you are an *americano*, you might get a smirk and the comment *Yo también* ("Me too") in return. Incidentally, in the Spanish-speaking world the correct way to refer to "the Americas" is in the singular: *América.* Schoolchildren are taught that, from the Bering Strait to Tierra del Fuego, it is but one continent.

Oddly enough, there really is no perfect way for U.S. citizens to state their origin in Spanish. *Norteamericano* is the most common word, but technically it includes Canadians and Mexicans as well. *Estadounidense* has caught on of late, but besides being a mouthful it overlooks the fact that other countries (the United Mexican States, for instance) are also technically "United States." Even so, saying *Soy de los Estados Unidos* is probably the easiest way of explaining your plight.

This confusion, incidentally, goes a long way toward explaining why *gringo* is so common a word in countries like Mexico and why you yourself will probably start to use it after a short time in these places. The word can be used in an offensive way, but usually the word's negative connotation is a result of the tone of voice. In Mexico, especially, *gringo* is very commonly used as an adjective as well; imports from the United States can easily (if colloquially) be referred to as *productos gringos*.

ARGUMENTO A classic trickster. This word doesn't work well as "argument" in the usual sense of a "heated discussion" or a "quarrel." Instead, it should be reserved for prepared arguments (such as lawyers' summations), debates, and carefully reasoned, often written arguments. *Argumento* describes a logical process, not a rather illogical throwing of pans and vases. For that, use *pleito, disputa,* or *disgusto* (see below), roughly in descending order of intensity. Perhaps the best all-purpose translation of "argument" is another trickster, *discusión*, which refers to a far more heated exchange than what we consider a "discussion" in English.

ASISTIR Not "to assist" but "to attend" or "to be present at." *Asistencia* is the proper word for "attendance" (see *atender* and *audiencia* below), and an *asistente* is technically just someone who is attending something. Nonetheless, you may come across *gerente asistente* as a way of saying "assistant manager," though you'll probably come across it at a local branch of a U.S. company. A more natural Spanish construction would be *subgerente*. For "to assist," use *ayudar*.

ATENDER Not "to attend" (see *asistir* above) but "to attend to"—a significant difference. Remember, you can *atender* a patient but you can't *atender* a concert.

AUDIENCIA Another word in the "attendance" versus "assistance" imbroglio. Correctly, an *audiencia* is usually a private interview granted to you by someone more important than you. In this sense, it is usually used with *conceder: El ministro nos concedió audiencia* = "The minister granted us an interview." This meaning is still in use in English, but it is usually reserved for the pope. In Spanish the town sewage commissioner can grant you one. *La audiencia* can be used for "the audience"—in a concert hall, for instance—but *la asistencia, el auditorio,* and *el público* are all preferred.

BALDE This doesn't refer to hair loss but to a bucket. It's also commonly seen in the expression *en balde*, which means "in vain." For "bald," you can use either *calvo* (polite) or *pelón* (irreverent).

BALÓN The common word for "ball," from about grapefruit size on up. Smaller balls are called *bolas* or *pelotas*. "Balloon" is *globo*, just so you know.

BILLÓN A false cognate that many overlook. *Un billón* is 1,000,000,000,000, or 10 to the twelfth power (10^{12}). It is equal to the U.S. "trillion." (In England, this quantity is a "billion.") To convey the U.S. "billion," or 10 to the ninth power (U.K. "milliard"), you must say *mil millones*, or "a thousand millions."

BIZARRO A fairly archaic term for "chivalrous" or "brave" (not "bizarre" in the sense of "peculiar"). Both "bizarre" and *bizarro* come from the Basque word for "bearded," which apparently suggested strangeness to some and gallantry to others. You don't need to know *bizarro* to speak Spanish, but you should be aware that it doesn't mean "bizarre" if you tend to translate your thoughts fairly literally from English to Spanish. For "bizarre," use *raro* or *extraño*.

"CAPABLE" This word doesn't even exist in Spanish, but if you were to use it, it would be understood as "castratable." Saying someone is *un hombre capable*, therefore, does not mean he is "capable" but rather in imminent danger of being rendered "incapable." The right word for "capable" is *capaz*; "incapable" is *incapaz*, which covers "incompetent" as well.

CARGO Almost works but not quite. *Carga*, with the feminine ending, is the right word for "cargo." *Cargo* in Spanish generally means "job position" or "post." *El encargado* is "the guy in charge."

CARPETA Usually a "portfolio" of the sort for keeping and carrying papers. It could also be a simple manila folder or a file. It is never a "carpet," which is covered by *tapete* or *alfombra*. Nonetheless, thanks to the influence of English, it is said (perhaps apocryphally) that Spanish-speaking residents of the United States say things like *Voy a vacunar la carpeta* for "I'm going to vacuum the carpet." In fact, this statement means "I'm going to vaccinate the portfolio." (See Appendix B for more English-influenced words and phrases.)

CHOCAR A tricky trickster. This word has long existed in Spanish to mean "to crash," as in what happens to a car that is driven recklessly. A few hundred years ago, though, the English word "shock" began to take on some trendy new scientific meanings, and a handful of these were assigned to the old standby *chocar* and its derivatives. Thus while *un choque* has always meant "a crash," in recent years it has been expanded to cover "a state of shock" (such as the driver's condition after the car's *choque*). It is also in widespread use for a powerful electrical shock, though *chocar* as a verb is not used for "to shock (electrically)." For that, use *dar choque* or, in many countries, *dar toques*. (Generally, *un choque* will kill you and *un toque* won't.) *La lámpara me dio toques* = "The lamp gave me a shock." To confuse matters more, sometimes *shock* is used instead of *choque*.

CHOCANTE As an adjective, this works pretty well as "shocking" but usually conveys a distinct disapproval that isn't implicit in the English word. In some contexts, especially in reference to people, it comes close to meaning "offensive" or "rude." *Me choca*, by extension, is a common colloquial way of saying you strongly dislike something: *Me choca el chocolate* = "I hate chocolate."

COMPLEXIÓN Not your skin texture, as in English, but your general physical structure and shape, or "build"—in other words, fat, skinny, pear-shaped, or just about right. Government forms in Spanish-speaking countries often ask about your *complexión*, and as long as you remember not to put "cleared up years ago," you'll be fine. For skin condition, stick to *piel* (all skin) or *cutis* (especially facial skin). "You have a nice complexion" is expressed by *Tienes buen cutis*.

COMPROMISO   Yes, it works as "compromise," but a far more common usage is to mean "commitment." The verb *comprometer* is similarly double-edged. *Me comprometo con las mujeres* could be a politician's way of saying he or she is committed to his or her female constituents and connotes no "compromising" situations. The same sense of obligation is present in the common marketplace remark *sin compromiso*, which means you can try on a blouse, for instance, "without committing" yourself to buy it. *Compromiso* is also an "appointment" or "engagement." *Tengo un compromiso después de la comida* = "I have an appointment after lunch." "Commitment" can also be used this way, but it sounds a bit like power-breakfast English, whereas in Spanish it is an everyday expression.

COPA   If you ask for your "cup of coffee" as a *copa de café* in the Spanish-speaking world, don't be surprised if you're served your coffee "Irish" or with a coffee liqueur. In general usage, a *copa* is a stemmed glass or goblet of the sort used for wine or champagne. Thus *copa*, in a restaurant setting, almost always suggests an alcoholic beverage of some sort. Just as you wouldn't think of asking for coffee in a goblet, your waiter won't think of serving something in a *copa* without a little booze in it. *Taza* is the correct word for a coffee-style "cup."

CORRIENTE   This word is only partly tricky, but when it's tricky, it's dangerously so. Basically you can use it safely as a noun to mean "current"—any sort of electrical, river, or political currents— but not as an adjective. As a modifier, *corriente* suggests "cheap" or "trashy"; when used for people, it is a definite insult, equating with "rude" or "vulgar." To convey "current" in the sense of "now in progress," you should take care to use *presente* or *actual* (see above).

DECEPCIÓN   A classic trickster. *Decepción* means "disappointment" or "disillusionment," often with no suggestion whatsoever of deceit. Likewise, *decepcionar* means "to disappoint," and *decepcionado* means "disappointed." *Me decepcionó su novio* means you were unimpressed by someone's boyfriend, not that he talked you out of your inheritance. For "to deceive" and its derivatives you're better off with *engañar*. *Defraudar* can work either way: "to defraud (monetarily)" or "to disillusion," "to let (someone) down."

DISGUSTAR   Not "to disgust" but "to cause displeasure"—a subtle but important difference. Turned around, with the speaker as the indirect object (as with *gustar*), it means simply "to dislike." *Me disgustan los pepinos* means you don't like cucumbers, not necessarily that they make you sick. For "to disgust," *asquear* or *dar asco* is appropriate: *Los pepinos me dan asco*. Similarly, "disgusting" would be *asqueroso.* Used to describe a person, it conveys the idea of extreme sleaziness. *Es un tipo asqueroso* = "He's a real slimeball."

"DUM DUM DA DUM DUM, TUMP TUMP" A non-verbal trickster of the most dangerous sort. It's hard to convey the sound pattern in writing (one rendering, perhaps from vaudeville days, is "shave and a haircut—two bits"), but the pattern is familiar to everyone. Imagine yourself knocking it on a door or tapping it out on your car horn. Got it? Now consider that in certain Latin countries, Mexico especially, what you've just said is, essentially, "Fuck your mother." Knock that on a door in Mexico and be prepared to see someone with a shotgun open it; tap it on your car horn and you'll have twenty vehicles gunning for you. Tap it on your car horn when there's a police car in front of you and you've got serious problems.

EMBARAZADO The most famous trickster of all, leading to all sorts of colorful anecdotes from travelers. The word actually can mean "embarrassed" in certain contexts and in certain expressions, but it also means "pregnant." By using it, even correctly, you open yourself to no end of silliness and smirks. Better to stick to the common ways of saying "embarrassed": *apenado* and *penoso*, both from the word *pena* (see below). *Dar pena* is good for "to embarrass." If you don't want to speak in public because it embarrasses you, bow out with a *Me da pena.* For "How embarrassing!" (as in "What a fool I've made of myself!"), a simple *¡Qué pena!* will suffice. A stronger concept like "shame," often with moralistic overtones, is covered by *vergüenza.* *Pena* is more the embarrassment that comes of shyness or prudishness.

EN ABSOLUTO Not "absolutely" but the opposite—"absolutely not." If you want to avoid using it altogether, that's fine, too. Use *claro* for "absolutely" and *claro que no* for "absolutely not." But learn the correct meaning of *en absoluto* for those times when it's used on you.

ENFRENTE DE A sneaky trickster and one that can cause crossed signals with the best of them. It means "in front of" in the sense of "across the way (or street) from" or "facing." Thus, if you tell your friends to pick you up *enfrente del cine* and you're waiting in front of the movie theater, expect to see your friends waiting across the street. *Frente a* is equally misleading, meaning the same as *enfrente de.* For "in front of" as we use it in English, try *en la puerta de* ("at the door of") to avoid any misinterpretations. *Al frente de* can also be used, but why risk the confusion? (See also Chapter 11 under "Front.")

EXCITADO An easy one to slip in unawares, this trickster probably conveys more than you bargained for. The English translation is "aroused," sexual overtones included. For "excited," use *emocionado*; for "exciting," *emocionante.*

ÉXITO   Not "exit" but "success." In the music industry *exitos* are "hits," lest you think *Los grandes éxitos de Frank Sinatra* refers to his greatest stage exits. "The exit" is *la salida*.

FÁBRICA   Not "fabric" but "factory." This is a good one to remember if you're going to get involved in business in Latin America, as a lot of people are these days. If you're looking to buy fabric, on the other hand, the word you want is *tela*.

GENTIL   Not really "gentle" but "kind" or "courteous." *Qué gentil* is a somewhat stuffy (and often ironic) way of saying "How nice" or "That's great." To say "gentle," you'll want to use *cuidadoso* or even simply *cuidado: Mucho cuidado por favor con esa caja* = "Please be gentle with that box." A "gentle" wind might be *suave*, while a "gentle" person would be *tierna*.

INFORMAL   This word has come to have pretty much the same meaning as its English cognate, with one important exception: when used to refer to people, *informal* means "unreliable." It's the word you use to refer to the plumber who swore that he'd be by last Thursday to unstop your drains, only to vanish from the face of the planet instead. To say that someone is "informal"—i.e., "laid-back"— you could use *relajado* ("relaxed") or *despreocupado*. For uses other than personal ones, *informal* is widespread, though purists tend to dislike it. *Fue una reunión informal* = "It was an informal get-together."

INJURIA   An "injury," yes, but a moral and psychological one—better known in English as an "insult" or "offense," and usually a real dinger of one at that. Don't use it for "injury," which, if major, is the noun *herida*. If it's a small injury (a sprained ankle, for example), the verb *lastimarse* is more appropriate. Why is Pablo limping? *Es que se lastimó el pie jugando tenis* ("He hurt his foot playing tennis").

INTOXICADO   Unless it's a real binge you're talking about, this word doesn't work for "drunk." It means "poisoned"—unintentionally, as a rule—and covers food poisoning, industrial toxins, overdoses, and the like. Another whole book could be written on how to say "intoxicated" in the sense of "drunk" in Spanish. *Ebrio* is the best equivalent for "intoxicated," while *borracho* is closest in tone to "drunk."

INTRODUCIR   You'll be tempted to use this for "to introduce," but don't. It means "to introduce" only in the sense of "to insert" or "to add something in." Often it is used as a fairly fancy substitute for *meter*, or "to stick in." For "to introduce to" with people, always use *presentar. Ven, quiero presentarte a un amigo* = "Come on, I want to introduce you to a friend of mine."

LARGO   Not "large" but "long." Just a reminder.

LIBRERÍA   Not "library" but "bookstore." Another reminder. A "library" is a *biblioteca*.

MEDIA   In Spanish, this (presumably) has nothing to do with your favorite newscaster. It means "stocking," and in the plural, "pantyhose." In math it means "mean." "Media," in the collective sense of newspapers, magazines, radio, and television, is usually covered in Spanish by *los medios (de comunicación)*.

MOLESTAR   In Spanish this word carries no sexual overtones whatsoever. It's perfectly safe and extremely common for "to bother." *No me molestes* = "Don't bother me." As an adjective, it works well as "upset," "angry," or "uncomfortable." *¿Estás molesto por algo?* = "Are you upset about something?"

ORDINARIO   Be careful using this term in regard to people. Far from meaning "ordinary," it means "vulgar," "rude," and "crass." *Es un tipo muy ordinario* = "He's a slob." To describe an average, run-of-the-mill person just like you and me and a million other people, use *normal* or *común: Es un tipo normal. El hombre común* is a good translation of "the man in the street." (See also Chapter 4.)

PARIENTES   Not "parents," though they're *parientes* too, but "relatives"—all of them, from your grandparents and children to in-laws and cousins. What you share with these people is called *parentesco*, or "kinship."

PENA   Not "pain" (the physical kind) but "sorrow" and "embarrassment." *Pena* is the word you want to learn so as to avoid using *embarazado* (see above). "Pain" is usually handled by *dolor*, as is "ache." A "headache" is a *dolor de cabeza*. In the figurative sense of a "pain in the neck" (or even lower), a good equivalent is *lata. ¡Qué lata* = "What a pain!" *Dar (la) lata* = "to be a pain," "to pester." To people who are bothering you, you can say *No des (la) lata* ("Stop being a pain").

PRIMER PISO   If you're used to thinking of the ground floor as the first floor, be prepared to think again in Spanish, where *primer piso* means "one flight up." The ground floor is usually called *la planta baja*, or *PB* in the elevators.

QUITAR   You may try to use this for "to quit," especially since Spanish at first glance doesn't seem to have a good word for "to quit." Unfortunately, *quitar* isn't that word either. It means "to take (something) off," "to take away." The word you need for "quit" depends on what you're quitting: if it's your job, the word is *renunciar*; if it's smoking or some other activity, *dejar de*. To "quit" a computer program, most translated software programs simply use *salir*.

REALIZAR   There is some overlap with this word and its English cognate. But for the most common use of "to realize" in English, *realizar* does not work. The correct phrase is *darse cuenta (de)*. "I realized too late he had a gun" is expressed by *Me di cuenta demasiado tarde de que traía pistola*. "Realize" in the common English sense can often be handled perfectly competently by *saber* ("to know") in Spanish. "I realize you're busy" thus becomes *Sé que estás ocupada.* "I didn't realize you were married" would be *No sabía que estabas casado.*

RECETA   Almost always a medical prescription or a cooking recipe in Spanish. It is never a "receipt," which would be *recibo* or *nota.*

ROPA   Not "rope" but "clothes." "Rope" is usually either *soga* or *cuerda.*

SANO   This goes beyond mental health to cover all aspects of health. In other words, it means "healthy." The word for "sane" is *cuerdo.* For "insane," use *loco.* It's a bit unscientific and insensitive, but then so is "insane."

SENSIBLE   It means "sensitive," not "sensible." For "sensible" you should use *sensato.* *Una persona sensible* is "a sensitive person." This is one of those confusing words you'll just have to remember.

SOPA   Not "soap" but "soup." Creamy soups are simply called *cremas,* as in *crema de champiñones* ("cream of mushroom soup"). "Soap" is *jabón.*

SOPORTAR   A common word in Spanish for "to tolerate," though it is more frequent in the negative in the sense of "can't stand." *No soporto la televisión* = "I can't stand television." Mixing it up will get you some funny looks: *Mi familia me soporta* doesn't mean your family pays your bills but that your family tolerates you (barely). For "to support" in the bill-paying sense use *mantener.* In the sense of physically supporting something (what a wall does for the ceiling, in other words), *sostener* is more accurate.

SUMAR   This verb may pop into your mind as a neat translation for "to sum up," but you should pop it right back out of there if you want to be understood. *Sumar* is the word for "to add" or "to add up." *¿Cuánto suma?* = "How much does that add up to?" For summaries and summations, stick to the verb *resumir* (*para resumir* = "to sum up," *en resumen* = "in sum"), although *en suma* is safe for "in sum" as well.

SUPLIR   Not "supply," as you might think. Instead, it means "to substitute" or "to fill in for." *Suplo en la oficina a mi hermana cuando está de viaje* = "I fill in for my sister at the office when she's out of town." A *suplente* is a "substitute"—a substitute teacher, for instance. *Substituto* and *substituir* also exist and mean about the same thing, but *suplir* and its derivatives are more frequent (and far easier to pronounce).

TREMENDO   Often a close fit for "tremendous" but not always. *Tremendo* often comes closer to "outrageous" and can mean "outrageously bad," "terrifying," or "terrible" as well as "outrageously good" or "tremendous." The word is especially tricky around children, it seems. *Es un niño tremendo* describes a monstrous child capable of the worst mischief. In short, be aware of the negative connotations that frequently surround this word.

TUNA   Here's a real menu trickster. *Tuna* is not the fish but the fruit of the prickly pear cactus, or *nopal*—that is, the "prickly pear" itself. "Tuna" is *atún*. Both are perfectly edible, but if you have your heart set on a tunafish sandwich, a serving of prickly pears may not quite fill the bill.

ÚLTIMAMENTE   In correct usage not "ultimately" but "recently." *Ultimamente ha estado enferma* = "She's been sick of late." For "ultimately," use *al final* or *a fin de cuentas*. *A fin de cuentas, es su decisión* = "Ultimately it is his decision."

VACUNAR   See *carpeta* above—and fast!

VAGO   This word means "vague" when applied to things, but it means "bum" or "tramp" when used for people. "Vagabond" is a good cognate for this usage. To express "vague," use *vago*, carefully, and use *impreciso* when referring to people or when there's any chance of being misinterpreted.

VOLUBLE   Those of you who studied your vocabulary lessons in high school will remember that this means "talkative." In Spanish, though, it means "unreliable," "flighty," or "fickle" and is a good deal more common than its English cognate.

ZORRA   "Foxy lady," even before Jimi Hendrix's time, has been a slangy way to refer to an attractive female. And "a fox," by itself, means much the same thing for either men or women. Slang is a dangerous thing to translate literally, however, and there is no better example of this than the Spanish word *zorra*, or "fox" (i.e., a canine of the genus Vulpes). When applied figuratively to human beings, it means "shrew," "slut," or "prostitute." What better way to learn your tricksters than to get a slap in the face? If you must use corny come-ons, stick to *guapo* and *guapa*.

4 OUR FELLOW HUMAN BEINGS

As we go about our daily lives, we are often put to the task of describing our fellow human beings. And the vast range of personalities these humans represent requires an equally vast vocabulary of descriptive terms. Rare is it indeed to encounter a person whose behavior can be wrapped up in so simple a concept as "good" or "evil." Instead, human behavior runs the gamut from charming to wicked, honest to malicious, overbearing to submissive, and happy to forlorn—sometimes even on the same day. For each of these many states and traits, you will need words in Spanish.

Of course, learning all of the epithets employed to describe human personalities would be the intellectual equivalent of memorizing a thesaurus. You could do that, naturally, but since you'll be wanting to save a little brain space for such things as nouns and verbs, it's better to concentrate on a few common ways of referring to other individuals. Thus what follows is by no means an exhaustive list of all Spanish words describing people but rather a collection of some of the most useful ones—ones you will probably hear, and may even be called, in the company of Spanish speakers.

Where appropriate, rough English equivalents are provided. The translations serve more to highlight the Spanish word's relative strength and connotations than to provide a literal translation. As in any language, you should choose your words carefully when referring to other people. When in doubt, a good rule is to use them for the first time when the person being described is not within hearing range. Outside of a language-learning context, of course, this is called gossip. But since you're still learning, it's allowed.

THE GOOD

Unless you are at a particularly low point in a mood swing, you will probably concur that when all is said and done, there are still a few good people out there. And with luck and perseverance, you may even meet one of them. When you do, it's important to be ready with the appropriate verbal match for your smile and that warm feeling in your belly.

A good way to convey this sensation is by telling a person you like them. Conveying this in Spanish, though, requires careful attention to differences in degree and intensity of the words. If you guide yourself by the dictionary, for instance, you will think that *querer* means "to like." This is true—up to a point—but what a dictionary often doesn't tell you is just how strong the "liking" reflected by *querer* really is. The distinction is important, since saying *te quiero* to someone whom you just "like" could provoke a considerably stronger reaction than you bargained for. *Te quiero* means "I love you"—in some contexts even "I want you"—and is virtually synonymous with the magic words *Te amo*. Suppose someone asks, "What do you think of my boyfriend?" If you try to say "I like him" with a response like *Lo quiero*, expect to be misunderstood: what you are really saying is "I want him," as in "I want him for myself." Such slips of the tongue could prove fatal.

So how do you say "Hey, you're not such a bad bloke" in Spanish? The simplest formula throughout the Spanish-speaking world is to use *caer bien*—literally "to fall well." *Ese señor me cae bien* is the common, colloquial, and nonintimate way of saying "I like that fellow." It is equally safe in direct speech. *¿Sabes? me caes bien* = "You know, I like you." This useful phrase will never fail to get your message across loudly, clearly, and without confusion and misinterpretation.

But, you say, my dictionary also says to use *gustar* for "to like," as in *Me gustan las tortillas*. True—up to that point, again. *Gustar* with people is a slightly different matter. *Me gusta Paco* does mean "I like Paco," but it carries many of the connotations and commitments implied in *Quiero a Paco*. "I fancy Paco" might be a good English equivalent. If you're male and you say *Me gusta Paco*, expect to receive funny looks. *Paco me cae bien* is presumably what you want to say.

As long as you're looking through the dictionary, you may also discover *agradar*. This verb does work for "I like you" (*Me agradas*) without the romantic overtones, but it can sound a little forced or formal.

Presumably your descriptions of others will occasionally go beyond the fact that you like them or dislike them. You'll want to describe, for the benefit of your listener, what kind of person Juan or Juanita is. If Juan is a "nice guy," for instance, you could say *es un buen tipo, es buena persona,* or *es buena gente* (closer to "he's good people"). These work with Juanita as well, with one important exception: when referring to women, note that *tipa* is derogatory. Thus *Es una buena tipa* sounds inherently contradictory—kind of like saying "She's a nice bitch"—and should be avoided. Regional expressions of general approval abound. In Mexican slang a likable person will often be described by saying simply *Es buena onda,* roughly "He's (or she's) cool."

Once you've mastered how to say you like a person, you'll want to delve deeper and learn words for specific personality traits. For the purposes of learning some of these, we'll divide positive personality traits into four entirely arbitrary groups: the *amables,* or "nice" people; the *simpáticos,* or "cool" people; the *listos,* or "sharp" people; and the *serios,* or "solid" people. Try to learn at least one description from each, and you'll be well on your way to explaining why exactly a given person "falls well to you."

Note as you go that all of these words, unless otherwise stated, should be used with *ser.* In fact, using some of these words with *estar* can lead to confusion and may change the meaning altogether. Where this is the case, it is noted.

THE *AMABLES*

Let's face it: some people are just downright nice. God knows how they got that way or how they manage to stay that way, but the fact is that they are kind, warm, and caring. And—why not admit it?—we like them. On the other hand, they may never become our best friends, and our dealings with them may never transcend the simply social. In Spanish such a person could be called *amable,* equating with "kind." *Amable* is a useful, generic, and somewhat bland word, perhaps most common in the stock phrase *gracias, muy amable. Gentil* is used in much the same way, though it rings more formal. Note also that *gentil* is a trickster (see Chapter 3); it can mean "gentle," but it often covers much more.

Here are other commonly used favorable descriptions that fall roughly in this category:

GENEROSO   Works safely as "generous."

BONDADOSO   Comes closer to "charitable" and "giving."

DESPRENDIDO   A nice, multisyllabic word for "generous" in the sense of "disinterested."

ATENTO   Means "thoughtful."

DETALLISTA   Means "thoughtful," too, but goes further and is used for the sort of people who send thank-you notes and tasteful, personalized gifts. It's the same in the masculine and feminine.

CORTÉS   Means "courteous" or "polite." A common maxim in Spanish is *Lo cortés no quita lo valiente,* which, very loosely translated, means something like "Real men can be polite, too."

UNA PERSONA CONSIDERADA   A very safe cognate for "a considerate person."

UNA PERSONA COMPRENSIVA   Similar to *una persona considerada* but distinct, referring more to a very "understanding" or "compassionate" person.

DULCE   Means "sweet," a good word for some people.

ES UN ALMA DE DIOS and *ES UN PAN DE DIOS*   Expressions for extremely good-hearted people, of the sort who have never had a harsh word for anyone.

Also falling into the *amable* category are a number of words and phrases typical of polite society:

UNA FINA PERSONA   Suggests a kind, considerate person. Turned around, *una persona fina* is a well-bred, "fine" person.

EDUCADO   Often used much like *una persona fina.* Remember in passing that *educado* has a far broader meaning in Spanish than "educated" does in English (see Chapter 2). Sometimes *educado* comes closer to "classy" or "a class act" in English.

UNA PERSONA CULTA   Goes a step further, describing a dignified, tasteful individual.

THE *SIMPÁTICOS*

This is the category that would include your best friends, and the most descriptive word for them is *simpático.* This word is also a trickster, looking like "sympathetic" but meaning something quite different. A single English word doesn't really do it justice; probably you would say something like "He (or she) is great!" The younger set might find "cool" a close equivalent. Easier than translating the epithet is imagining the sort of person who would be worthy of it: a happy, friendly, attractive, charming, witty, altogether likable person.

About the only quirk to be noted about *simpático* is its use with the verb *estar,* especially in reference to members of the opposite sex and babies. In these contexts *está simpático* can sound like a backhanded compliment. For babies, it would be like saying, "What an interesting-looking child." For members of the opposite sex, especially "eligible" ones about your own age, it's on a par with saying "Well, he (or she) certainly has a good personality." Perhaps a parallel English word would be "cute," in cases when it's understood that you're deliberately not using a more flattering word. If you're trying to be nice, use *simpático* with *ser*.

If you want to pin down a *simpático*'s personality further, there is a wealth of words at your disposal:

ALEGRE   Covers "happy," "happy-go-lucky," "outgoing," and the like.

AMIGABLE   A safe cognate for "friendly," but the Spanish word is less common and more specific.

ATRACTIVO   A straightforward cognate of "attractive." Like the English word, it stresses the person's physical charms.

ENCANTADOR   A close fit for "charming."

RELAJADO   Describes a *simpático* who is "relaxed" or "laid-back."

SOCIABLE   Means "sociable" and is used to describe the outgoing, partying type.

GENIAL   A useful word, though it almost ranks as a trickster. It usually means "clever" or "great" when referring to things or ideas, and "a character" or "a wild-and-crazy guy (or gal)" when referring to people. It is usually a favorable assessment. For "genial," rely on *amable* or *amigable*.

THE *LISTOS*

Some people rank high in our esteem because they are notably "clever," "sharp," or "bright." Calling them that presupposes some intelligence on their part, but it's not the same thing as calling them "smart" or "intelligent." "Witty" might come closer, in some cases. A catch-all Spanish word for these people is *listo*, used with *ser* (with *estar* it means "ready"). This is the word for people who appeal to you on an intellectual level, people who enlighten, challenge, and entertain, people you generally like to have around.

Not all bright and witty people are likable, of course, but the ones who are can merit additional words:

GRACIOSO and **CHISTOSO**   Stress the humorous aspect of the person's personality.

ASTUTO and **ÁGIL**   Emphasize sheer mental acumen.

DESPIERTO   A close fit for "bright," suggesting one part "brilliant" and one part "bright-eyed and bushy-tailed," "lively," "energetic." Used with *estar*, of course, *despierto* simply means "awake."

THE *SERIOS*

Some people we like simply because they seem to be "good people." They are honest, forthright, hard-working, and guileless. What you see is what you get. These people tend to be our most esteemed co-workers and our counselors in times of trouble, and the best word for them in Spanish is *serio*, used, as usual, with *ser. Es una persona seria* = "He (or she) is a real straight-shooter" or "He (or she) has his (or her) act together" or even is a "together person." *Serio* does not necessarily convey the idea of a droopy-faced soul or a rigid, unyielding sort (although with *estar* it can). Instead, it refers to a reliable, trustworthy, solid individual. *Formal* means much the same, but is more, well, formal.

Since *serio* is often used to describe the ideal qualities in a professional colleague, many words in this category pop up frequently in reference to the workplace:

CAPAZ Means "capable." (Remember that *capable* is a dangerous trickster; see Chapter 3.)

TRABAJADOR Means "hard-working."

RESPONSABLE and **DEDICADO** These are our old friends "responsible" and "dedicated."

CUMPLIDO An extremely useful word for "reliable" or "competent." Saying *Es muy cumplida* about someone means "She gets the job done."

Some other qualifiers are slippery and should be used with care:

MUY VIVO Sounds very complimentary—especially considering the alternative—but this somewhat slangy expression hints that the person is "clever," "nobody's fool," and perhaps even a tad "shady," "underhanded" or "crooked." *Despierto*, noted above, is a safer choice.

MOVIDO Suffers the same fate as *muy vivo*. It refers to a very active person—a real "go-getter"—but on the downside it can imply that you're never really sure where this person is "moving," with whom, or according to whose rules.

Other "serious" words stress moral rectitude and solidness of judgment:

RECTO Highlights the person's basic decency and honesty.

HONESTO Includes "honest" but often covers a wider range of moral traits; "decent" might be a better translation. For simply "honest," *honrado* is more accurate.

UNA PERSONA DE CONFIANZA A common way to say a person can be trusted or confided in, either in the sense of personal honesty or competence.

SENSATO   Means "sensible" and is a good word to describe someone's sound judgment and solid character.

THE BAD

All of us know that if you don't have anything nice to say about a person, you shouldn't say anything at all. None of us practices this belief, though, which is why this section is needed. For unless you lead an extraordinarily blessed existence, you will probably find yourself in need of one or more of the following words sooner or later. After all, even if you don't take pleasure in verbally thrashing your fellow human being, you'll still need a few good words to describe those who do.

Spanish, alas, is a rich language for belittling others. The range of words, phrases, and expressions that can be employed to this end is practically infinite and, furthermore, varies widely from region to region. Not all of these epithets fall within the range of dignified abuse, of course, and some are so harsh and vulgar that they can reflect as poorly on the person using them as on the person for whom they are intended. For crude, harsh, and undignified abuse, flip ahead to Chapter 10.

In this section, we'll concern ourselves with descriptions for people whom you simply don't like. These people, in Spanish, can be said to "fall badly to you": *te caen mal*. The converse of *caer bien, caer mal* is the safest and most universal way of expressing dislike in Spanish. A watered-down version is *no caer bien. Pedro no me cae bien* = "I not too fond of Pedro." A "watered-up" version is *no caer nada bien. Pedro no me cae nada bien* = "I don't like Pedro at all." In many countries, local and colloquial modifications of *caer mal* have been invented. In Mexico it is common to hear that so-and-so *me cae gordo*: "falls fat to me," literally. *Me cae pesado*, or "he falls heavy to me," is the same idea. Remember to use the correct gender depending on who is "falling to you": *él me cae pesado* but *ella me cae pesada*.

As when expressing your likes, you are on shaky ground using the verb *querer* to convey dislike. *No lo quiero* means "I don't love him" or "I don't want him"—leaving a lot to the imagination of the listener. *Gustar* is also dubious. *No me gusta* suggests "He (or she) is not for me" or "is not my type."

To capture what it is about a person that "falls badly" to you, you will need to enter the world of words for negative personality traits. Again, we can divide them into four arbitrary groups: the *pesados*, or "obnoxious" people; the *imbéciles*, or "jerks"; the *malvados*, or "mean" people; and the *cochinos*, or "slobs." Remember that while these words are less likely overall to provoke a brawl than their four-lettered cousins in Chapter 10, you should still use them advisedly. Pay attention to such intangibles as tone and situation. The same word said lazily to a friend can offend or inflame a stranger. Unless otherwise noted, these epithets are best used with *ser*.

THE *PESADOS*

This group covers the obnoxious boor, and *pesado* is the word we've chosen to carry the banner. *Una persona pesada* can be anyone from a nagger to an intolerable snob. What all *pesados* have in common is that they get on our nerves after a while—in many cases after a very short while. They are not really malicious; they're just underequipped in the personality department.

Pesados tell crude jokes when no one wants to hear them, make repeated passes at the same woman, use foreign words that nobody understands, drop names, sneer at your wardrobe, flaunt theirs, gossip a lot, argue about everything, and never accept their mistakes. Thank God we're not like them! In a lighter vein, you can use *pesado* among friends or family to tell someone to behave themselves or to "lighten up." *No seas pesado*, said without much conviction, carries the same message as "Don't be a pain."

Other words explore the *pesado* phenomenon in more detail:

PEDANTE For intellectually snobbish people (the ones who use those foreign words). When we were kids, we called these people "know-it-alls." Some people may refrain from correcting your Spanish for fear of appearing *pedante*. The word can be generalized to cover anyone who has a higher opinion of himself or herself than others do. "Stuck-up" comes to mind in English.

PRESUMIDO The word you've been searching for to say "show-off." Kids who stick their neat toys in your face but don't let you play with them are *presumidos*. Ditto for adults with fancy cars.

PREPOTENTE Implies a powerful person who abuses his or her authority to the detriment of others. It's a good word for cops, judges, politicians, and bosses, providing they don't overhear you. A good English equivalent doesn't really exist.

ARROGANTE Safe for "arrogant," "excessively proud."

VANIDOSO Means "vain" but is more commonly used than its English equivalent.

SNOB or **ESNOB** This term, for better or worse, is creeping into Spanish. You may hear it, but try to use a Spanish equivalent to avoid being taken for one yourself.

CREERSE This verb, along with an appropriate adjective, will deflate a pretentious person in a hurry. Someone who tells bad jokes *se cree chistoso*; someone who wears fancy clothes *se cree elegante*; someone who uses foreign phrases *se cree inteligente*; and so on. *Se* *cree mucho*, by itself, covers the lot of these people. In other words, they believe themselves to be "great shakes," but this opinion is not widely held.

Regional words and slang expressions to cover snootiness are frequent and often the most colorful. In Mexico *sangrón* is widely if somewhat slangily used to convey "obnoxious." In Mexico, too, you can say of a snob, *Le echa mucha crema a sus tacos*, or "He (or she) puts a lot of cream on his (or her) tacos." Once I heard, in reference to a particularly stuck-up young man, that *se cree la última Pepsi del desierto* ("he thinks he's the last Pepsi in the desert"). Keep your ears open, wherever you are, and you should be able to add fun new descriptions to the stock you acquire here.

THE *IMBÉCILES*

As a rule, none of us likes stupid people. It's not a matter of their I.Q.—in fact, they may be quite intelligent—but we call them "stupid" nonetheless. These are people who do stupid things and make stupid comments. Sometimes they make us wonder how on earth anyone can be so downright, undeniably, irretrievably STUPID!

When you reach that point in your regard of a fellow human being, the word you want is *imbécil*. In truth, *estúpido* exists and is widely used as well, but it lacks the punch that *imbécil* packs. Say it with heavy, accentuated, spitting scorn on the middle syllable: *im-BE-cil*. Now throw your hand in the air as you say it, as if casting this person from the planet: *¡im-BE-cil!* Isn't this fun?

Imbécil, like "stupid," doesn't necessarily mean that the object of your scorn is unintelligent. This is a good thing, because it means you can use it on an even wider range of people: college graduates, college professors, or even college presidents, if you like. An English equivalent might be "jerk" or perhaps "stupid jerk" or even "You stupid jerk!" depending on the amount of spit and scorn you want to add. It is a multipurpose, and strong, pejorative. I once watched as an unseemly man pestered a young, well-dressed blonde woman on the subway in a major Latin American city; taking her for a tourist, he kept asking her "Whey a you from?" in barely pidgin English. Finally the woman got fed up with this harrassment, turned on the man, and spit *De aquí, ¡imbécil!* in his face. The man slinked off, humbled, and the crowd was delighted. *Estúpido* just wouldn't have worked.

The *imbécil* category includes a number of other useful descriptions for those who make a distinctly bad impression on us:

IDIOTA   Similar to *imbécil* but perhaps a shade weaker. Still, native English speakers should be warned that this word is not used nearly as casually in Spanish as in English—as in "Oh, don't be an idiot" or "What a blunder! I feel like an idiot!" Same in masculine and feminine: *él es un idiota, ella es una idiota.*

INFELIZ Less a "jerk" and more a "klutz" or a "schmuck." It is used to describe a sort of hapless clod whose luck is mostly bad, at least in part because of a lack of willpower to make it better. An *infeliz* is not necessarily a scoundrel or even an entirely unpleasant person, but you probably wouldn't want to have one as a friend. To soften the blow, qualify it with *pobre. Un pobre infeliz* = "a poor sap," "a loser," a real "sad sack."

TONTO Works as "silly" or a watered-down "fool."

PAYASO Means "clown" and is a stronger word for "fool," particularly a clumsy, oafish one.

BABOSO Less harsh than *payaso* but no less clear in its implications (it comes from *babear*, "to slobber").

TARADO A handy word suggesting that something crucial to cerebral functioning may be missing; "moron" might fit.

TARUGO A term that means "a block of wood." Applied to people, it equates nicely with "blockhead."

BURRO Meaning "donkey," the word calls to mind "dumbbell" or "dunce" and, like those words, is a favorite among schoolkids.

BOBO In the same class as *burro*, suggesting "dummy."

IGNORANTE and **CRETINO** Safe cognates that are heard on occasion.

SIMPLE Mostly a false cognate, especially when talking about people; it means "simple-minded" or "simpleton" more than "simple." If "simpleton" is the word you seek, *simplón* is even more expressive.

TORPE Means "clumsy oaf" or "klutz."

NECIO A useful word that refers more to stubbornness than stupidity, though the two often go hand in hand; "jackass" may be a good equivalent.

THE *MALVADOS*

In this group we lump people whom we consider mean, offensive, malicious, or simply "bad" people. *Malvado* is a good catchall to describe these people, especially if they have done us some harm. *Maldito* is stronger, though without being crudely so, and is invariably the word chosen in subtitled films to translate "bastard." (In Spanish *bastardo* is usually reserved for persons born out of wedlock and thus works poorly as a general-purpose insult.) Here are some other useful descriptions of this type:

MAL PARIDO and **MAL NACIDO** Meaning literally "born bad," these phrases convey the same ignominy as *malvado* but sound a bit snazzier.

SINVERGÜENZA   Literally meaning "without shame" or "scoundrel," the word suggests that this person actually enjoys being offensive. Very commonly used. Same form for masculine and feminine.

CANALLA   Refers generally to men, often a man who mistreats women. It works well for "lout." Same form for masculine and feminine.

DESGRACIADO   A common term of generic opprobrium, generally meaning an unpleasant person who has tried to do us some wrong. It also implicitly tries to write the person off as trivial and unworthy of genuine scorn. It equates fairly well with "wretch" or "sap" in English.

INFAME   A good strong word used to describe someone who, by his or her actions, has earned everlasting infamy—at least in our eyes. Murderous tyrants are *infames*; so, by extension (and slight exaggeration), is anyone who causes you genuine harm with malicious intent.

MENTIROSO   A strong word, stronger even than "liar." It suggests the person is a habitual liar and uses lies to defame and gain advantage. Be careful using it.

MALÉFICO   Describes a real evil sort, a pernicious "ne'er-do-well."

MALVIVIENTE   Literally meaning "bad-liver" (one who lives badly), the word suggests an incorrigible rogue with a long police record.

DELINCUENTE   Much the same as *malviviente*, the term means "delinquent" but stresses the criminal lifestyle that such a person has chosen. As a result of increasing drug use and the crime that goes with it, words like *mariguano* are coming into vogue to mean the same thing. To an English speaker the word calls to mind a fading hippie, but in Spanish it describes a dangerous "druggie" and is becoming the common word for scandalous and vandalous teenagers.

THE *COCHINOS*

For uncouth, classless slobs, *cochino* is the word. It is one of four common Spanish words for "pig" (the animal)—*cerdo, puerco,* and *marrano* are the others—and all work well for the human equivalent. If you dislike someone because he or she throws trash out of car windows, takes up three train seats, or burps at the dinner table, this is the category you should check. (You should be aware that the word *marrano* has a long anti-Semitic history, though it is rarely used that way today.)

GROSERO   The catchall word for "rude." *Se portó bastante grosero* would be the common way of saying "He acted quite rude," "He treated us badly."

VAGO Describes an unkempt person or "bum." (It is also the word for "vague"; see Chapter 3.)

BAJO Widely used in the phrase *un tipo de lo más bajo*, a strong denunciation that translates well as "a low-life," "creep," or even "scum." Note, however, that *Es un tipo bajo* usually just means "He's a short guy."

A number of other common words refer to general "low-class" behavior. Though most modern-day English speakers are not accustomed to think of behavioral traits in class terms, in much of the Spanish-speaking world the class distinction is still a strong one. Words like *corriente, vulgar,* and *ordinario* denote little more than "common" or "characteristic of the masses," but all three connote "uncouth," "slobbish," or "classless" (as in "he has no class") when used to refer to people. *Un hombre corriente* can be expected to meet his dinner guests unshaven, in boxer shorts and scratching his paunch. *Inculto* falls into this group as well. It means "uncultured" but is much broader and more frequently heard than its English cognate; an *inculto* not only doesn't appreciate Mozart but plays his radio too loud.

THE INDIFFERENT

We have looked at the human race from both sides now. We have met the lowest of the low, the snobs and scoundrels, and learned what to call them. We have also been introduced to the crème de la crème, the well-bred gentlefolk, and have had a few charmed words with them. But what about the rest of the world's inhabitants—that gray, faceless mass that hovers uncertainly between good and evil? What do you say to describe a "nowhere type," a fair-to-middling sort, a person who's nothing to write home about and just like the next guy, only less so? What do you say about people when there isn't much to say about them one way or the other?

A number of unspectacularly adequate Spanish words rise humbly to the task. *Regular, normal,* and *común* all make the grade, though you should be alert to their idiosyncrasies. *Regular* with *estar*, for example, is a notch or two below "regular" on the scale of descriptive tags; whereas in English it means "average," in Spanish it is closer to "fair" or even "not so hot," especially when referring to objects. *Está regular el camino* does not mean "It's an average road" but rather "It's a pretty lousy road." "Regular" in the sense of "consistent" is *regular* with *ser*. Be alert to the distinction: *Es un cliente regular* would be "He's a steady customer," while *Ese cliente está regular* suggests the customer is a lousy tipper or otherwise "fair." Using *asiduo* instead of *regular* to describe the steady customer can avoid a potential misunderstanding and win you brownie points for using a good Spanish word.

Normal is the best all-around word for the "nothing-special" category. *Mediocre* carries a clear connotation of insufficiency, as does its cognate in English. Other words—specifically *corriente* and *ordinario*—are listed in dictionaries as synonyms for "normal" or "ordinary," but in fact can be charged with negative meaning when used to label people, as noted above. *Común* works in the expression *un hombre común*, meaning "common folk" or "the man on the street." *Común y corriente* is a good translation for "run-of-the-mill," without the negative connotations of *corriente* by itself. Still, your safest bet in almost every circumstance involving people is *normal*.

In situations where physical appearance is being commented on, a different set of words takes over. A person whose looks are "nothing special" could be described as *pasadero* or *pasable*, meaning "acceptable" or "tolerable" in the sense of "if nothing better comes along." A useful, if regional, slang phrase for "not bad" (or "not great") is *dos tres*; it works equally well for people, places, and things and sounds, to my ear, a lot better than *así así*, which every textbook will tell you means "so-so." *Más o menos* (technically, "more or less") is also commonly used in Spanish, even when there's no indication of what is being compared: *¿Qué tal la película? Más o menos.* = "How was the film?" "Not bad." Sometimes in slang *más o menos* gets shortened to *ma' o meno'* in this usage.

Some fun expressions for saying "nothing special" employ neither-nor constructions. A Peruvian, for instance, might say someone is *ni chicha ni limoná*, where *chicha* is a local alcoholic drink and *limoná* is "lemonade." The idea is that the person is neither alcoholic nor nonalcoholic—that is, isn't anything well-defined. "Neither here nor there" comes out as *ni de aquí ni de allá. Ni pinta ni da color* means that someone (or something) "neither paints nor adds color," suggesting that there is no real reason for this person or thing to exist at all.

Another common way of saying "no great shakes" is *nada del otro mundo* (literally, "nothing from the other world"). Another handy phrase is *Es cosa de cada domingo* ("It's an every-Sunday thing"), equating with "a dime a dozen" and showing that you are distinctly unimpressed. *No es nada fuera de lo común* is good but a bit stilted for "It's nothing out of the ordinary." When you are completely unimpressed by something or someone, but still unwilling to turn it or them down, resort to *peor es nada*—the correct rendering for "better than nothing."

TEMPORARY STATES

Since we've spent so much of this chapter name-calling, it's only decent of us to finish by noting that most bad traits are only temporary and that most people, if we'd only give them time and get to know them, would soon return to being their real sweet, lovable selves. With this is mind, you'll need the proper vocabulary to describe these warm and caring individuals who just happen to be acting like miserable worms at the moment.

One way to get this across is by using *estar*, the Verb of Temporary States, but not simply as a substitute for *ser*. Instead, by inserting *de* between *estar* and your adjective, you change "He's an S.O.B. (or whatever)!" to "He's being an S.O.B.!" Thus *Es un grosero* describes a permanently rude, coarse, and unpleasant man; *Está de grosero* describes a man who is acting rudely. *Es un presumido* = "He's a show-off"; *Está de presumido* = "He's showing off."

This construction is especially useful for capturing moods. For instance, *Está de pesado* = "He's in a lousy mood." Two other key phrases for moods employ the generic terms *buenas* and *malas*. *Está de buenas* means someone is "in a good mood." *Está de malas* is the dreaded opposite.

Estar de can also be used instead of *ser* for ironic effect. For instance, *Está de generoso* suggests that someone who usually isn't generous is for some reason suddenly giving away the store. Saying that a child *está de obediente* suggests that the child's obedient behavior is indeed most unusual. *Estar de* can likewise be used to explain away behavior as a temporary aberration: *Estoy de tarado* = "I'm acting a little stupid." It should be noted that some adjectives by their very meaning resist the *estar de* construction; it is hard, for instance, to imagine someone being *infame* for only a few minutes or so.

5 THE SECRET LIFE OF VERBS

Many students of Spanish can still recall their first encounter with Spanish verbs. Often the reaction was something like, "What do you mean it has different endings in every tense? What on earth for? Aaaarrgh!"

Alas, for verb endings there is little alternative but to buckle down and memorize them. But even when you've managed to separate -*aban* from -*aron*, another unappetizing task awaits: using each ending and each tense and mode in the right situation. To English speakers the idea of an imperfect tense is unfamiliar, while the notion of a frequently used subjunctive mode can seem downright perverse. Can't verbs be made just a little easier?

The answer is yes. There are several pointers on the use of the tenses that will make learning them a less doleful task. And there are a couple of obvious pitfalls that anyone wandering into the world of tenses should be alert to. This chapter presumes you have some background knowledge on the use of tenses in Spanish; even so, I'll try to summarize some of the basics of tense usage to refresh your memory.

THE PRESENT

The present is the most straightforward of tenses in Spanish and corresponds almost perfectly to the present tense in English: *bailo* is "I dance," *estoy bailando* is "I am dancing," and so on. For the English compound present ("I do dance"), in Spanish you can slip a *sí* ("yes") into the phrase. "He does eat a lot" = *El sí come mucho*. "But, honey, I *do* love you" = *Pero cariño, sí te quiero.* Note that in English the present progressive is used far more than in Spanish. Thus "She's going" should almost always be rendered *Se va* and only rarely *Se está yendo.*

One tip on the present tense: it is used much more in Spanish for future events than its English equivalent. For instance, the common way to ask "Are you coming tomorrow?" is simply *¿Vienes mañana?* "We'll see you later" often gets rendered *Nos vemos*—literally, "We see each other." This trick works even when you're specifying a future time or date. *Te lo doy el martes* = "I'll give it to you Tuesday." In Spanish the context makes it clear that the future is being referred to. Compare these examples:

> *Te cuento.* = "I'll tell you (now)."
> *Te contaré.* = "I'll tell you (someday)."
> *Mañana te cuento.* = "I'll tell you tomorrow."
> *Mañana te contaré.* = "I shall tell you tomorrow."

THE FUTURE

The future is not a particularly hard tense to learn, and when to use it is pretty obvious. Still, it can be simplified considerably by remembering the following rule: ignore it.

What? Just forget about the future? Well, maybe not altogether. There are a few uses for the future in common spoken Spanish. But most of the time you can avoid it outright, and you'll even sound more fluent by doing so.

The two most frequent substitutes for the future tense in Spanish are the "present-as-future," discussed above, and the compound future using the verb *ir* ("to go"), just as in English. *Mañana voy a llamar a mi hermano* = "Tomorrow I'm going to call my brother." In common Spanish usage, one of these two constructions almost always replaces the future tense, although the future can be used and is certainly understood: *Mañana llamaré a mi hermano.* Sometimes, though, the future sounds formal, stiff, and even awkward. *Vuelvo en seguida* = "I'll be right back." *Volveré en seguida* = "I will return promptly."

One special use of the future that anyone aspiring to fluency must learn is what is called the "future of uncertainty." It is a very common construction that has no real equivalent in English—which is why many students shudder at the mere thought of it. The best way to get a grip on it is by example. You often hear it, for instance, when someone knocks unexpectedly on the door. "Who could that be?"

you'd blurt out in English. *¿Quién será!* you'd say in Spanish. Other examples: *¿Habrá más!* = "Might there be more?" *¿Estará en casa!* = "Do you suppose he's at home?" And so on.

The future of uncertainty, applied to the past, uses the compound future perfect tense. That sounds difficult, but really it works out to sticking *habrá* or an equivalent in front of the past participle of your choice. *¿Quién habrá sido!* ("Who might that have been?"), you might wonder on hearing a strange voice on your answering machine. *¿No habrán querido asustarme!* = "You don't suppose they wanted to scare me, do you?"

THE CONDITIONAL

The conditional is a very predictable tense, conveying thoughts in Spanish that in English rely on the auxiliary "would." It's an easy tense to understand intuitively. "I'd like to eat now" is expressed as *Me gustaría comer ahora.* "You would have liked it" = *Te habría gustado."*

One special warning applies for the conditional: note that in English we occasionally use "would" for repeated past actions, as in "His father would eat every night at seven sharp." This construction in Spanish calls for the imperfect—in fact, it's a textbook example of when the imperfect is needed: *Su padre cenaba todas las noches a las siete en punto.* If you think about it long enough, it becomes clear why this is not a true conditional, in either English or Spanish. But if you're simply translating your "woulds," it's easy to make this mistake.

THE PRETERIT VERSUS THE IMPERFECT

This face-off is one of the trickiest in Spanish, mostly because in English we often gloss over the distinction. We do have the progressive past, of course, in such constructions as "He was flying a kite," but not all "ongoing" past activities use it. In many cases, you'll have to slow your translating computer down a few megas and think about exactly what kind of past action you are describing.

Basically the Spanish imperfect covers two constructions:

1. The progressive past, including actions that are taking place over a period of time in the past, usually in relation to some other action that happened suddenly. For example, "He was sleeping when the alarm went off." Or "She was overseas when the new president was elected." Keep your eye (and your mind's eye, if you're speaking) out for these juxtapositions; they represent one of the most common uses of the imperfect. Because of the explicit juxtaposition, these are also the easiest situations to recognize as an opportunity for the imperfect.

2. Actions that took place over a period of time in the past, often keyed to the English constructions "used to" and, on occasion, "would" (see "The Conditional" above). This second common use of the imperfect is indispensable in describing the way things were: "I used to work nights" is expressed as *Yo trabajaba de noche.* The key words aren't always present, though. "When I was a kid, the teachers beat the students" would be *Cuando yo era niño, los maestros golpeaban a los estudiantes.*

The problem of the disappearing key words can be seen in the following sentences. Just as you could say "My father ate at seven every night," "My father used to eat at seven," or "My father would eat at seven," you could just as easily state, pure and simple, "My father ate at seven." Grammatically this last example is correct, but it is confusing without a clarifying context. Did he eat at seven o'clock just once, or did he always eat at seven? Spanish lets you make the distinction in the verb itself: *cenó a las siete* is clear in communicating that he ate at seven on a certain occasion; *cenaba a las siete,* using the imperfect, indicates that it was his custom to eat at seven night after night.

Understanding this distinction will clear up a lot of the conflicts between imperfect and preterit, but incorporating that knowledge into your storytelling skills will take some time and practice. Often, when relating a story, you'll have to jump nimbly back and forth from imperfect to preterit, and this requires analyzing each action as it pops up.

Let's say this father usually ate at nine, but on one particular night he ate at seven; while he was eating, he found a fly in his soup and fainted. What tenses will make this meaning clear in Spanish? First, we have to explain that the father used to eat or usually ate (*cenaba*) at nine; on the night in question, though, he ate (*cenó*) at seven. While he was eating (*cenaba*—the imperfect again), he found a fly in his soup (*encontró una mosca en la sopa*—preterit) and fainted (*se desmayó*—also preterit).

Sometimes, the differences between past and imperfect are subtle to the point of near invisibility. In these cases, native Spanish speakers will sense the distinction, but they have a hard time explaining it you. Let's say you answer the phone and your boyfriend is on the other end. He could ask, *¿Qué estabas haciendo?* Or he might ask, *¿Qué estuviste haciendo?* What's the difference? In the first example, using the imperfect in the auxiliary, he is asking what you were doing in relation to a sudden action—presumably, the ringing of the phone. That is, "What are you doing right now (besides talking on the telephone)?" In the second example, he is asking what you were doing, with the idea that you may have finished by now. "What have you done all day?" or "What have you been up to?" is closer. Of course, if he wanted to be completely clear, he could ask ¿Qué hacías or ¿Qué hiciste hoy? or ¿Qué has estado haciendo? and so on. But where's the romance in that?

The important thing in these borderline cases is not to learn the "right" form. (In fact, your boyfriend would probably just ask ¿Qué haces?) The important thing is to search for the distinctions in these close cases to get a feel for past tenses that will serve to guide you when no key words or juxtapositions are there to help you along.

Let's take a final borderline example. You were at home last night. But do you use the imperfect or the preterit to convey that to your listener? Again, it depends. Both could be correct, but estaba en casa suggests you were there for the duration and something sudden or specific happened during this time: Estaba en casa cuando se fue la luz ("I was at home when the lights went out"). The juxtaposition may be implied, not stated, but you create the expectation of one by using the imperfect. In other words, Estaba en casa anoche in effect prompts the question "And what happened?" Estuve en casa is a much more basic, self-contained, declarative sentence. It just says you were at home, period. In this sense, it's a safer, more all-purpose choice than estaba.

SPECIAL CASES

In Spanish the tense of certain verbs is almost as important as word choice in getting your point across correctly, and students of the language are generally unaware of the subtle twists they can give these verbs by their choice of tense. Yet by manipulating the tenses well, you can discover ways to express familiar English phrases in correct, colloquial Spanish.

For instance, querer ("to want") changes its meaning on the trip from preterit to imperfect. Consider the case of quisieron (preterit) and querían (imperfect). Both mean "they wanted," but a native Spanish speaker hears a difference. The former suggests that they wanted to do something (and they did it). Thus their "wanting" came to an end, at least for a while, so the verb goes into the preterit as a done deal. Querían, the imperfect, suggests they wanted to do something and, evidently, they still want to. That is, they wanted but were unable to do something. Thus, Quisieron ir al cine and Querían ir al cine both mean "They wanted to go to the movies," but with a difference. The preterit conveys the idea that they wanted to go the movies, so they went. The imperfect suggests that they wanted to go the movies but didn't—maybe after seeing the ticket prices.

The imperfect can also be used to say that they wanted to do something and perhaps eventually did do it, but not before something else intervened making that possible. For example, *Querían ir al cine, y los mandé* ("They wanted to go to the movies, so I sent them"). The use of *quisieron* implies that they would have gone without waiting for someone to send them. As in the earlier example about being at home, an imperfect on its own almost seems to raise the question *¿Y qué pasó?* It is, so to speak, the tense in which the other shoe is always waiting to drop.

In the negative, the preterit-imperfect distinction is sharper still. *No quería ir a la fiesta* implies "I didn't want to go to the party (but I went along anyway)," perhaps to avoid offending the host. *No quise ir a la fiesta* says bluntly "I didn't want to go to the party (so I didn't)." Very often, *querer* in the preterit and negative translates best as "to refuse." *No quisieron dar sus nombres* = "They refused to give their names."

Similar changes occur to the verb *poder* ("to be able") when it makes the switch from preterit to imperfect. *Mi hermano podía romperme la cabeza* suggests "My brother had the physical force necessary to bust my head," while *Mi hermano pudo romperme la cabeza* suggests that on the occasion in question he put this theoretical force to the test. In the preterit, in other words, *poder* means you not only could do something but actually did do it. *El podía nombrar todas las capitales del mundo* ("He could name all of the world's capitals") might be said of a smart lad. *El pudo nombrar todas las capitales del mundo* means the tyke was actually put to the test—and succeeded ("He was able to name all of the world's capitals").

As with *querer*, the distinction is sharper in the negative. *No podía caminar* might mean that your feet hurt after a long hike and you spent a day cuddled up on the couch watching sitcoms. *No pude caminar* suggests you actually tried to walk and fell on your face. In general, the preterit with *no poder* implies a fairly formidable obstacle and suggests that an unsuccessful effort was at least made. The imperfect with *no poder* is much less definite and does not hint that an effort was made. To take an extreme example, *No podía volar del techo de la casa* is stating the obvious: "I wasn't able to fly off the roof of my house." *No pude volar del techo de la casa* are words that, if uttered at all, would most likely be uttered in an ICU ward by a sheepish lunatic—that is, after trying to fly and failing.

The last common verb whose meaning varies significantly between the imperfect and the preterit is *saber* ("to know"). In fact, this variation causes students of Spanish no end of confusion. It seems unjust that such everyday statements as "I didn't know that!" and "Did you know he was coming?" require a brain-racking choice of tense.

In fact, with *saber* the difference is usually quite clear-cut. Here's a rule of thumb that works well most of the time: use the imperfect. In the preterit *saber* usually means "to find out." Some examples are in order. *No sabía eso* = "I didn't know that." *Sabía que llegarías* = "I knew you'd show up." *¿Sabías hablar español cuando llegaste aquí?* = "Did you know how to speak Spanish when you got here?" In the preterit, in contrast, *saber* generally refers to sudden knowledge about a specific event. *Supe que habías llegado* = "I heard (I found out, word reached me) that you had arrived." *¿Supiste . . . ?* in particular is almost always used for "Did you hear . . . ?" and implies some new gossip, revelation, or fast-breaking news. *¿Supiste que gané la lotería?* = "Did you know (hear) that I won the lottery?"

SER VERSUS ESTAR

In Spanish the question is not so much "to be or not to be?" but "to be (*ser*) or to be (*estar*)?" These two verbs are the source of constant headaches and frequent errors for even intermediate and advanced students of Spanish. Native Spanish speakers intuitively choose the correct form without so much as a thought. You should be so lucky.

One modern Spanish dictionary, in its introduction, makes this very point (and rather smugly, I thought): "[Foreigners] should know, so that they realize that the distinction between *ser* and *estar* is clear and precise and that it is just a matter of managing to penetrate the distinct nature of both verbs, that Spaniards, even the most uncultured ones, never use them wrong."*

As a foreigner, of course, you will use them wrong, and about 10 percent of the cases will still seem mystifying to you even years after you learn the common usages. But in at least 90 percent of the cases the distinction between *ser* and *estar* is "clear and precise"—or at least pretty easy to guess. As for that other 10 percent, well, you gotta leave something to learn as you get older!

THE EASY ONES

Ser is the verb "to be" for things that are That Way, period. They're not that way in relation to something else, or at certain times

---

*Maria Moliner, *Diccionario de uso del español* (Madrid: Editorial Gredos, 1990), 1:1219.

of day, or in the spring or the fall, or only in election years. They are that way because they were born that way and they will presumably remain that way until the day they die. *Ser* is a solid, upstanding verb—one that you can rely on to give you the same answer time and time again.

Estar, in comparison, is a flake. It is the variable, flighty, here-today-gone-tomorrow verb "to be." *Estar* covers personality traits that are ephemeral and ethereal. It describes things that change from one minute to the next. It's an all-over-the-place, outta-control kind of verb. It's untrustworthy. It's slippery. You would never buy a used car from a verb like *estar*.

Let's take an example. Say your boss is a fool. *Es una tonta*, you might say (though perhaps not to her face). But let's also say that she spent all morning collecting mud samples and is now absolutely filthy. *Es una tonta* and *está mugrienta*. What's more, in a moment of inspired honesty, you told her that she looked like something that just crawled out from under a rock, and now she's mad—*está enojada*. Just like her to get so upset about a casual observation, you think. She's so sensitive—*es tan sensible*.

As you can see, we're getting a good picture of your boss: *es una tonta* and *es muy sensible* (all the time), and *está mugrienta* and *está enojada* (this afternoon). Probably not the best time to be kicking back and reading a book, come to think of it.

Some words flat out change in meaning depending on whether they are governed by *ser* or *estar*, and they can help us "penetrate" those "distinct natures" we've been told so much about. Here's a rule that can be applied in most cases: if you can add a "now" or "at the moment" to your description, you should be using *estar*. If not, leave it to *ser. Es un borracho*, for instance, means that someone is a "drunkard"—a habitual drunk or a wino. *Está borracho*, on the other hand, means "He is drunk (at the moment)." *Es callado* refers to a man who is "quiet," not at any given moment but as a way of life—it's his nature; he is a person who keeps to himself and speaks softly and rarely. To say of another man *está callado* means something quite different: he is quiet—now. We are given no insight to his overall personality; we just know that in this place and at this time, he's keeping his mouth shut.

Learning and reviewing examples is a good way to absorb the essential difference between *ser* and *estar*. But a few other specific tips may be helpful as well.

1. Use *ser* for general, permanent physical appearance: tall, dark, handsome, short, light-skinned, ugly. (An exception will be dealt with in a moment.) Use *estar* for any temporary physical condition: pale, flushed, disheveled, unshaven, and so on.

2. For quantities, numerical or otherwise, always use *ser: somos veinte personas, es mucho, era poco, son dos.*

3. For possession, use *ser: es mío, es de él, son de las señoras, son suyos.*

4. Location is always the province of *estar.* This might throw you if you think of the location of, say, a building as fairly unchanging. But location is an implicit recognition of an object's relation to other things—not a reflection of its indelible self—and thus is a job for *estar.*

5. With all adverbs, adverbial expressions, and present participle forms or gerunds (the "-ing" form), use *estar: está bien, están en buenas condiciones, está lloviendo, estoy nadando.*

6. With all nouns, use *ser.* If you have trouble recognizing nouns, a good device is to key on the presence of the indefinite article (*un, una, unos, unas*). Thus *es un doctor, eres una tonta, es un santo,* and so on. When the article is missing, as it often is in Spanish (that is, *es doctor*), you'll just have to remember that it could be used in that situation and therefore it's a noun that requires *ser.*

GETTING TRICKY: THE PAST PARTICIPLES

With past participles (the "-ed" form in English, the *-ado* and *-ido* forms in Spanish), things start to get tricky. Both *estar* and *ser* can be used, but they mean different things. With *estar* the participle is generally being used as an adjective and to describe a passing state. *Estaba agotado* means "He was worn out (at that moment)."

With *ser* the past participle is generally used to form a passive construction or a predicate noun. In the case of the passive, you implicitly ask (and often must explicitly state) "whodunnit?"—that is, who or what caused the action. *Fue agotado,* for instance, means "He was worn out," meaning something or someone wore him out. A few past participles are used with *ser* without any explicit causal agent, including *conocido, sabido, tardado,* and *parecido.*

Some examples may help clarify the distinction between *ser* and *estar.* Say you went on an expedition to a remote patch of rainforest. When you got there, though, you found that it had recently been bulldozed. On your return, someone may ask, "How was the forest?" You could reply using either *Estaba destruído,* referring to its destroyed state, or *Fue destruído,* meaning essentially "It has been destroyed" and calling attention to the fact that someone or something destroyed it. In English both senses can be covered by "It was destroyed." Spanish makes a finer distinction.

Another example: you can say both *Las tiendas son cerradas a las nueve* and *Las tiendas están cerradas a las nueve.* What's the difference? With *ser* you are saying that the stores are physically closed by someone at nine 'o clock sharp. That is when the doors are shut and the keys turn in the locks. With *estar* you are saying that if you go to the commercial district at nine you will find the stores closed. They may have been closed at eight, or at six, or at five minutes to nine, but in any case you will find that they are closed at nine. In other words, *Son cerradas a las nueve* = "They close at nine"; *Están cerradas a las nueve* = "They are closed by nine."

Finally, an example you will want to study assiduously if you are of the married persuasion: *soy casado* versus *estoy casado*. Some will argue that there's no big difference here. Others will say there's a world of difference. Basically, *soy casado* is "I'm a married man." It describes a permanent state. *Estoy casado* means "I'm married," but some feel it implies "for the moment" or "at present," something akin to "I am passing through a married phase at the moment." (*Estoy de casado* would say that unambiguously.) Nonetheless, a man wouldn't say *soy casado con* (wife's name) but *estoy casado con* (wife's name). In the past tense, the distinction becomes very clear: *Fui casado con María* means "I was (forcibly) married to María (and may still be)." *Estuve casado con María* means "I was married to María (who is now my ex-wife)."

Look at the following examples and practice separating them in your mind:

> *Fue cambiado.* = "It was changed (by someone)."
> *Estaba cambiado.* = "It was (looked) changed."
> *Fue dormido.* = "It was put to sleep."
> *Estaba dormido.* = "It was asleep."
> *Fue roto.* = "It was broken (by someone)."
> *Estaba roto.* = "It was (already) broken."

THE HARD ONES: DESCRIPTIVE ADJECTIVES

Don't worry about mastering the gray areas between *ser* and *estar* from the start. It's enough to know why the differences exist so as to incorporate them intuitively as you go along. With practice, the light gray areas will get progressively lighter and the pitch-black regions will soon turn a sort of dark gray. Examining examples and asking yourself why? is the best way to start shedding light on the matter. Some dubious cases of *ser* versus *estar* follow. Absorb them at your own pace.

Perhaps you've noticed in your dealings in Spanish that to compliment someone on, say, his beauty, you use *estar: Estás guapo*. But aren't you in a sense suggesting that his beauty is just a temporary state, that you're saying, "You are beautiful today (but not as a general rule)?" Some compliment! There's a kernel of truth in your suspicion, but perhaps because of human vanity, such a comment is generally taken favorably to mean "You look especially beautiful today."

Compliments highlight one of the largest zones of overlap between *ser* and *estar*, the descriptive adjectives. For instance, if someone is tall, they are presumably tall all the time, and we would correctly expect *es alto* to convey that. So what the devil are we to make of *está alto*, which you will undoubtedly come across sooner or later? Certainly you can't temporarily be tall?

In general, using *estar* with adjectives is a way of highlighting the immediate and subjective nature of a perception—"This is my impression" or "This seems especially that way to me now." *Es alto* means "He is tall." *Está alto* means, more or less, "He's so tall," "He's much taller than I thought," "Gosh, he's tall." To say "He's tall for his age," for instance, you would use *Está alto para su edad*. If he were tall, period—in other words, a tall person—you would simply say *Es alto*.

Let's take another adjective. *Es feo* would be "He is ugly"—no debate permitted or even needed. Look up "ugly" in the dictionary and you'll find his picture alongside. Follow him home and he'll have ugly parents. So what's left for *Está feo*? It could mean "He's temporarily ugly"—because of a horrible haircut, for instance. Or it could suggest "He sure looks ugly to me" or "He really is ugly."

Becoming adept at making this distinction is a matter of time and exposure. What's the difference, for instance, between *es difícil* and *está difícil*? Roughly, *es difícil* describes something that is always difficult and notoriously so: say, swimming the English Channel or learning Chinese. *Está difícil* suggests that something that has come up is difficult or that something is harder than was expected. *Es difícil aprender la diferencia entre* ser *y* estar = "It is difficult to learn the difference between *ser* and *estar*." *Está difícil aprender la diferencia entre* ser *y* estar = "I'm having real trouble with this *ser* and *estar* business."

Now how about *es viejo* versus *está viejo*? The first example means someone is old, period—a senior citizen. The second, with *estar*, is much more subjective and can cover a wide range of English translations, including "He feels old," "He looks (seems) old," and "He is too old (for some specific task)." A similar case is *ser joven* versus *estar joven*. *Soy joven* means "I am young (i.e., a member of the group of young people)." *Estoy joven* covers anything from "I feel young" to "I'm young (for my position)" to "I'm still young" (a washed-up pitcher to his coach), and so on. Note the difference in the past: *Cuando eras joven* = "When you were young (a youngster)." *Cuando estabas joven* = "When you still had some pep (weren't over-the-hill)."

How about *es buena* versus *está buena* in reference to, say, a film? Again, the key is in the subjective appreciation. After seeing it

and liking it, you might say *Está buena la película* to communicate
your personal approval. You could use *Es buena*, too, but there you'd
be declaring "It is a good film"—well done, professionally made, with
good actors, and the recipient perhaps of several awards. If after seeing
the film you say *Es una buena película*, you are subtly implying "It
was good, but . . . . " In my experience, people seem to say *Es una
buena película* in reference to arty films—ones they presume to be
"good" but didn't understand or particularly enjoy.

Some final examples will call attention to an advanced aspect
of the distinction with descriptive adjectives. If a person has a permanent physical illness (polio, for instance), he or she can still be described using *está enfermo* or *está enferma*. *Está enferma desde niña* =
"She's been ill since childhood." Likewise, the adjective *loco* is generally used with *estar*, even when referring to someone who has spent
fifty years in an insane asylum. You would say *está loco* of this person,
less commonly *es loco*. Why? Because illness and insanity, as in these
cases, are not an essential part of the person's character but an excep-
tional, uncharacteristic condition. That is, it is not in their very nature
as people to be sick; it is a condition, a state, an exception. When adjectives like *enfermo* and *loco* are made into nouns, though, they are
used with *ser*—but usually only with a preceding indefinite article: *Es
un enfermo* = "He's sick (a sick person)."

The extreme application of the "essential nature" principle is
está muerto and *está muerta*, which is the only way to say "He (or
she) is dead." Students, understandably, balk at this one, since for most
of us death is considered a fairly permanent state, worthy of *ser*. Actually, the use of *estar* makes sense if you take the perspective of the
individual involved: being dead may be a lasting experience, but it's
not an essential aspect of the individual's nature. When the person is
remembered and eulogized years later, people won't say "He (or she)
was a good person, a kind person, and a dead person." Besides, *Es
muerto* means "He is killed"—the use of *ser* and a past participle in a
passive construction. An illustrative if redundant example containing
both would be *Fue muerto a tiros, y ahora está muerto*, literally "He
was killed by shots, and now he's dead."

SORTING OUT *SER* AND *ESTAR*
IN THE IMPERATIVE

Imperatives are a source of some added confusion with *ser* and
estar. I've never found a good rule governing their usage in the imperative, so I'll invent one: avoid using either of them in the imperative,
but if you must, always use *ser*. It's a fairly drastic rule, and exceptions
can of course be found if you want to get picky. But it will do for the
most part.

Why avoid imperatives with the "to be" verbs? Because Spanish, unlike English, does not lend itself to them as a rule. In English you can without hesitation say "Be good," "Be on time," "Be there," "Don't worry, be happy," and so on. To translate these constructions into Spanish, you would almost always resort to a verb other than the "to be" verbs: *Pórtate bien, Llega a tiempo, Asiste, Anímate.* If you insisted on using a "to be" verb in Spanish, you would almost always use *ser*, even when referring to a transitory state: you would say *Sé amable,* for instance, to express "Be friendly," even if you meant it only for a short while. *Sé amable con tu abuela, sólo nos visita de vez en cuando* = "Be friendly to your grandmother, she only visits us from time to time."

Encouraging you to avoid using "to be" in the imperative in Spanish is not to say that you won't hear it. It's not an especially common construction, but neither is it rare. Here are some examples you may run across:

>   *Sé puntual.* = "Be on time."
>   *Sé buena gente.* = "Be a nice guy (or gal)."
>   *Estate quieto.* = "Be still." (said to children)
>   *Estate callado.* = "Be quiet." (said to children)

The imperative with both *ser* and *estar* is much more frequent in the negative in Spanish:

>   *No seas malo.* = "Be a pal."
>   *No seas tonto.* = "Don't be a fool."
>   *No seas imbécil.* = "Don't be a jerk."

With *estar* the negative imperative almost always is constructed with the present participle:

>   *No estés molestando.* = "Quit bugging me."
>   *No estés gritando.* = "Quit shouting."

Even in the negative, though, imperatives tend not use a "to be" verb at all, as we have seen:

>   *No te enojes.* = "Don't be mad."
>   *No llegues tarde.* = "Don't be late."
>   *No te aloques.* = "Don't be crazy."
>   *No hagas ruido.* = "Don't be noisy."

For the student, the *ser-estar* confrontation is a real and constant struggle. Penetrating these verbs' distinct natures can be time-consuming and, frankly, a real pain in the backside. Effort is definitely required, but it is also repaid, since the intuitive understanding of Spanish you gain in separating *ser* from *estar* will prove indispensable to true fluency. As that dictionary quoted above goes on to say about the *ser-estar* problem: "If [foreigners] feel irritated with Spanish for this difficulty, they should consider that the differentiation between the essence and the state of things in everyday speech is but one more demonstration—perhaps the most brilliant one—of the logical sense of this language."*

A MATTER OF PERSPECTIVE

Learning how to make your English turn into correct Spanish is sometimes a matter of mastering the vocabulary and sometimes a matter of mastering a concept. But sometimes—rarely—it's a matter of mastering a whole new way of looking at things. It's a matter, in short, of effecting a change of perspective. Long after basic fluency has been achieved, many foreigners still have trouble remembering to make this change. Most foreigners, it could honestly be said, never make the change completely.

Nowhere does this perspective problem crop up with greater frequency than with the indispensable verbs *llevar* and *traer*. The key to getting this distinction right is to remember and implement a very basic rule: in Spanish you can't "bring" something from where you are to where you aren't. If you are going to a dinner at a friend's house, you must ask if you should "take" (*llevar*) something (a salad, a bottle of wine, etc.). "Bringing" is only for cases when something away from the speaker is being moved toward the speaker.

In English we tend to play loosely with what is essentially the same rule. That is, we use "bring" regardless of whether the implied movement is toward the speaker or away from the speaker. If we are going to a party, we will offer to "bring" a salad; we will "bring" a cooler with us when we go on a picnic. In Spanish you have to "take" the salad and "take" the cooler.

Imagine the following phone conversation:

JOSÉ: "Hey, Carlos, I think I left my wallet at your house last night. Could you *bring* it over today?"

*Ibid.

CARLOS: "Sure. I'll *bring* it over in the afternoon."

Now, in Spanish:

JOSÉ: Oye, Carlos, creo que dejé mi cartera en tu casa anoche. ¿Me la puedes *traer* hoy?

CARLOS: Claro, te la *llevo* por la tarde.

It's important to pay attention to the distinction not just to sound better but to avoid sounding rude and demanding when you're not. Imagine, in our phone conversation, that Carlos had no reason to go by José's house that afternoon—in fact, imagine that it was an hour out of his way. Imagine further that they have a class together at five o'clock at the university. Now José, by asking Carlos to *traer* the wallet, is being dreadfully uncouth. José is saying, in effect, "Bring it to me here at my house" when he may have meant "Take it to me there at school"—in which case he would have to say ¿*Me la puedes llevar hoy?*

The same problem of perspective comes into play with *ir* and *venir*. In English we can call home and ask if the plumber "came" that day; we can say we'll fix the sink when we "come" home; when we are called to the phone, we say "I'm coming." In all of these cases in Spanish, however, you have to use *ir* ("to go"), not *venir* ("to come"). To rephrase the *llevar-traer* rule, you can't "come" (with *venir*) to a location that is somewhere other than where you are at that moment. *Venir* can only refer to your present location—where you are sitting or standing or, in a larger sense, to the city or country you are in. ¿*Fue el plomero hoy?* = "Did the plumber come today?" *Arreglaré el lavabo cuando vaya* (or *llegue*) *a casa* = "I'll fix the sink when I come home." *Voy* = "I'm coming (to the phone)."

THE TWILIGHT ZONE 6

First, an explanation. Why title this chapter, which is about the subjunctive mode in Spanish, "The Twilight Zone?" The answer is simple and twofold. First, the concept of a hazy, ephemeral Twilight Zone accurately conveys the spirit of the subjunctive. And, second, if it were called "The Subjunctive Mode," no one would read it.

What is it about the subjunctive that inspires such fear and loathing in students of Spanish? Mostly, it is the task of retraining the mind to recognize a concept that has no readily obvious equivalent in English. After all, it's bad enough that Spanish puts different endings on its verbs to denote mode, tense, and person. But to invent a whole new mode outright—one that needs endings all its own—is nearly criminal.

Spanish, of course, did not invent the subjunctive. In fact, the subjunctive is widely used in English, though not nearly as frequently as it is in Spanish. Take, for example, a sign hanging in the Sears restrooms in Waco, Texas: "It is important to us that our restrooms be clean." A nicer, neater subjunctive was never seen.

But in Spanish it's often hard to get a grasp of why the subjunctive is needed and when. Thus "The Twilight Zone." For that, essentially, is what the subjunctive is: the Twilight Zone of the verb universe. The subjunctive gets the job of describing "could-have-beens," "might-bes," and "maybe-never-weres." Anything that has happened, is happening, or may happen on the borders of our consciousness gets handled by the subjunctive. Without the subjunctive, García Márquez would read like Hemingway. The subjunctive is more than a verb mode; it is a complete separate reality.

Although beginning and intermediate students of Spanish find it difficult to believe, many English speakers who have learned to live with the Spanish subjunctive will tell you that it can actually be quite enjoyable. With the mere flick of a verb ending you can cast doubt or aspersions, relegating a simple occurrence to a different realm of understanding. It is a realm you can flirt with and explore, avoid when you want (sometimes), and revel in at will. Almost certainly you will find yourself wanting it more and more as you explore the Spanish-speaking world. Magical realism finds its home here, as does the seeming surrealism of much of daily life in the Spanish-speaking world.

So how do you go about learning it? Basically, there are two equally important approaches. One approach is to learn the rules—especially with the Twilight Zone concept in mind. A second approach is to learn the common cues for the use of the subjunctive. Practice both, and the subjunctive will appear to you one day—perhaps even in a dream. From that day forward, it will be your constant companion, your escape hatch into the unreal. Signpost up ahead: Subjunctive Mode!

THE RULES

INDIRECT COMMANDS (SHALLOW TWILIGHT)

This group covers giving orders, asking others to do things, and engaging in other bossy behavior. Thus in a sentence like "Tell the mariachis to go away," the English infinitive "to go away" must be rendered in the subjunctive in Spanish. Why? Because the action of the mariachis going away doesn't become a reality until they actually go away. Until then, it must be considered an entirely suspect notion, lurking off in the unknown: Will the mariachis go away? Will they stay? How about if we pay them to go away?

We can lump implicit indirect commands in this category, including "wishing" and "hoping" that the mariachis will go away. "I hope the mariachis go away" is, after all, nothing more than a cowardly version of "Tell the mariachis to go away." And, as in the first example, simply hoping that they will go away is no guarantee that they will actually do so. They may want to sing "La Bamba" again. You have no way of knowing, so you have to rely on the subjunctive. In passing, note that you won't always have an obvious "telling" or "hoping" verb directing the action. Sometimes, the order is implicit or impersonal, and it often begins with *que* all by itself: *Que se vayan los mariachis* = "Have the mariachis go away." Similarly, *ojalá* will often initiate a wishing construction: *Ojalá que se vayan los mariachis* = "I sure hope that the mariachis will leave."

THE ETERNAL MYSTERY (DEEP TWILIGHT)

For this category, we must venture even further into the Twilight Zone. This is the realm of doubt, uncertainty, suspicion, and downright disbelief. For example, *Es posible que los mariachis se vayan* ("It's possible that the mariachis will go"), *Dudo que se vayan* ("I doubt that they will go"), *No creo que se vayan jamás* ("I don't think they are ever going to go"), and so on. In each of these cases, we return to the elemental problem of the mariachis' departure as a mystery, an eternal uncertainty, an action belonging to a separate realm.

Statements of negation also lurk in this shadowy world. At first, their presence here confounds us: aren't they statements of fact and thus perfect candidates for the indicative? On closer examination, however, we can see why they are here. Negations are declarations of something that never happened, actions that only exist in somebody's mind. Here, with a little study, we can see the careful distinction that turns a harmless indicative statement into an unruly, ethereal subjunctive. *No asalté el banco* = "I didn't rob the bank." Straightforward and indicative: I didn't do it. But when the sentence structure forces us to make the action of bank robbery stand alone, it acquires its true character—that of an action that was not. *Niego que haya robado el banco* = "I deny that I robbed the bank." Here "I robbed the bank" is a non-event, an untrue claim, a load of nonsense. It simply didn't happen— I swear! And since it didn't happen, it must be exiled to that world where all the things that never happened—the "could-have-beens," "might-bes," and "maybe-never-weres"—reside. In short, it must go to the Twilight Zone.

A similar treatment awaits things you "don't believe" or "don't think." Since you don't believe them, you certainly don't have to consider them real. *No creo que esté aquí* = "I don't think she's here." Her presence here is something that for you, the speaker, doesn't belong in your universe of hard facts. Thus into the subjunctive it goes.

THE CUES

QUE

By now, being a sharp reader, you will have noticed that every use of the subjunctive so far has been preceded by a certain word: *que*. And you're thinking, "Hey, maybe I'm on to something." In fact, you are—sort of. *Que* is a good cue for using the subjunctive, though not an entirely reliable one. That is, almost every time the subjunctive appears, there will be a *que* preceding it. But *que* will not always be followed by the subjunctive every time it appears. Still, if you pay attention to when you use *que*, you will be on your way to spotting opportunities for showing off your subjunctive.

The context surrounding *que* is the deciding factor in whether the subjunctive should indeed follow. And often this context is little more than the proper combination of words with *que*. Thus certain impersonal expressions followed by *que* almost invariably take the subjunctive:

> *Es posible (probable, factible, concebible) que*
> *Es mejor (conveniente, preferible, oportuno) que*
> *Es importante (necesario, preciso, urgente, obligatorio,*
>   *forzoso) que*

As a matter of fact, only a handful of common adjectives can be placed between *es* and *que* and still produce the indicative. Some of these exceptions are *claro, obvio, evidente,* and the like, which stress that a fact is a fact is a fact. *Es obvio que estoy aquí* = "It's obvious that I'm here." So obvious a fact certainly has no business in the Twilight Zone.

Many of the adjectives in the *es* + adjective constructions used above also have verb forms. With our old friend *que* these verbs also take the subjunctive:

> *Urge que*
> *Conviene que*
> *Precisa que*
> *Prefiero que*

Along these lines are other impersonal expressions that take the subjunctive:

> *Más vale que*
> *Lástima que*

So do certain "impersonalized" or reflexive constructions:

> *Se espera que* (always)
> *Se cree que* (sometimes)

If you change these constructions from impersonal to personal, in most cases you will still need the subjunctive. Some common verbs that, when followed by *que*, usually require the subjunctive include *esperar, sentir, querer, pedir, mandar, dejar,* and *permitir*.

Note that when there is no change in subject, the infinitive can be substituted for the subjunctive clause, as it is in English. These are the constructions you won't have any trouble with:

> *Quiero ir.* = "I want to go."
> *Esperan ganar.* = "They hope to win."

Changing the subject of the second clause will require the subjunctive, however:

> *Quiero que vayas.* = "I want you to go."
> *Espero que gane ella.* = "I hope she wins."

With some indirect command verbs, especially *mandar, permitir*, and *dejar*, the imperative can also be rigged together with the infinitive to avoid the subjunctive altogether:

> *Manda traer el dinero.* = "Send for the money to be brought."
> *Déjale traer el dinero.* = "Let him bring the money."

A more natural-sounding construction in these and other cases of indirect commands is simply starting your sentence with *que* and following it with the subjunctive, as in the earlier example *Que se vayan los mariachis*. This equates with the English "Have . . . ," which is one of the most common indirect command forms in English.

> *Que traiga el dinero.* = "Have him bring the money."
> *Que venga a las seis.* = "Have her come at six."

Que is also a reliable cue for the subjunctive when paired with other words to form certain conjunctions. Most textbooks will give you a laundry list of these conjunctions, half of which you will probably never need. Here are the important ones to remember:

> *para que* = "so that," "in order that"
> *a menos que* = "unless"
> *a pesar de que* = "despite," "even though"
> *antes de que* = "before"

NON-*QUE* CUES

Another common use of the subjunctive is generally not introduced by *que*, so you'll have to be alert for it. Instead, it uses *cuando, donde, como*, and other adverbs. The best guide in this case is the English translation. When you could substitute "-ever," as in "whenever," "wherever," or "however," follow the adverb with the subjunctive in Spanish. If it helps you remember, memorize one of the classic lines used to challenge someone to a fight in Spanish: *Cuando quieras, donde quieras, y como quieras* ("Whenever you want, wherever you want, however you want"). (The expression is reputedly in use as well as a "pick up" line, so make sure the person you use it on knows whether you're a lover or a fighter!) Most likely, though, you will be called upon to use this subjunctive construction in these more mundane situations:

> *¿Cuándo quieres ir? Cuando tú quieras.* = "When do you
>   want to go?" "Whenever you want."
> *¿Adónde vamos? Donde quieras.* = "Where are we going?"
>   "Wherever you want."
> *¿Cuándo me vas a dar el dinero? Cuando yo quiera.* = "When
>   are you going to give me the money?" "Whenever I
>   feel like it."

THE SUBJUNCTIVE WITH *SER: SEA*

Ser is also commonly used in "-ever" constructions, and expressions with *sea* are good to slip into your conversational Spanish. *Cuando sea, como sea, donde sea*, and *quien sea* are equivalents for "whenever," "however," "wherever," and "whoever" when used alone. Often more common in English is to use an "any-" word—"anywhere," "anyhow," and so forth:

> *¿Con quién quieres ir al cine? Con quien sea.* = "Whom
>   do you want to go to the movies with?" "With
>   whomever."
> *¿Dónde quieres comer? Donde sea.* = "Where do you want to
>   eat?" "Wherever (anywhere)."
> *¿Cómo quieres la carne: con salsa, sin salsa, con papas, sin
>   papas, término medio, bien cocida? Como sea.* =
>   "How do you want your meat: with sauce, without
>   sauce, with potatoes, without potatoes, medium, well
>   done?" "Any ol' way will do."

Often, the best English translation of expressions using *sea* would be a slangy expression like "It's up to you," "You name it," "I don't care," or "It doesn't matter." All of these can be conveyed by the Spanish subjunctive.

Although *ser* and *querer* are the two commonest verbs used in "-ever" expressions, virtually any verb can be used:

> *¿Cuándo vas a llegar a la fiesta? Cuando pueda.* = "When are
> you going to get to the party?" "Whenever (as soon as)
> I can."
> *Yo quiero salir ahora. Bueno, lo que tú digas.* = "I want to
> leave now." "Okay, whatever you say."

Once you get a feel for the *cuando quiera– donde quiera–
como quiera* complex, you'll be close to mastering one of the trickiest uses of the subjunctive: a clause containing the adverb plus the
subjunctive to refer to the future. Here you should keep the Twilight
Zone idea in mind. In Spanish, for instance, you would say *Cuando
termine el libro, te llamaré* for "When I finish the book, I'll call you."
In this case, *cuando* is followed by the subjunctive because it refers to
an event in the future that may never happen. A meteor could strike
the reader one page from the book's end, so the notion of "when I finish the book" must be considered uncertain.

Only when you are referring to a habitual action should you
use the indicative. In these cases, note that you are not so much referring to the future as to the past. *Cuando termino de leer en las ma-
ñanas, voy a la tienda* = "When I finish reading in the morning, I go
to the store." Here the indicative is safe because presumably you have
done this sort of thing before and thus know that it can happen and has
happened.

THE TRAVELER'S SUBJUNCTIVE

A final note on the subjunctive is especially useful for those
traveling in the Spanish-speaking world. A common question format
for lost, bewildered, or just-curious travelers goes as follows: "Is there
a such-and-such near here that does such-and-such?" For instance, you
might want to ask, "Is there a store near here that sells wine?" or "I'm
looking for place where I can leave my luggage." In all cases like these
you must use the subjunctive in Spanish, since the place you are seeking may or may not exist. Or, put another way, it won't exist until your
question is answered, "Yes, there is such a place." Until such an answer is given, the place belongs in the never-never world of the Twilight Zone. *¿Hay una tienda por aquí que venda vino? Busco un lugar
donde pueda dejar mi equipaje.* The same logic applies when you ask
about people. *¿Hay alguien aquí que hable inglés?* = "Is there anyone
here who speaks English?"

When the answer is in the negative, the place remains nonexistent and therefore must still be referred to in the subjunctive. *No hay*

una tienda cerca que venda vino = "There is no store nearby that sells wine." This is, after all, but a simple statement of negation, like the ones we saw above. Ditto for nonexistent people: *¡No hay nadie en esta ciudad que me entienda!* = "There's no one in this city who understands me!"

SIXTY-FOUR VERBS, UP   **7**
CLOSE AND PERSONAL

Pocket dictionaries will generally give you simple, one-word equivalents for Spanish verbs. Better dictionaries will give you a list of other possible meanings and maybe some examples. But rarely is the dictionary reader given guidance on what usages are common—i.e., worth the bother of learning—and which are poetic or archaic and thus irrelevant. And besides, who wants to read a dictionary?

What follows is a pared-down list of sixty-four Spanish verbs whose basic meaning you probably already know, but whose inner secrets and common usage go far beyond that. The list cuts through the clutter and highlights unexpected usages that a native English speaker may not be on the lookout for or that are "out of character" for a given verb. Each section also explains a chosen few idiomatic expressions, selected for their frequency in everyday spoken Spanish. There's a lot to absorb here, but the alphabetical listing will allow for hour after hour of repeated consultation. Take heart—it could be worse. You could be reading the dictionary!

ACABAR

This is a synonym for *terminar* and, like that word, is a good equivalent for most uses of "to end" and "to finish" in English. Used with *con* as an intensifier, both verbs work well for "to finish off": *Acabé con la leche.* Often you will hear *acabarse* in the reflexive to mean "to run out of." *Se nos acabó el dinero* = "We've run out of money." *Se acabó* by itself, meanwhile, means either "It's over" or "I'm out of it." You'll hear it a lot in stores, at newsstands, and the like when what you want to buy is no longer in stock. *Terminar* is likewise used this way; *agotar* is also heard, especially in the phrase *Está agotado* ("We're out of it"). *Está acabado* usually isn't used in this sense, since its meaning is closer to "It's finished" or, colloquially, "He's washed up." *Acabar* has one other very common use that *terminar* doesn't have: in the present tense, with *de*, it means "to have just," as in *Acabo de comer* ("I've just eaten"). Used in the imperfect, it becomes "had just." *Acababa de comer cuando llegaste* = "I had just eaten when you arrived."

AMANECER

This somewhat uncommon word, which means "to dawn," is included here because of one expression that has perplexed generations of language students, especially those who live for a time with a Spanish-speaking family when studying abroad. The expression is *¿Cómo amaneciste?*—which translates literally as "How did you dawn?" but which means "How did you sleep?" The answer is (usually) *Bien, gracias*. A fun Spanish expression for "to die in one's sleep" uses this verb: *Amaneció muerto*; if it translates at all, it would have to be rendered "He woke up all dead."

ANDAR

Dictionaries say it means "to walk," which of course it does, but that won't help you when you hear *anda corriendo* or *anda en coche* for the first time. In English we would probably be inclined to say "go around" for most uses of *andar*. *Pedro anda gritando tu nombre* = "Pedro's going around shouting your name." *Andar* also covers slangy expressions like "to hang out" or "to hang around." *Ya no ando con ellos* = "I don't hang around with them anymore." *¿Por dónde andas?* works well for "Whereabouts are you?" or the colloquial "Where are you at?" And in some countries *anda* lends itself to the common idiomatic expressions *¡Ándale!* and *¡Anda!* Said with vigor, they mean "Let's get a move on!" or "Way to go!" Said in passing, they mean the same as "okay" or "all right." In Mexico, for instance, you'll hear *ándale* all the time for "that's fine," "that's right," and even "good-bye": *Nos vemos mañana. Ándale.* Throw a *pues* on the end and you'll be saying nothing at all but will sound very fluent: *Ándale pues* ("Have a nice day"). Remember as well the use of *andar* for "to run" or "to work" in reference to objects. *¿Qué tal anda tu coche?* = "How's your car running?" (literally, "How's your car walking?"). Some wags have even argued that the different conception of time in Spanish-speaking countries is due to the fact that in Spanish clocks walk rather than run!

ANTOJAR

Used generally as a reflexive (*antojarse*), this is an exceptionally common verb and one that you should get to know well. To translate it, dictionaries offer "to long for" or "to desire earnestly," but its use in Spanish covers a lot more ground than that. Closer to the mark would be "to get a hankering for" or simply "to feel like." An *antojo* is a "craving" or an "urge" and covers both intense longings (like the kind that make pregnant women eat pickles) and simpler pleasures. You'll probably run across the verb frequently in these same situations. Some examples: *Se me antoja una pizza* = "I'm dying for (could go for) a pizza." *¿Por qué no vas a ir al cine? Porque no se me antoja.* = "Why aren't you going to the movies?" "Because I don't feel like it." *Déjame una dona; luego se me va a antojar* = "Leave me a doughnut; I'll probably feel like having one later."

BAJAR

This verb means "to go down," "to put down," "to get off," and so on. Most of its uses are predictable, but a few that may not be include "to go downstairs," "to get out of a car (bus, train, etc.)," and "to lose weight" (*bajar de peso*). It also means "to get (something) down," as when you ask someone to get your suitcase down off the rack (*¿Me baja la maleta, por favor?*). *Bájale*, by itself, is usually "Turn it down," referring to the volume or the general noise level; in the right context, it can also mean "Slow down."

CABER

An irregular verb that you should learn. It means "to fit," but only in the sense of "fit into" or "fit onto." It is not used for clothing. In the first-person present, it's *quepo*, and you're likely to hear it in

¡*Quepo yo!*—meaning "Will I fit?" or "Is there room for one more?" Otherwise, you may run into it in set expressions like *cabe decir* ("it's worth mentioning") and *no cabe duda* ("there's no doubt").

CAER

It means "to fall," of course, and "to drop" when used reflexively (*caerse*): *Se me cayó el vaso* = "I dropped the glass." It's also very frequently heard in the phrases *caer bien* and *caer mal* to express likes and dislikes (see Chapter 4). You may also run across *caer* for "to visit unexpectedly" or "to drop in on." *Te caigo en la tarde* is an informal way of saying "I'll drop in on you in the afternoon." Sometimes it's used to suggest that someone's arrival was not only unexpected but also unwelcome. "What are your in-laws doing here?" might be answered by *Es que me cayeron* ("They just kind of showed up").

CAMBIAR

Meaning "to change" as well as "to make change" in the sense of "Can you change a twenty?"(¿*Me puede cambiar un billete de a veinte?*), *cambiar* also crops up in a number of common expressions. These include *cambiar de idea* or *cambiar de opinión* ("to change one's mind"), *cambiar de ropa* ("to change one's clothes"), and *cambiar de casa* ("to move").

COGER

This is one of those words that many dictionaries handle with more discretion than clarity. The simple fact is that *coger* is a vulgar term for "to fornicate" in several countries (Argentina, Mexico, Uruguay, and others), where as a result it is rarely used in proper company (see Chapter 10). That said, it is also one of the most commonly used verbs in some other countries (especially Spain). What's a poor student to do when faced with the choice? That will depend on where you are learning the language and with whom you expect to be communicating. But if you want to use substitutes for *coger* right from the start— in the sense of "to get," "to take," "to grab"—it may not be such a bad idea. The word that usually replaces it is *tomar*, as in *tomar el tren*. In Mexico, particularly, *agarrar* is often heard. Both substitutes are understood even where *coger* is used, and both can save you considerable embarrassment.

CONOCER

This verb is often confused with *saber* by students of Spanish; both mean "to know," but *conocer* is used in the sense of "to be familiar with." A limited rule of thumb: use *conocer* for proper nouns and all specific people, places, and things; use *saber* for everything else. Do you know Paris? *Conocer.* Do you know the French Quarter? *Conocer.* Do you know the old lady there who sells flowers on the street? *Conocer.* Do you know her name? *Saber.* Do you know what flowers she sells? *Saber.* Do you know what she's saying about you? *Saber.*

Conocer also means "to meet," but keep in mind that it only works for the first time you meet someone. English speakers use "to meet" to describe routine encounters, such as "I met my mother at the train station." They also tend to say *la primera vez que lo conocí* to convey "the first time I met him" (instead of the less redundant *cuando lo conocí*). In Spanish you can only *conocer* someone once, and needless to say it would be difficult (not to mention dramatic) to *conocer* your mother at a train station. Finding the right Spanish word for "to meet" in these other situations will give you an idea of how overworked this poor verb is in English. When you are referring to a first meeting, as noted, use *conocer. Lo conocí en París* = "I met him (for the first time) in Paris." All chance encounters after that are handled by *encontrar. La encontré en el cine* = "I met (ran into) her at the movies." Meeting a plane or a train would be covered by *recibir. Me recibieron en la estación* = "They met me at the station." For a planned get-together you would use *quedar en verse con* or *quedar en encontrarse con: Quedé en verme con unos amigos en el centro* = "I met (up with) some friends downtown."

CREER

It means "to believe," but it is also almost always the word you want for "to think." Beginning students, incorrectly, often prefer *pensar* (see below). The distinction is subtle, but it works out roughly as follows: if the emphasis is specifically on the thought process or the act of thinking, use *pensar.* If you're stating a personal belief or opinion, use *creer.* Thus *Creo que tienes la razón* = "I think you're right." *Creer* is also used in many interjections and phrases, such as *¡Qué* *crees?* ("Guess what?"), *Créeme* ("Trust me"), *¿Tú crees?* ("You really think so?"), and so on. A good phrase to learn is *ni creas*, which could be translated as "don't expect" or "no way." *Ni creas que te voy a ayudar* = "You're crazy if you think I'm going to help you" or "Don't expect me to help you." *Creo que sí* and *Creo que no*, finally, should be on the tip of your tongue for "I think so" and "I don't think so."

CUIDAR

Technically, this means "to care for," though in English we would generally use some other word to translate it. *Ana se quedó para cuidar a los niños* = "Ana stayed home to watch (take care of) the kids." *Cuide su cartera en ese barrio* = "Watch your wallet in that neighborhood." *Cuídate* is "Take care of yourself" or, slangily, "Take it easy"; it is sometimes used as a parting comment. *Cuidar* in general is the word you want for asking someone to "watch over" or "to keep an eye on" something, as when you want to leave your luggage in the bus station for a few minutes (not a recommended practice). *¿Me puede cuidar la maleta unos minutos?* = "Can you keep an eye on my bag for a few minutes?" See also *guardar.*

DAR

"To give" and much more. A common additional meaning of *dar* is "to hit," giving rise to a number of expressions. *Dar en el blanco* is "to hit the bull's-eye" and is often heard for "to guess right," "to hit the nail on the head." *Dar en la torre* is a common idiomatic expression that covers physical beatings as well as more metaphorical thrashings. "How did the Cubs do against the Mets?" *Le dieron en la torre* ("They beat the pants off 'em"). *Dále*, by itself, is "Hit it" (or "Hit him," "Hit her"); you can let off steam by shouting it at boxing matches. More metaphorically, it means "Give it your best" or "Give 'em hell." Often, in this sense, it's paired with *duro* and said to give encouragement: *¡Dále duro, Juan!* ("Give 'em hell, Juan!"). By the same token, you can use *dándole duro* to convey the intensity of an action or an effort. "How are you coming with the term paper?" *¡Dándole duro!*

Here are other *dar* expressions you'll want to know:

> *dar a la calle* (*al patio, a la alberca*, etc.) = "to face the street (the patio, the pool, etc.)"
> *da igual* or *da lo mismo* = "it's all the same to me" or "it doesn't matter"

dar coraje = "to make mad"
dar (la) lata = "to pester" or "to be a pain"

Dar is also used in some parts of the Spanish-speaking world for "what's on"—in the sense of showings on television or at the movie theater. *Están dando la segunda parte de* Arma Mortal = "They're showing the second part of *Lethal Weapon*." (See also *pasar*.) Finally, though you won't find it in the dictionary, an increasingly common expression in American Spanish is *dar chance* for "to give a break." *Vamos, oficial, dénos chance* = "Come on, officer, give us a break." Purists will tell you that this is a horrible barbarism and that you should say *denos una oportunidad* instead. But purists should consider cutting their losses, since more and more speakers of slang are already bypassing *dar chance* in favor of *dar un break*, which is more barbaric yet.

    Darse, the reflexive form, is also used for a few handy phrases, such as *darse cuenta de*, which means "to realize." *Perdón, no me di cuenta de que estaba estacionado en su pie* = "Sorry, I didn't realize I was parked on your foot." *Darse por vencido* is the phrase you want for "to give up," "to surrender." To say "I give up" in response to a riddle, for instance, you can even use *Me doy* (more formally, *Me rindo*) all by itself.

DECIR

    "To tell" or "to say." You'll probably also be using it a lot in the phrase *querer decir*, or "to mean." *¿Qué quiere decir esa palabra?* = "What does that word mean?" *Decir* also pops up in a lot of cute little phrases, such as *No me digas* ("You don't say"), *Díme* ("Tell me" or simply "Yes?"), and *¿Qué decías?* ("What were you saying?"—after an interruption). You should also be alert to *Díle* (and *Dígale*) as a typical preface to an indirect command, and thus the subjunctive. *Díle que venga* = "Tell him to come here." If you're stating a fact instead of issuing a command, it takes the indicative. *Díle que estamos aquí* = "Tell him (or her) we're here."

DEJAR

    Meaning "to leave" or "to let," this verb is often found in other expressions and is not always a reliable vehicle for English "let" phrases. For example, *Déjenos entrar* means "Let us in," but *Entremos* (or *Vamos a entrar*) means "Let's go in." *Dejar* is heard in such phrases as *Déjame en paz* ("Leave me alone"), *Déjalo* ("Leave it" or "Drop it" or "Skip it," often referring to a sensitive topic or one best dealt with later), and *Deja ver* or *Déjame ver* = "Let me see."

DISFRUTAR

"To enjoy." Only mentioned here to dissuade you from saying *Disfrútense* for "Enjoy yourselves." It does mean this, but probably not in the way you intend. "Have fun with yourselves" or "Take pleasure in yourselves" would probably be a more accurate translation. Instead, you should say *Que lo disfruten*, usually in reference to a specific event. For the best translation of "Enjoy yourselves," forget about *disfrutar* altogether and use *divertirse: Diviértanse* or *Que se diviertan*.

DORMIR

Dormir is "to sleep" while *dormirse* is "to fall asleep." Just a reminder: "sleep," the noun, has to be expressed by *sueño* (see *soñar*).

DURAR

This is one of the words you will need to ask how long things take (movies, bus rides, flights, speeches, etc.). You can think of *durar* as a generally safe translation of "to last." *La fiesta duró toda la noche* = "The party lasted all night." Generally *durar* is used for things that have a specific duration—or *dura*tion, if it helps you remember. (See also *tardar* and *hacer*.)

ECHAR

Echar is one of those words that take up about three pages in the dictionary. Not all of those expressions are that common or useful, though. Almost all of them have to do with a forcible casting out or expulsion. File away this division of labor: *meter* is for putting in, *sacar* for taking out, and *echar* for kicking out, more or less. Buses *echan* smoke, teachers *echan* students, and so on. An unexpected use of *echar* is for "to pour," as with a liquid into a glass or from a pitcher. Some of the idiomatic expressions using *echar* are very handy. *Echar de menos a* is "to miss (someone)" (though in the Americas you are more likely to hear *extrañar*). *Echar a perder* is "to spoil," be it children or food in your refrigerator. *Echar ganas* is a very common expression for "to show enthusiasm" or "to give it a good effort: "Mom, I can't understand my math homework." *Vamos, échale ganas, hijo.* *Echar una mano* is the expression you will need for "to lend a hand," and *Échame la mano* is "Gimme a hand." *Echar un ojo* is "to have a quick look," and *echar la culpa* is "to blame."

ENCARGAR

This verb, meaning "to entrust" or "to commission," is far more common than these awkward English translations suggest. Almost always it conveys some notion of "charge"—to take charge, to be in charge, to charge, and so on. With *de*, for instance, it means "to take charge of" or "to put someone in charge of" something: *Yo me encargo de la ensalada* = "I'll be in charge of (take care of) the salad." *El encargado* is the all-purpose word for "the guy in charge." Without the *de*, *encargar* means "to entrust" but often with more colloquial English equivalents. For example, if someone's going off to the store, you might say *¿Te encargo unas aspirinas?* ("Can you get me some aspirin?"). Many usages could almost be translated "to order." *Le encargué dos litros al lechero* = "I ordered two liters from the milkman." Sometimes, what you're ordering or entrusting is not spelled out, and "to count on" would make for a better fit. If someone offers to fix your car by nightfall and you plan to leave town that very night, you might say to the mechanic, *Se lo encargo mucho* ("I'm really counting on you").

EQUIVOCAR

Used as a reflexive (*equivocarse*), this is the common verb for "to make a mistake" (although *estár equivocado* works as well). Usually used with the preposition *de*, it means "to get something wrong." For instance, when you've dialed the wrong number, you would say, *Perdón, me equivoqué de teléfono* (or *número*). If Pedro shows up on the wrong day for a party, you would tell him, *Te equivocaste de día.* And so on. As a subtle distinction, *estar equivocado* generally suggests someone is mistaken; *equivocarse* means he or she has made a mistake.

ESPERAR

Meaning both "to hope" and "to wait," the verb will usually take the subjunctive in both senses. *Espero que venga* = "I hope he (or she) comes." *Estoy esperando que regrese* = "I'm waiting for him (or her) to get back." Unless the context makes it clear, you would use the preposition *a* with *esperar* to say "to wait for." Thus, *Espero a que regrese* = "I'll wait for him (or her) to get back." (*Esperar por* or *esperar para* should never be used for "to wait for.") *Esperar* is frequently heard in the imperative for "Wait a minute" or "Hold on." *Espérese, por favor* is the form you're most likely to hear. In familiar usage it's *Espérate*, which often comes out sounding like *'pérate*.

ESTAR

The other verb for "to be"—the one that covers transitory states. The *ser* versus *estar* confrontation was covered in detail in Chapter 5. So here it's enough to glance at one use of the verb you might not have been expecting—about the only one that is out of character for it from the standpoint of an English speaker—*estar* when used to ask "What's today's date?": *¿A qué estamos hoy?* or *¿A cuántos estamos?* The answer is phrased *Estamos a* and the number: *Estamos a 25*, for example. Remember too that *estar* + *de* is used for moods and inclinations. *El está de malas* = "He's in a bad mood." (This use is covered in Chapter 4.)

ESTRENAR

This is not the commonest of verbs, nor is it one that you desperately need to learn. It means to use or display something for the first time—to "debut" something, as it were. *Juan está estrenando su nuevo coche* = "Juan is trying out his new car." *Voy a estrenar la camisa que me regalaste* = "I'm going to wear (for the first time) the shirt that you gave me." *Un estreno*, referring to films and theater, is a "premiere" or "opening"; referring to an artist, it would be a "debut."

GUARDAR

Meaning "to guard" or "to save," this is the common verb to use for telling someone to "hold on to" something or "put (something) away." *Guardar* is usually used when you give someone something that you want them to put away until you need it again. If you're going swimming and don't want to take your traveler's checks into the pool with you, you might hand them to a friend and say *¿Me los guardas?* *Guardar* is also commonly used by parents to tell their children, "Put it away" (*Guárdalo*), be it in their closet or in their pocket. *Guárdame un poco* is "Save a little for me," said of a favorite foodstuff, for instance. (See also "Save" in Chapter 11.) The word is a little tricky to use in the sense of its English cognate. *¿Me guarda la maleta?* could be "Keep an eye on my suitcase" but also something like "Put my suitcase away"; so if you tell someone to "guard" it and they walk off with it, you'll know why. Use *cuidar* (see above) for "to keep an eye on," "to watch."

HABER

This is one of the megaverbs, with more uses than you might ever be inclined to learn. Some are indispensable, though. *Hay*, of course, is the way to say "There is . . ." and "There are . . . ." Say it with a lilt and it becomes the questions "Are there . . . ?" and "Is there . . . ?" *No hay* is the typical curt response to questions about availability: *¿Hay café? No hay. ¿Hay cuartos? No hay. Hay que* is the impersonal way of saying "to have to"—that is, when it's not obvious exactly who has to do something. *Hay que ir a España para aprender español* = "One has to go to Spain to learn Spanish." The imperfect and preterit forms of *haber* are *había* and *hubo*, respectively. *Había* is the more commonly used of the two. *Había veinte personas en el coche* = "There were twenty people in the car." *Hubo* is for something that was there all at once or not for long. *Hubo un choque en la carretera* = "There was an accident on the highway." Remember never to use *habían* or *hubieron* for "there were," regardless of the number of persons or things involved: *Había una monja en la lancha* and *Había dos monjas en la lancha*.

HABLAR

A straightforward word for "to talk" or "to speak," but keep it in mind for use on the telephone, where its use is rampant. It's not hard to imagine a phone conversation going something like this: (R-i-i-i-ing.) *Hola. ¿Quién habla? ¿Con quién quiere hablar? Habla Juan. ¿Puedo hablar con Fred? El habla. ¡Ah! ¡Hablas español!* Of these, the *El habla* (or *Ella habla*) response is the most important to get straight. It will spare you countless episodes of saying *Soy él* (or *ella*) or *Hablando*, both of which are incorrect when you mean "This is he (or she)" or "Speaking."

HACER

Hacer means "to make" or "to do," but you know that already. Where English speakers have to remember to use *hacer* is in the many weather-related expressions that in English are covered by "to be." Some of the things that "make" in Spanish are *frío, calor, viento,* and *sol* ("cold," "hot," "windy," "sunny"). *Hacer* is also the way to say "ago" in Spanish: *Hace dos años nació mi hijo* ("My son was born two years ago"). When did they leave? *Hace un rato* ("A little while ago"). To say "We did it!" or "We made it!" in Spanish, you say *¡Lo hicimos!* With *la* instead of *lo* and intensified with *ya,* it becomes a colloquial *¡Ya la hicimos!* ("We've got it made!"). Don't trouble your mind searching for an antecedent to *la*—there is none. A very useful phrase with *hacer,* finally, is *Hazte de cuenta* (or *Haz de cuenta*), which introduces a thought with "Pretend . . ." or "Let's say . . . ." (See also Chapter 8 under *"Haz de cuenta que."*)

Hacerse, in the reflexive, also turns up in a lot of unexpected expressions. It's a common way of translating "to become" and is also common idiomatically for "to make like" or "to act like." *El se hace el payaso* = "He's acting like a clown." *Se hace el loco para no ir a la carcel* = "He's pretending to be crazy to avoid going to prison." You'll often encounter this expression in the negative as an exhortation. *No te hagas tonto* = "Don't play stupid." *No te hagas la víctima* = "Don't play the victim." In Mexico especially you'll encounter *No te hagas* all by itself, with the predicate understood. This is a good translation for common interjections like "Come off it!" or "Don't gimme that!" or "Cut it out!"

IR

The verb for "to go" comes into play in many situations that parallel English usages, but you'll have to be on the lookout for them to learn to use them well. It's widely used, for instance, for negative imperatives, otherwise known as warnings, equating approximately with the English "Don't go . . . ": *No te vayas a meter en líos* = "Don't go getting yourself in trouble." *No le vayas a decir* = "Now don't go telling him" or just "Don't tell him." In many compound verb forms, *ir* is extremely useful to get your point across. It's used, as in English, in the future (*Voy a llamar* = "I'm going to call") and in the imperfect (*Iba a llamar* = "I was going to call"). And *Vamos a* means "Let's . . . ." Other common expressions with *ir* include *irle a* ("to root for," as in *Yo le voy a los Orioles*), *ir por* ("to go get" or "to go for," as in *Voy por el coche*), and *Ahí te va* (meaning "Catch" or "Your turn").

Vaya by itself is "All right" or "Omigosh," depending on tone and context. *Vaya, vaya, vaya* is the common way to say "Well, well, well," as in "What have we here?" *Vaya* plus a noun is the equivalent of the sarcastic comment "Some . . . !" If you return home to find the plumber has managed to flood the entire basement, you might say sarcastically *¡Vaya plomero!* ("Some plumber!").

LOGRAR

This is the word you want for "to manage" when used with another verb in the infinitive. *Logré reparar la tele* = "I managed to fix the television." *Si logro salir de esta reunión, estaré en casa en media hora* = "If I manage to get out of this meeting, I'll be home in half an hour."

LLEVAR

Llevar means "to carry" or "to take" and is often used for "to bring," as we saw in Chapter 5. Here we'll concern ourselves with *llevar* in those expressions you'll want to have handy in your daily doings. One common one is *llevar* for expressions of time. A good way to answer the inevitable question heard abroad, "How long have you been here," is to say *Llevo* + the number + *meses (años, días) aquí.* The question, in fact, will often be phrased *¿Cuánto tiempo lleva (usted) aquí?* Once you get a feel for this usage, you'll find yourself needing it more and more. *Llevo dos días en cama* is much smoother and more colloquial than *He estado en cama durante* (or *desde hace*) *dos días* for "I've spent two days in bed." *Llevar* is also useful for "to wear" or "to have on." *Es el señor que lleva lentes* = "He's the man with the glasses on."

Llevarse, the reflexive, is also handy for a couple of expressions. A common one is for "to get along." *Ella y yo no nos llevamos* = "She and I don't get along." *No me llevo con ellos* = "I don't get along with them." Another one you'll need, especially for shopping, is *llevarse* for "to take" something (after paying for it, naturally). It means the same as *llevar* essentially, but the reflexive is added for emphasis. *¿Dos mil pesos? Me lo llevo* = "Two thousand pesos? It's a deal." *Me llevo dos* = "I'll take two." *Llévatelo* is "Take it," pure and simple. Any usage that translates as "to take along" gets the reflexive as well: *Me llevo un suéter por si hace frío* = "I'll take a sweater in case it gets cold."

MANDAR

Meaning "to send" or "to order," this word can cause problems because of other words that can get the same message across. Most uses of "to send," for instance, work better with *enviar*, and "to order" in a restaurant is *pedir* or (increasingly) *ordenar*. *Mandar* is used for real orders, of the sort that generals and bosses give, and you'll come across it a lot in conjunction with a second verb. In these cases it works as "to send out for" or "to have done." *Manda hacer unas copias* = "Have some copies made." It usually implies an order to an underling, so don't use it freely unless you are in a position either to give orders or to take orders. If you go to Mexico, your first encounter with *mandar* may be the ubiquitous expression *¿Mande?* for "What?" or "You called?" It's considered polite, but many foreigners (especially from other Spanish-speaking countries) seem to think it servile and demeaning. If you feel that way, you can substitute *¿Cómo?* or even the brusque *¿Qué?*—but you'll hear *¿Mande?* just the same.

METER

Meter, meaning "to put (something) in," is used in a far wider range of circumstances. It's the common way of saying "to go inside" (*Vamos a meternos* = "Let's go inside") or "to go in" (*Vamos a meternos al agua* = "Let's go in the water"). It can even be used for "to get in" a car (as in *Métete al coche*), but *subirse* is preferred. The reflexive form *meterse* is also a good translation for "to get involved in" or "to get mixed up with." *No te metas* = "Don't get involved." *No te metas con mi hermana* = "Don't mess around with my sister." *Meterse en líos* takes the idea further and means "to get mixed up in problems," "to get into trouble." If you get caught in the middle of a family squabble and find opposing sides of the squabble looking to you for support, you might throw up your hands and say *Yo no me meto* ("I'm not getting involved in this").

NOTAR

This verb is worth learning in the reflexive form (*notarse*) to express "I can see that" or "It shows." It's a nice, dry comment that says that you, too, can perceive the obvious. If someone in the midst of a downpour reminds you that it's the rainy season, you might respond *Se nota* ("I figured that out" or "But of course"). Adding the personal pronouns *me, te,* or *se* personalizes the phrase. Your friend, screaming, tells you she's angry. You say, *Se te nota* ("So I see," literally "One notes that in you.") *Notar*, incidentally, is not a good word for "to note something down" or "to make a note of." For that, use *anotar* or *apuntar*.

PARAR

"To stop." *Pare el mundo, quiero bajarme* = "Stop the world, I want to get off." *¿Dónde para el tren?* = "Where does the train stop?" And so on. *Párale* is sometimes employed to say "Stop it" or "Cut it out," as when someone is talking too much or the kids are screaming. In most of the Americas (and even parts of Spain), the reflexive *pararse* means "to stand up," and *parado* is "standing up." Travelers will sometimes ask if there is room on a train or bus and be told *Si quiere ir parado* ("If you want to travel standing up"). *Párate que nos vamos* would be a colloquial way of saying "Get up, we're going." Learn to distinguish between *parar* and *pararse* for "to stop." The reflexive form is appropriate for stopping unassisted, whereas *parar* suggests something stopping something else. *Paré el coche* is "I stopped the car." *El coche se paró* is "The car stopped."

PARECER

Meaning "to seem," this verb is more frequently encountered than its English equivalent. One of the most common ways of conveying likes and dislikes in Spanish, in fact, is with *parecer*. Here are some typical usages: *¿Qué te parece?* = "What do you think?" or "How does that strike you?" *¿Te parece?* = "Is that okay with you?" *No me parece* = "I don't like it." *Me parece bien* = "Fine with me." The reflexive *parecerse* is "to look like" or "to resemble." *Me parezco a mi madre* = "I take after my mother." "To look like" in the sense of "to look as if" requires *parece que*, not the reflexive. *Parece que va a llover* = "It looks like (as if) it's going to rain."

PASAR

One of several options for "to happen" (see Chapter 11), *pasar* is also usually safe for most uses of "to pass," although it's a bit slangy at the dinner table (*Pásame la sal*). One use you may not be expecting: in some Latin American countries, *pasar* is the verb to use when asking "what's on" television or at the local theater. *¿Qué están pasando* *en el 8?* = "What's on Channel 8?" *Están pasando la nueva película de de Niro en el Cine Colón* = "They're showing the new de Niro movie at the Cine Colon." In South American countries the verb of choice here would be *dar*, usually in the phrase *estar dando*.

As a colloquial greeting, both *¿Qué pasa?* and *¿Qué pasó?* are used, though individual countries tend to have a preferred form. In most situations, *¿Qué pasa?* implies that something is wrong or abnormal; this is the question to ask when there are police cars parked in front of your house. In Mexico, where *¿Qué pasó?* is the preferred greeting, saluting someone with *¿Qué pasa?* may prompt raised eyebrows and the question *¿Por qué?* So much for starting a pleasant conversation.

Using *pasar con* conveys "to happen to" in the sense of "to become of." *¿Qué pasó con Juan?* = "What's become of Juan?"—that is, why is he late? In the present tense *¿Qué pasa?* with an indirect object pronoun (*me, te, le, nos,* or *les*) is like asking "What's (my, your, his, her, our, their) problem?" In fact, *¿Qué te pasa?* is roughly equivalent to "What's bugging you?" In the past tense, this same construction means "What happened to (me, you, him, her, us, them)?": *¿Qué le pasó?* = "What happened to him?"—for example, why are they carrying him off on a stretcher?

Pasarse, the reflexive form, plus the preposition *de* is very handy in expressions meaning "to go too far," figuratively speaking. *Se pasó de listo* means someone "was too clever" or "was too sneaky," and implies that the person got caught at it. Sometimes it can be translated as "to get carried away." When a person *se pasa de listo* (*lista*) with another person, it can mean that he or she is making unwelcome sexual advances. *Ese señor se pasó de listo con María* = "That guy made a (rude) pass at María." The formula *pasarse de* can be used with almost any adjective or quality, positive or negative. *Usted se pasa de generosa* = "You are being overly generous." *Te pasaste de imbécil* = "You were even stupider than usual."

PEDIR

"To ask," "to ask for," and the correct verb for "to order" in a restaurant (although *ordenar* is gaining ground). *Pedir* should make you think of indirect commands and the subjunctive: *Pídele que se vaya* ("Ask him to leave"). It is also used in a number of stock phrases, quite a few of which you are liable to need in the course of your dealings in Spanish. Some common ones include *pedir permiso* ("to ask permission"), *pedir perdón* ("to apologize"), *pedir informes* ("to ask for information"), and *pedir ayuda* ("to ask for help"). *Pedir prestado* is the correct phrase for "to borrow," but you'll often find *prestar* (see below) handier. A rule of life for some in the Spanish-speaking world is *Es más fácil pedir perdón que pedir permiso,* or "It's easier to ask forgiveness than permission."

PENSAR

The verb for "to think," though often *creer* (see above) is preferred. To the extent that there is a rule for distinguishing them, use *pensar* when you might use "to have been thinking" or "to be thinking about" in English. If it's just a simple statement of opinion, use *creer*. *Pienso que debes irte* = "It is my feeling that you should go." *Creo que debes irte* = "You should probably go." Sometimes the two are interchangeable. A usage of *pensar* you should become very familiar with is *pensar* plus the infinitive to mean "to plan on" or "to intend." *Pienso irme mañana* = "I plan to go tomorrow." *Pienso quedarme unos días* = "I intend to stay a couple of days." *Pensar + en* is "to think of" or "to have in mind." *Pensar + sobre* (or *acerca de*) works as "to think about" or "to consider" something. *Pensar + de* is "to think of," in the sense of an opinion, and is a lot like *creer*. *Estoy pensando en nuestras vacaciones* = "I'm thinking of (remembering, daydreaming about) our vacation." *Todavía estoy pensando sobre* (or *acerca de*) *nuestras vacaciones* = "I'm still thinking about (considering, analyzing) our vacation." *¿Qué piensas de nuestras vacaciones?* = "What do you think of our vacation (so far)? Stock phrases with *pensar* include *¡ni pensarlo!* ("no way," "it's out of the question"), *pensándolo bien* ("on second thought"), and *sin pensar* ("without thinking," "unintentionally").

PODER

Meaning "to be able," this is in general a predictable word. Aside from its quirks in the past tenses (see Chapter 5), it's just a matter of mastering a few stock phrases to get a hold on *poder*. One such phrase is *poder + con*, which means something like "to handle" or "to deal with." Examples will be useful here. A student who has trouble learning biology might lament, *No puedo con la biología.* In the sports pages, you'll often come across headlines saying things like *Los Leones No Pudieron con Los Toros* ("The Lions Couldn't Handle the Bulls"— that is, the Bulls beat the Lions, pure and simple). A Cuban postrevolutionary chant intones *Fidel, Fidel, ¿qué tiene Fidel, que los americanos no pueden con él?,* which means "Fidel, Fidel, what does Fidel have, that the Americans can't handle (defeat) him?" Depending on the context, *poder* + *con* can also mean "to tolerate," and in this sense is nearly synonymous with the verb *aguantar*. *¡Ay, no puedo con mi hermano!* = "Arrgh, I just can't stand my brother!" A fun way of describing an extremely irritating person is to say *No puede ni consigo mismo* ("He can't even stand himself"). Other phrases using *poder* that you'll want on the tip of your tongue: *¿Se puede?* ("May I?"), *Puede ser* ("Could be" or "Maybe"), and *Puede que* plus the subjunctive ("It could be that . . ." or "Maybe . . . ").

PRESTAR

Prestar, "to lend," works for just about anything you might want to borrow, just as "to lend" does in English. Thus *Préstame tu pluma* = "Lend me your pen." (For "lending a hand," though, you would probably use *dar* or *echar: Oye, échame una mano.*) What is difficult for many English speakers is to switch between "borrow" phrases and "lend" phrases in Spanish. This sometimes leads to convoluted constructions with *pedir prestado*, like *¿Puedo pedir prestada tu pluma?* Much more natural in Spanish is to turn it around (i.e., saying "you lend" instead of "I borrow") and use *prestar* by itself. If *Préstame* is too tactless for your tastes, say *¿Me presta?* or *¿Me prestas?: ¿Me prestas tu pluma?* In very slangy speech you might hear *Presta para acá* or *Presta pa'cá* for "Hand it over" or "Give it up." The latter example has sexual overtones, as it does in English.

Prestar is also used for "to pay attention," which, if you think about it, is much more realistic than the English concept (we don't really "pay" attention, we just lend it out). *¡Niños, presten atención!* = "Children, pay attention!" *Prestarse*, the reflexive form, can be quite useful for "to lend oneself," though it sounds much more idiomatic in Spanish than in English. *¿Tú crees que Juan nos deje copiar en el examen? No, él no se presta a eso.* = "Do you think Juan will let us copy his exam?" "No, he doesn't lend himself to that."

QUEDAR

A megaverb that you'll want to have on your side as quickly as possible. Its most straightforward uses revolve around "to stay" or "to remain." *Aquí me quedo* is "I'm staying here" and is sometimes used as a name for cantinas. *Quédate aquí* = "Stay here." Other uses require "to have left" in English. *Sólo me quedan treinta dólares* = "I only have thirty dollars left."

A host of other expressions with *quedarse*, the reflexive, are better covered in English by "to keep." *Me quedé con treinta dólares* = "I kept thirty dollars." *Quédese con el cambio* would be "Keep the change." *Quédatelo* = "Keep it." For use in shopping, *quedarse* is a lot like *llevarse* (see above). *Me quedo con el azul* = "I'll take the blue one." Often *quedarse* suggests a final or resultant state of affairs. *Me quedé helado* is, literally, "I was left frozen" and suggests you were frozen with fear. *Me quedé en blanco* is to say "I ended up blank" or "I didn't understand that at all." If someone asks you whether you understood an explanation of the theory of relativity, you could answer, *Para nada. Me quedé en blanco.* In English slang the equivalent might even be "I spaced." A stock phrase you should remember for personal dealings is *¿En qué quedamos?* to mean something like "What's the agreement, then?" or "So what's the deal?" Use it toward the end of conversations to establish clearly the next step, be it the signing of a multimillion-dollar merger agreement or a date to sip margaritas under the stars.

Along these same lines of final or resultant states are the everyday expressions *quedar bien* and *quedar mal*. Like many of the expressions using *quedar*, these seem to defy a simple English translation, but the idea is "to end up well (or badly) with someone." Their use is similar to *caer bien* and *caer mal*, and often they can be translated with "impress," though that's a little strong. "To get on someone's good side" might come closer for *quedar bien*. *Se puso corbata para quedar bien con los suegros* = "He put on a tie to get on his in-laws' good side." For *quedar mal*, an example will be more helpful than an English equivalent. *Quedé mal con él porque no lo saludé* = "I've gotten on his bad side (i.e., he's mad at me) because I didn't say hello to him."

Finally, *quedar* has a couple of common uses that you should be alert to since they don't fall into the "stay" or "remain" categories. It is the common word for "to fit," for clothes and everything else. Remember to use it with the indirect object pronouns *me, te, le*, etc. *Este saco no me queda* = "This coat doesn't fit." Also, and more natural to a Spanish speaker, *Este saco me queda grande* (or *chico*) = "This coat is too big (or small) for me." *Quedar* also comes into play for describing locations. As a tourist, especially, you will hear it (and can even use it!) a lot. *Perdón, ¿donde queda la plaza? Adelante, a tres cuadras.* = "Excuse me, where is the plaza?" "Three blocks up." *Queda cerca* and *queda lejos* are both handy phrases for travelers. *¿Queda cerca la plaza? No, queda lejos.*

QUERER

An absolutely vital word, and one this book gives a lot of space to so you can get it right. It means "to like" or "to want" and, with people, "to love" or "to want" (see Chapter 4). Like *poder* and *saber*, this verb acts a little strangely in the past tenses (see Chapter 5). Otherwise it's trustworthy, though it's worth rehashing a few tips for using it well. *Querer* performs many interesting tricks when paired with an adverb and in the subjunctive. Before you faint, remember that we already went over that (Chapter 6) and you survived it quite nicely— *cuando quieras, donde quieras, como quieras,* and so on. We've also gone over how to say you "want" something (using *traer*) without dragging *yo quiero* into your speech habits (Chapter 2). Another option is to use *quisiera* ("I'd like"). *Querer* is also, in the phrases *con querer* and *sin querer,* your best ticket for handling "on purpose" and "by accident" (Chapter 12). *Mamá, metí al gato en la piscina. ¿Fue con querer o sin querer?* = "Mommy, I put the cat in the swimming pool." "Was it on purpose or by accident?"

REPETIR

"To repeat," of course, but also "to burp" or "to provoke burps." The proper word for "to burp" is *eructar,* which covers most every burp, while *repetir* is for those little, barely perceptible, good-eatin' burps. Just thought you'd want to know.

ROMPER

Remember that *romper* is "to break intentionally": *Rompí el vaso tirándolo contra la pared* = "I broke the glass by throwing it against the wall." *Romperse* is "to break" in the sense of an accidental act: *Se me rompió el vaso cuando lo estaba lavando* = "The glass broke (on me) when I was washing it." In this construction the literal meaning is "such-and-such broke itself to me (or you, him, her, us, them)." The distinction is not dogma, but you should try to stick to it. *Romper con* is "to break up with" in the sense of lonely hearts and whatnot.

SABER

A sometimes complicated verb, *saber* bears watching for its trickery in past tenses (Chapter 5) and in contrast to *conocer* (see above). An imperfect but useful rule of thumb: use *conocer* with proper and specific nouns and *saber* or *saber de* with the rest of them and most clauses. *¿Conoces París?* but *¿Sabes dónde comen los parisinos?* and *¿Sabes de su historia?* An exception to this rule are the names of languages, which take *saber: ¿Sabes inglés?* Another more sweeping but also far-from-perfect rule: more often than not the word you want for "to know" is *saber. Saber* is frequently followed by verb infinitives; *conocer* never is. *Saber* carries with it the idea of "to know how," so you don't have to say *saber como. ¿Sabes esquiar? No, pero sé caerme.* = "Do you know how to ski?" "No, but I know how to fall down."

A few of the many stock expressions using *saber* include *¿Sabes qué?* ("Know what?"), *No sé* ("I don't know"), *¿Quién sabe?* ("Who knows?"), *¡De haberlo sabido!* ("If I had only known!"), *¿Yo qué sé?* ("What do I know?" or "Don't ask me!"). *Un sabelotodo* is "a know-it-all," and a useful phrase for "as far as I know" is *que yo sepa.*

Finally, and just possibly to confuse you further, *saber* is also the word for "to taste," as in how something tastes to you. *La sopa sabe bien* is "The soup tastes good." In the first person (for use after kissing or among cannibals), the correct form is *sé,* but colloquially you might hear *sepo. ¿Qué tal sé (sepo)? Sabes a pepinillos agrios.* = "How do I taste?" "You taste like pickles." For the transitive "to taste"—that is, to taste something—you need to use *probar.*

SEGUIR

"To follow," yes, but also frequently "to continue" or "to keep (on)." The most common formula is *seguir* plus the infinitive: *Sigue viniendo* ("He keeps coming"), *Sigues comiendo* ("You keep eating") *Sigo llorando* ("I keep crying"), and so on. *Seguir* also works to translate a lot of the uses of "still" in English. In fact, using *seguir* frequently sounds more natural in Spanish than using *todavía,* which is what native English speakers tend to resort to: *Sigue creyendo en Santa Claus.* = "She still believes in Santa Claus." *Sigo enfermo* = "I'm still sick." For the negative, you can use *seguir* + *sin* and sound very "Spanish" indeed: *¿Sigues sin creer en Dios?* = "Do you still not believe in God?" *Seguir sin* and *seguir con* are also useful constructions with a noun tacked on instead of the infinitive. *Sigue sin trabajo* = "He still doesn't have a job." A few odds and ends to take note of: *Síguele* is a handy phrase for "Keep it up" in both its genuine and ironic senses; *¿Quién sigue?* = "Who's next?"; *¿Cómo sigues?* as a greeting means "How are you getting along?" and implies that a person has been sick or afflicted by some sort of trouble, even if it's only Spanish grammar exercises.

SENTIR

Sentir means "to feel" and is a transitive verb used with direct objects—that is, things you feel. Sentirse, the reflexive, is used with adjectives to express how you feel. Thus *Siento frío* is "I feel cold" but *Me siento bien* is "I feel fine." *Siento asco* is "I feel nauseous," and *Me siento mal del estómago* is "I feel sick to my stomach." *Lo siento*, keep in mind, is "I'm sorry," and *Lo siento mucho* is "I'm very sorry." In case you need to explain further, you need only add *haber* and a past participle, dropping the *lo*. Try to learn a couple of these by heart and keep them at the ready: *Siento haber llegado tarde* = "Sorry I'm late." *Siento mucho no haber podido ir* = "I'm very sorry I couldn't come (or go)."

SER

Except when you need *estar* (Chapter 5), *ser* is used for "to be." It is the verb of permanent states, of the way things are, of telling it like it is. There are a billion or so expressions using *ser*, but most of them are predictable and translate as "to be" in English. A few to watch: *¿De quién es?* = "Whose is it?" *¿De qué es?* = "What is it made of?" Like *querer*, *ser* in its subjunctive forms can be employed to form "-ever" words or to say "any": *cuando sea, donde sea*, and so forth. This is covered in Chapter 6, but a few examples here can't hurt. Usually you employ *que sea* after someone has already fed you the antecedent. It's better not to repeat the antecedent but think fast to get the right gender. If someone asks, "What brand of beer do you want?" you can answer *La (marca) que sea*. "In what restaurant do you want to eat?" *En el (restaurante) que sea*. It's worth a little extra work to get these expressions down pat, since otherwise you'll be inclined to say ghastly things like *Cualquier hora que quieres*, instead of the pure and lilting *Cuando sea*, for "Anytime."

SERVIR

"To serve," yes, but how often do you say "to serve" in an average day? "After I serve dinner, if it serves you, m'lord, I'll serve you poisoned coffee and it'll serve you right!" In Spanish *servir* is much

more commonly heard for "to work" in the sense of "to function."
No sirve mi teléfono is "My phone doesn't work." *¿Para qué sirve?* is
"What is it used for?" or even "What good is it?" When *servir* is used
for "to serve," it is often dressed up in the stock phrase *¿En qué le
puedo servir?* ("May I help you?"). *Sírvase* (or *Sírvete*), finally, can be
used for "Help yourself," but a Spanish speaker would probably say
Tome lo que quiera instead.

SOLER

There is no English equivalent for this word among the verbs,
which is odd considering how often you'll find yourself needing it. *Soler* (meaning "to be in the habit of," "to be accustomed to") is useful to
describe something you usually do and is stuck before another verb
in the infinitive, making it a snap to use. *Suelo comer a las dos* = "I
usually eat at two." *Suele ir al cine saliendo del trabajo* = "He usually goes to the movies after work." See Chapter 12 (under "Usually")
for other ways to handle this concept.

SONAR

"To sound" or "to ring." *Suena el timbre* = "The doorbell's
ringing." *Eso suena dudoso* = "That sounds dubious." *Sonar* is also
the verb to use to say "to ring a bell," as in what happens in your
memory when something sounds familiar. "Do you know Juan Pérez?"
No, pero el nombre me suena ("No, but the name rings a bell"). *Sonarse*, incidentally, is "to blow one's nose," and *sonarse a alguien* is
"to smack someone."

SOÑAR

Meaning "to dream," the verb is used with *con*. *Sueño con serpientes* = "I dream about snakes." Here's something worth remembering: *sueño*, the noun form, means both "dream" and "sleep." *Una
falta de sueño* = "A lack of sleep." *Soñado*, the adjective form, is a
fun word for "dreamy" or "ideal": *la playa soñada* = "the beach of
your dreams."

SUBIR

The polar opposite of *bajar* (see above), *subir* works conversely
for gaining weight, getting on a bus, and so on.

TARDAR

Tardar works well for "to take" in time expressions. *Durar* (see above), on the other hand, generally works better for "to last." *Tarda el tiempo que quieras* = "Take as much time as you want." *¿Cuánto tardará en venir?* = "How long will he take in coming?" Since we sometimes use "to take" and "to last" loosely in English, there can be confusion in the correct Spanish choice. *El avión tarda media hora en venir de allá a acá.* = "The plane takes half an hour to get here from there." *El vuelo dura media hora* = "The flight lasts half an hour." As a rule, use *durar* whenever "to last" could work, and use *tardar* otherwise. *Tardar* also means "to take time" with the suggestion of "to take too much time," "to dally," "to be late." *Tardé en llegar porque había mucho tráfico* = "I took a long time getting here (I'm late) because there was a lot of traffic." *El tren está tardando en llegar* = "The train is taking too much time (is late) arriving."

TENER

A megaverb, *tener* is almost worthy of a chapter of its own. Many of its uses are predictable renditions of "to have" in English, including the indispensable *tener que* for "to have to": *Tengo que irme* = "I have to go." It can also be used by itself in the negative to say "I don't have any" when the antecedent is understood. *Dame dinero. No tengo.* = "Give me money." "I don't have any." *¿Dónde está su boleto? No tengo.* = "Where's your ticket?" "I don't have one." Another common use of *tener* with an implied complement is the question *¿Qué tienes?* (or *¿Qué tiene?*), which can translate as "What's your (or his, her) problem?" or "What's the matter with you (or him, her, it)?" Another example: "I don't like the house they've picked out for us." *¿Qué tiene?* ("What's wrong with it?")

Where you will have to pay special attention to *tener* is in the thousand and one expressions in Spanish that use *tener* plus a noun for what in English would be "to be" plus an adjective. In English, for instance, you "are cold," whereas in Spanish you "have cold." Common examples of this construction include *tener hambre* ("to be hungry"), *tener sed* ("to be thirsty"), *tener frío* ("to be cold"), *tener calor* ("to be hot"), *tener sueño* ("to be sleepy"), *tener paciencia* ("to be patient"), *tener cuidado* ("to be careful"), *tener razon* ("to be right"), *tener prisa* ("to be in a hurry").

There are also another thousand and one expressions, many of them quite colloquial, using *no tener*. Here are some you should learn:

No tiene sentido. = "It doesn't make sense."

No tiene caso. = "There's no point" or "What's the point?"
(indicating futility)

No tiene chiste. = "It's boring" or "What's the point?" (indicating insipidness)

No tiene (nada) que ver. = "That has nothing to do with it" "That's irrelevant."

No tiene vergüenza. = "He (or she) is shameless."

No tiene lógica. = "It's illogical" or "It doesn't make sense." (indicating incredulity)

No tiene ni pies ni cabeza. = "I can't make heads or tails of it."

No tiene en donde caerse muerto. = "He (or she) is flat broke."
(literally, "doesn't even have anywhere to drop dead")

No tiene remedio. = "There's no way out" or "There's nothing to be done."

No tiene (ni la menor or *ni la más mínima) idea.* = "He (or she) hasn't got the faintest idea" or "He (or she) hasn't got a clue."

TIRAR

The common verb for "to throw," though *aventar* and *arrojar* are also used quite a lot regionally. *Tirar* also has the implication of "to throw away" or "to throw out." *Tira esa basura* = "Throw that worthless thing out." It is also used for "to knock over," as in *Tiré el vaso* ("I knocked over the glass"). To convey "to toss," as in "Toss me a pen," you could use *aventar* (in the Americas) or *echar* or even *tirar*, but mostly you wouldn't use anything because it's considered rude in the Spanish-speaking world to toss things (see Chapter 2). Unless you're especially keen on seeing a particular object in flight, stick to *Préstame* (see *prestar* above).

TOCAR

"To touch," of course, but also "to play" (a musical instrument) and "to knock" or "to ring" (at someone's door). In *Casablanca* Bogie would have told the pianist, *Tócala, Sam.* An extremely common use of *tocar* that is often glossed over in textbooks is for "to experience" or "to be one's turn." A simple and good translation is elusive, but examples will get the point across. *Me toca.* = "My turn." *¡A* *quién le toca?* = "Whose turn is it?" *A mí no me toca decirle.* = "It's not up to me to tell him." *Al dueño le toca arreglar la casa.* = "It's up to the owner to fix the house." Sometimes the best translation involves "to get": *¿A quién le toca la última rebanada?* = "Who gets the last slice?" *A ti te tocó la más guapa de las hermanas.* = "You got the prettiest of the sisters." *A mí me tocó el más feo de los hermanos* = "I got (stuck with) the ugliest brother." *No me ha tocado verlo en concierto* = "I haven't had (gotten) a chance to see him in concert." And so on. A final note on *tocar*: its past participle, *tocado*, is a common synonym for *loco*—as in the English sense of being slightly "touched" in the head. Children often adapt it to *toca-toca*, translating perhaps as "cuckoo."

TRAER

Traer is straightforward for "to bring," except when "take" and "bring" (*llevar* and *traer*) get mixed up (see Chapter 5).

TRATAR

"To treat," of course, but far more commonly encountered with *de* and meaning "to try." For some reason, though, many Spanish-English dictionaries refuse to acknowledge this fact, leaving the student to choose among *ensayar, procurar, intentar,* and *pretender.* These are all worthy and acceptable verbs, of course, and someday you might even want to learn them. But for now, remember: *tratar de* = "to try." *Traté de dormir* = "I tried to sleep." *Tratamos de llamarte* = "We tried to call you." *Trata de venir antes de las once* = "Try to come before eleven." Only when you're using "to try" in the sense of "to sample" or "to test" should you abandon *tratar de;* the correct verb here is *probar.* An awkward but illustrative example: *Trata de probar el vino blanco 1985.* = "Try to try (i.e., make an effort to sample) the 1985 white wine."

Tratarse, the reflexive form, is a useful verb for "to have to do with" or "to be about." *¿De qué se trata?* is the common way of asking "What's it about?" (in reference to a film, a book, a scuffle, an argument, and the like). "To treat" in the sense of "to pay for someone else" is usually handled by *invitar. Yo invito* = "I'm treating."

VALER

Meaning "to be worth," this verb is frequently encountered in the stock phrases *vale la pena* ("it's worth it") and *no vale la pena*

("it's not worth it"). In addition, you may find *valer* handy for asking
prices. *¿Cuánto vale?* = "How much is it?" Another good use of *valer*,
preceded by *más*, is to translate English phrases that use "better" or
"had better." *Más te vale irte* = "You'd better get out of here." *Más
vale preguntar* = "We'd better ask." And there's the old standby *Más
vale tarde que nunca* ("Better late than never"). In Spain and less so
elsewhere, *vale* by itself is a common interjection for "all right" or
"okay." In Mexico, especially, *valer* with an indirect object pronoun
is a somewhat crude way of saying "couldn't care less." *Me vale* = "I
couldn't care less." *Le vale* = "He doesn't give a damn." Its crudeness
comes from the fact that it's a shortened and therefore euphemistic
form of another phrase, which you'll have to read about in Chapter 10.

VENIR

Meaning "to come," naturally, and sometimes difficult to distinguish from "to go" (see Chapter 5). This verb has some common
but unexpected uses, as in *No viene al caso* ("That's beside the point").
Que viene is especially worth learning in stock phrases like *la semana
que viene* ("next week") and *el año que viene* ("next year"). *Venirse*,
the reflexive form, is usually an innocent intensifier for *venir*, but it
has sexual overtones in some countries and should be used with care.

VER

As "to see," this is a pretty straightforward verb. It can sometimes be confused with *mirar*, since *ver* also works as "to look at" in
many cases where you might be tempted to use *mirar: Ese señor se me
queda viendo* = "That man keeps looking at me." *Estoy viendo tus
discos* = "I'm looking at your records." *Mirar* would work fine in the
first example, but in the second would suggest you are gazing at the
records as if waiting for them to do something. An extremely common
expression is *A ver*, which is simply "Let's see . . ." but which is used
mainly to buy time while you think of a clever response. *Vamos a
ver* means the same but is less common as an interjection or "crutch
word." *Tener que ver con* is the easiest way to translate "to have to do
with." *No tengo nada que ver con el asunto* = "I have nothing to do
with this business." *No tiene que ver* = "That's irrelevant."

Ver is sometimes used to express an opinion, in the sense of
how you "see" or "size up" a problem. *Lo veo difícil* = "It looks difficult to me." *Verse*, the reflexive, covers almost all uses of "to look"
that refer to the appearance of something or someone. You should etch

the phrase *se ve* onto the end of your tongue and have it ready for such common utterances as *Se ve bien* ("It/he/she looks good"), *Se ve difícil* ("It looks difficult"), *Se ve bonito* ("It looks nice"), and so on. *Se ve que* plus a clause is an easy way to communicate "You can tell that . . ." or "It's obvious that . . . . "*Se ve que no han cambiado el agua en la piscina* = "You can tell they haven't changed the water in the pool." *Se ve que son grandes amigos* = "You can tell that they're great friends."

VOLVER

In the sense of "to return" or "to come back," *volver* is interchangeable with *regresar*. *Volver* has another common use that you will want to learn, though—one that *regresar* does not share. *Volver* plus *a* plus an infinitive is frequently found as a substitute for "to repeat" or "to do again." It will take some practice before you start to use it properly—and as an alternative to *otra vez*—but it's worth the extra effort. Some typical examples of when to substitute: *Gracias, vuelvo a llamar más tarde* = "Thanks, I'll call back (again) later." *Si vuelves a pedírmelo, no te lo voy a dar* = "If you ask me for it again, I'm not going to give it to you." *Vuelve a intentar* = "Try again." *Volver* cannot be used transitively—to "return" a book to the library, for instance, or "to give back" a borrowed item. Use either *regresar* or *devolver* in these situations. *Devuélveme a mi chica* ("Give me back my girl"), for instance, was the name of a pop song and movie of a few seasons ago. *Volverse*, finally, is one of the common ways to handle "to become" (or "to get"). Skip ahead to Chapter 11 for details.

CRANKING UP
YOUR SPANISH

Not long ago, I owned a somewhat antiquated motor vehicle that in fits and starts, quite literally, became dear to me. It wasn't much to look at—antique buffs generally looked away instead—but it more often than not got me where I was going. The car's main flaw, and what finally led me to get rid of it, was its temperament on chilly mornings. Instead of responding to the turn of the key with a loud growl and churning pistons, it tended to respond with a weak series of hiccups and the grinding of metal. Once started, it sputtered, stuttered, gurgled, and spit. Only after a few minutes of this litany did it begin to growl a little roughly, then purr hesitantly, then hum.

Beginning Spanish speakers remind me of that car. Once warmed up, they chatter along merrily, constructing elaborate clauses and communicating their meaning. But getting warmed up is another story. Frequent false starts, "ums," hiccups, and the grinding of gray matter punctuate their speech, and English interjections pop in and out. It is obvious that they are still thinking in English and trying to translate, rather than thinking in Spanish.

What beginning students often lack are the appropriate words and phrases to start a sentence smoothly. As in English, these words don't always contribute a lot to the meaning of the sentence, but they do give the brain a chance to warm up and kick into gear. Skipping over them can make speech sound stilted and abrupt—sometimes even impolite or hasty. Even when you are past the beginner stage, you should pay attention to your "sentence starters." Learn a few well, get accustomed to using them, and your Spanish will sound more natural, flow more easily, and hum along to its desired destination.

BUENO

Bueno means nothing more than "well," but it is nearly indispensable to good spoken Spanish. It simply prefaces comments and tends to tone down their hastiness or prepare the listener for a message. The difference between *Ya me voy* and *Bueno, ya me voy* is subtle but noticeable. The first is "I'm going now" and comes across as a sort of dare to anyone who might try to stop you, while the second suggests "Well, I think I'll be going now" and sounds more laid-back and more polite.

Bueno often insinuates a "stop" into an ongoing conversation or activity. You might sit down to chat with friends for five or ten minutes and then simply say *bueno* to announce your imminent departure. Or you could sit down to talk business with colleagues and, after a few minutes of small talk and niceties, signal the beginning of the business talk with a *bueno*. If the person speaking before you at a conference decides to launch a vitriolic attack against everything the audience holds dear, you might begin your presentation with a sighed *bueno*; here it would convey "anyhow" or "as we were saying" or even "whew!" Usually it's much simpler: a pause while you get your thoughts together, a signal that you have the floor, an acceptance of what has gone before but a statement that you intend to begin something different.

PUES

Similar to *bueno* but simpler still. *Pues* means "well, then" but often replaces an English "ummm" or "let's see" It means, in short, that you are thinking about your response and would like your listener to hold on for a few seconds while you try to bring order to the mild chaos reigning in your head. Often, *pues* is accompanied by eyes rolling about, looking up, or darting off to some distant object and other telltale and foolproof signs of intense mental activity. "Wanna go to a movie?" *Pues* . . . ("Will it mean staying out late? Can I find a baby-sitter? What good movies are around? Shouldn't I be working on my taxes? Can I afford a movie these days?") . . . *sí, vámonos.*

You'll sometimes hear *pues* reduced to a shortened, or just more mumbled, form: *pos*, for instance, or *pus* or *pos'n*. In parts of Spain you'll hear an emphatic *¡pue!*; in parts of Mexico a barely audible *pss*. When a foreigner talks this way, it can sound very natural or very stupid, depending on the stigma (upper-class snob, lower-class slob, rural hick, urban gang, etc.) that accompanies a form in each given locale. Listen to how people around you speak, then contract your *pues* if you're so inclined.

ENTONCES

It means "then," but which "then"? Usually, *entonces* crops up in storytelling situations, as when you are relating what happened in chronological order. *Entonces yo llamé a la policía. Entonces Juan escondió la tú-ya-sabes-que. Entonces llegó la señora de los rifles . . . .* But you will also run across it in present-time situations where it translates more like "so" or "so then." *Entonces, ¿qué hacemos?* = "So what do we do?" *Entonces, yo voy por la Carretera 1* = "So then (what you're saying is that) I take Highway 1." *¿Entonces no van a querer pizza?* = "So you're not going to want any pizza?" *¿Entonces?* and *¿Entonces qué?* as questions mean "And next?" or "Then what?" Both are very common and, when reduced in a slangy context, can come out sounding like *¿'tons qué?* ("So what'll it be?" or "Now what?"). You may even hear *¿'tons?* by itself, but remember that these lazy shortcuts have their enemies among the more refined speakers of the language.

LUEGO

Luego is a lot like *entonces* in that it means "then" and is interchangeable with *entonces* in many cases. *Luego* generally tends to be reserved more for time constructions and often works better as "later" than as "then." A subtle distinction: *entonces* implies "and then (as a result)," whereas *luego* is often simply "and then (in sequence)." *Primero me voy a bañar, luego voy a la tienda, y luego a tu casa* = "First I'm going to take a bath, then go to the store, and then to your house." It works as "later" when you're putting something off into an indistinct future. The most familiar example of this is *Hasta luego* for "See you later." You can also say *Luego te hablo* ("I'll call you later"), *Termínalo luego* ("Finish it later"), *Luego voy* ("I'll go later"), *Luego te digo* ("I'll tell you later"), and so on. Note that regionally *luego luego* (paradoxically) means "right away" or "immediately," and not "later, later."

A PROPÓSITO

"By the way." As in English, this usually announces a change of subject or indicates that the speaker has been reminded of something else that needs relating. *Son las nueve. A propósito, ¿no ibas a llamar a Juan?* = "It's nine o'clock. By the way, weren't you going to call Juan?"

POR CIERTO

This also means "by the way." If there is a difference, this phrase is better for changing the subject when no apparent cause for it exists. In other words, if someone is talking about the philosophical implications of modern cinema, and you're hungry and want to talk about sandwiches, you could say *Por cierto, ¿nadie tiene hambre?* You'll still get a funny look, but you'll be more correct than if you use *a propósito*, which denotes "in reference to that."

ES QUE

This is an extremely useful sentence starter, and one you should learn and prepare to embellish. You won't appreciate the importance of *es que* unless you stop and think of all of the utterly useless words you tack on to the beginning of your conversational speech in English. Rarely, for instance, do we say "He doesn't want to go to the store." We say something like, "No, well, as it happens, he doesn't want to go to the store." Okay, I'm exaggerating, but pay close attention to how you speak and you'll see I'm not exaggerating much. Are you hungry? "No, it's just that I've got this craving for a Milky Way." Did you sleep well? "No, well, sort of, but the thing was, there were so damn many dogs howling that I kept waking up." It may not read pretty, but this is the way we speak much of the time. In Spanish you can add useless words and phrases to your speech, too, and sound more fluent in the process. The best all-purpose add-on is *es que*, which can be used in all of the comments used above. *No, es que no quiere ir a la tienda. No, es que se me antoja un Milky Way. No, bueno, más o menos sí, pero es que estaban ladrando tantos malditos perros que me seguía despertando.*

In these examples, *es que* introduces a negation or qualification of a preceding statement. It doesn't always, but it does require a preceding statement of some sort to build from. Once you get the hang of *es que*, you will find that just about any preceding statement at all will do:

"Why is Juan unhappy?"
Es que está enamorado de María.
"Why doesn't he tell her?"
Es que ella está hablando con ese tipo.
"And when she's finished?"
Es que Juan tiene miedo.
"Of what?"
Es que ese tipo está muy grandote.

       "So?"
Es que es el esposo de María.
       "Ah. So he'd better forget about María . . ."
Es que no puede.
       " . . . and find someone else."
Es que no le gustan las otras.
       "So he's got a problem."
Es que está loco.
       "And unhappy."
Es que está enamorado de María . . .

And so on.

LO QUE PASA ES QUE

Just like *es que*, only more so. This is a very typical, very natural, very unnecessary phrase to add on at the beginning of your thought to make yourself sound more fluent. It can be used in the same instances that *es que* can be used—which is to say practically anytime. Why is Juan unhappy? *Lo que pasa es que está enamorado . . .* and so on.

LA VERDAD ES QUE

This means something like "the truth of the matter is, "but you'll hear it—and need to use it—more often than that. In fact, this is often a good translation for "actually," which many English speakers use to start a sentence and which, as beginning Spanish speakers, they tend to translate as *actualmente*. Sadly, *actualmente* doesn't mean "actually" but "at present" or "currently." So you're left with *la verdad es que* or some other substitute. "Everything okay?" *Bueno, la verdad es que la sopa es un poco salada* ("Well, actually, the soup is a little salty"). "Can I drop by later tonight?" *Pues, la verdad es que pensaba ir al cine* ("Well, actually, I was thinking of going to a movie"). Note that *la verdad es que*, like "actually," is frequently used as a polite way to break some bad news or indicate disagreement.

RESULTA (QUE)

Here's the word you've been wanting for "it turns out (that)." *Fuimos al cine, pero resulta que cierran los viernes* = "We went to the movies, but it turns out that they close on Fridays." *Creía que Juan era un sinvergüenza, pero resulta que es muy amable"* = "I thought Juan was a jerk, but it turns out he's a nice guy." Often it is used to start off a sentence, especially in response to questions and quizzical expressions. You walk in, empty-handed, after going to the store. Your mother looks at you strangely. You say, prompted or un-prompted and a little peeved, *Resulta que ya no aceptan efectivo en las tiendas* ("It turns out that they don't accept cash anymore in the stores"). *Resultar que* can also be used for "to work out" in the sense of a mathematical result. *Resulta que nos debes dos mil pesos* = "It works out that you owe us 2,000 pesos."

Resulta without a *que* clause and with an adjective or a noun, and sometimes with *ser* thrown in for good measure, is also a common construction. Usually, it still translates well as "to turn out." *Resultó (ser) un desastre su fiesta* = "His party turned out to be a disaster." *Resultó (ser) agradable la visita* = "The visit turned out to be quite pleasant."

QUE

You know of course that *que* is a key element of speaking Spanish, and you even know where and when to use it—most of the time. But if you are like most native English speakers, you will have to train yourself to use *que* when answering questions that start with *¿qué?* "That" is not always used this way in English, though some-times it is. Say your Spanish professor calls you at home, and after the call your brother asks, *¿Qué pasó?* ("What's up?"). *Que mañana va a haber un examen* ("We're having an exam tomorrow"), you would an-swer. Or say the terrorists have taken hostages and sent a list of de-mands. Trying to read over the police chief's shoulder, you ask, *¿Qué quieren?* He would answer, *Que liberemos a cien prisioneros* ("For us to free a hundred prisoners").

Another case in which "that" is rarely used in English but *que* almost always is in Spanish is when you repeat something:

> *Juan no está en su casa.*
> *¿Qué dices?*
> *Que Juan no está en su casa.*

In some cases, as when repeating a direct command, you'll have to change from the imperative to the subjunctive (indirect command) the second time around. This extra hurdle, in fact, may explain why many foreigners don't take the trouble to learn this use of *que*:

> *Vete a tu casa.* = "Go home."
> *¿Qué dices?* = "What did you say?"
> *Que te vayas a tu casa.* = "I said for you to go home."

Note that the police chief also used the subjunctive as he transformed a direct command into an indirect command above.

ASÍ QUE

Generally, this is the phrase you need to translate "so" at the start of a sentence. "So you wanna be a rock 'n' roll star?" would be expressed as *¿Así que quieres ser una estrella de rock?* "So you're really leaving me?" would be *¿Así que de verdad me vas a dejar?* And so on. Note that *así que* does not, however, mean "So what?" For that, use *¿Y qué?*

FÍJATE (QUE)

Again, not a phrase that will boost the intellectual content of your comment, but one that will help you sound more fluent. It means something like "Look, . . ." and is used to call someone's attention to something. For some reason, I associate it with reading a newspaper and passing on bits of news to someone sitting nearby. It's used more than that, of course, but that's a good example of how it should be used. *Fíjate que van a cerrar la autopista mañana* = "Look, they're going to close the freeway tomorrow." *Fíjate que Robert Redford usa los mismos zapatos que tú* = "How about that! Robert Redford wears the same shoes as you." Sometimes it introduces a note of skepticism into what you are relating. *Fíjate que el presidente dice que ya no hay crisis económica* = "Whaddya know? The president says there's no more economic crisis."

Fíjate que plus the subjunctive means "make sure" and can be used instead of the barbarism *checar* to say "to check." *Fíjate que esté bien cerrada la puerta* = "Make sure the door's closed all the way." *Fíjate que no tenga gusanos antes de comerlo* = "Check to make sure it doesn't have any worms before you eat it."

Fíjate without the *que* is simply "watch out" or "pay attention." Parents tend to use this phrase to scold children who mindlessly wander into puddles, for instance. *¡Fíjate!* or *¡Fíjate donde caminas!* They also might use it to get a child to concentrate on an explanation of a math problem, say. *Fíjate, la dos pasa para allá* = "Look, the two goes over there." Finally, if you want to be as rude as the klutz who just bumped into you on the sidewalk, you can say *¡Fíjate, imbécil!*

MIRA

Meaning "Look!" or "Look here," this imperative can be used literally (*¡Mira! ¡No trae ropa!*) or figuratively (*Mira, yo no quiero problemas*). In the figurative sense, it almost always is used to set the record straight. *Mira, yo nunca dije que no pudieras irte* = "Look, I never said you couldn't go." If you're keen on sounding macho, it's also a good way to lead off a verbal assault, much like "Look here, . . . "*Mira, o te largas o llamo a la policía* = "Look here, either you get lost or I call the police."

HAZ DE CUENTA QUE

This phrase is mostly to be found in the world of kids, but grown-ups can use it, too. The best translation among kids is "Make believe . . . ," as in "Make believe I'm Spiderman and you're Godzilla." Since we grown-ups don't say things like that, in our mouths *haz de cuenta* could translate as "Imagine . . . . "*Haz de cuenta que sales del baño y hay un alacrán en tu toalla.* = "Imagine that you get out of the bath and there's a scorpion on your towel" *Haz de cuenta que eres el presidente, ¿qué harías?* = "Say you were the president. What would you do?" It can also be used to cover a lot of uses of "to pretend," which *pretender* is notoriously unfit to do. "Pretend I'm not here" = *Haz de cuenta que no estoy.* The formal form of this phrase, for the record, is *haga de cuenta*, while in the plural it is *hagan de cuenta*. Note also that sometimes it is used reflexively: *hazte de cuenta, hágase de cuenta, háganse de cuenta*.

NI MODO QUE

This expression isn't used everywhere in the Spanish-speaking world, but in Mexico, for instance, it's so common that you'll wonder how the other countries survive without it. It's a very handy expression, and one that can be considered "advanced" for beginners—especially since it calls for the subjunctive to follow it. But if you're feeling ready to flex some Spanish muscles, give it a go. *Ni modo que*, more or less literally, means "no way that." I say this reluctantly, because *ni modo* definitely does not mean "No way!" as in "No way, José" (use *para nada* for that). But *ni modo que* as a sentence starter can translate as "No way that . . . ." Better translations might be "Like hell . . ." or "You can't expect . . . ."

An example will help here. On your tax return you claim that you made only two dollars the previous year, despite working full time as an investment banker. A friend questions the ethics of your claim and you say, *¡Ni modo que les diga la verdad!* ("No way I'm going to tell them the truth!"). A few months later you get a call from an IRS agent who says she found some irregularities in your return and wants to talk to you. You grudgingly make an appointment. *Ni modo que me vaya a México* ("Well, I can't just run off to Mexico"), you shrug. The agent chats with you, then a prosecutor chats with you, and then all of a sudden a judge is chatting with you. *Ni modo que te dejemos libre* ("Well, we can't just let you go free"), he says. You make bail and decide to visit a travel agency, where you buy a one-way ticket to Cancun. *Ni modo que vaya a prisión* ("Like hell I'm going to jail"), you say. Months later, on the beach in Cancun, someone asks you why you came to Mexico. *Pues ni modo que me quedara ahí, con tanto crimen que hay* ("Well, you couldn't expect me to stay there, with all that crime"), you respond.

MENOS MAL QUE

Here's an extremely useful sentence starter that you should learn and use. The best translation is "good thing" or "it's just as well," and you'll find yourself needing it more and more as you become comfortable with it. *Menos mal que trajiste paraguas, porque va a llover* = "Good thing you brought an umbrella, because it's going to rain." *Menos mal que no fuiste, estuvo muy aburrida* = "Just as well you didn't go, it was very boring." Often it is used by itself, just like the English comments "Good thing" or "Just as well." *Juan no pudo venir. Menos mal. Me cae mal.* = "Juan couldn't come." "Just as well. I don't like him." *Este tren no para hasta San José. Menos mal.* = "This train doesn't stop until San José." "Good."

LO BUENO, LO MALO, LO INCREÍBLE, LO PEOR, ETC.

In English, it is common to begin a sentence by referring to an unspecified "thing." It may not be glamorous, but we do it. The good thing is that in Spanish there is an equivalent construction; the bad thing is that it is done differently; the only thing to remember is the word *lo*.

    Lo plus an adjective is the formula in Spanish for "the good thing," "the bad thing," "the only thing," and similar constructions: *Lo bueno, lo malo, lo único,* etc. This formula saves you from ungainly constructions such as *la buena cosa* or *la cosa mala,* which aren't natural to Spanish. Once you get the hang of this formula, I promise that you will wonder how you spoke Spanish so long without it. The usual formula is *lo* + adjective + *es que*. Here are some of the common adjectives to make use of this formula:

> *lo bueno* = "the good thing"
> *lo malo* = "the bad thing"
> *lo único* = "the only thing"
> *lo difícil* = "the hard thing"
> *lo peor* = "the worst thing"
> *lo mejor* = "the best thing"
> *lo raro, lo extraño* = "the strange thing"
> *lo chistoso* = "the funny thing"
> *lo increíble* = "the amazing thing"
> *lo (más) absurdo* = "the crazy thing"

The formula *es* + *lo* + adjective is also a handy one for quick and fluent comebacks, of the sort that are dealt with in the next chapter. For example, *Es lo raro* = "That's the strange thing (about what has just happened)."

A VER

    Either by itself or followed by a clause, *a ver* is a useful sentence starter that translates well as "Let's see . . . . "By itself, it is used almost as an interjection. "My computer is acting up." *A ver* ("Let me have a look"). "I can turn water into wine." *A ver* ("Let's see you do it"). "Do you have change for a dollar?" *A ver* ("Hold on, let me check"). The clauses that usually follow *A ver* begin with *qué* or *si* and translate as "Let's see if" or "Let's see what." Often it provides an easy, painless translation for "to check," similar to *fíjate* (see above) but usually implying that the speaker will help with the checking. *A ver si la puerta está bien cerrada* = "Let's check and see if the door's closed." *A ver si ya regresaron* = "Let's see if they're back yet." *A ver qué hacen los niños* = "Let's see (check on) what the kids are doing." When writing *a ver*, take care not to confuse it with its homonym *haber*.

CON RAZÓN

This is an excellent sentence starter that can be used, like *a ver*, either by itself or to introduce a clause. In both cases, its best translation is "No wonder!" or "Little wonder." "As a child, John was attacked by a Great Dane." *Con razón les tiene miedo ahora* ("No wonder he's afraid of them now"). "My car broke down." *Con razón llegaste caminando* ("No wonder you arrived on foot"). "I ate three chili dogs and now I'm feeling a little sick" *Pues con razón* ("Little wonder" or "Well, whaddya expect?"). This notion can also be rendered with *No es para menos*.

POR ESO

This phrase means "that's why" and frequently comes in handy, by itself or with a clause, to draw a connection that may not be immediately obvious. "I hear you're going to marry my daughter." *Sí señor, por eso quiero hablar con usted* ("Yes sir, that's why I want to talk with you"). "There's a lot of crime in this neighborhood." *Por eso tenemos triple candado en la puerta* ("That's why we have a triple lock on the door"). "You want to go outside? But it's pouring rain!" *Por eso. Quiero estrenar mi nuevo paraguas* ("For that very reason. I want to try out my new umbrella").

EN FIN

A close fit for "So anyhow, . . ." and very useful for leading off a summation or a conclusion or for steering a conversation back to its original point. *En fin, no puedo visitar ahora* = "So anyhow, I can't visit now." The phrase is usually used as a sentence starter after you've been talking for a while. For instance, after recounting all the different plates you sampled at the restaurant, you might finish your description with *En fin, comí bien* ("So anyhow, I ate well"). If you use it after someone else has been talking awhile, you're saying, in effect, "Yes, very interesting, but back to the subject at hand . . . ."

TOTAL

Total can also be used for "So anyhow, . . ." and can be paired with *que* to lead off a clause. *Total que nadie fue a su fiesta* = "So (as it turned out) no one went to his party." Or, slangily, *Total que fuimos*

y no había nadie = "So anyhow we went and there was no one there."
Both *total* and *en fin* sound more natural than the standard translations that dictionaries give for "anyhow" and "anyway": *de todos modos, de todas maneras, de cualquier modo, en todo caso*—at least at
the beginning of sentences. These translations are best saved for cases
where "anyway" or "anyhow" is used at the end of the sentence:
"He stole your car. *Pero lo quiero de todos modos* ("But I love him
anyway").

YA AND *TODAVÍA*

Beginning students often have trouble distinguishing these
two invaluable sentence starters. As a rule, *ya* means "already" and *todavía* means "still" or "yet." *Ya* in the negative can equal "no longer"
or "not . . . anymore."

> *Ya estoy comiendo.* = "I'm already eating."
> *Todavía estoy comiendo.* = "I'm still eating."
> *Ya quiero comer.* = "I want to eat already (now)."
> *Todavía quiero comer.* = "I still want to eat."
> *Ya no quiero comer.* = "I don't want to eat anymore,"
>   "I no longer want to eat."
> *Todavía no quiero comer.* = "I still don't want to eat,"
>   "I don't want to eat yet."

Let's say you're having a dinner party and the guest of honor is half an
hour late. You go to call his house and return with one of the following
messages:

> *Ya viene.* = "He's on his way," "He's about to leave."
> *Todavía viene.* = "He's still (planning on) coming (though not
>   immediately)."
> *Ya no viene.* = "He's not coming anymore."
> *Todavía no viene.* = "He still hasn't left."

To learn *ya* well, keep in mind that it is often used for emphasis with
present-tense verbs. Regionally in American English "already" is used
in the same way: "all right already," for instance. *Ya voy* = "I'm coming already." Sometimes "now" is the better translation. *Ya nos vamos*
= "We're going now." *Ya está la comida* = "The food's ready now."
Sometimes the added emphasis is in the tone. *Ya verás* = "You'll see."
Ya intensifies imperatives as well. *Cómete la fruta* would be "Eat your
fruit"; *Ya cómete la fruta* would be more like "Come on, eat your

fruit." Note that in most cases, *ya* indicates a change in the way things have been up to that point.

Ya que is also a common sentence starter that students seem to shy away from because "already that" doesn't ring any bells in their head. It means "since" or, even better, "seeing that" or "now that." *Ya que terminaste este capítulo, ¿qué vas a hacer?* = "Now that you've finished this chapter, what are you going to do?"

9   SNAPPY ANSWERS

Many native Spanish speakers will instinctively judge a foreigner's fluency in Spanish by the foreigner's ability to respond quickly and conventionally to a wide range of stock situations and comments. From such simple remarks as *Mucho gusto* and *¿Cómo estás?* to more complex utterances, many statements seem to have a traditional, almost automatic response built in. The sooner you master some of these answers, the sooner you will achieve an enviable degree of fluency in Spanish.

Mastering the comeback means having a handful of stock expressions on the tip of your tongue, ready to be activated by the right comment. *Mucho gusto*, someone says. A click goes off in your brain, synapses slap together, and your tongue utters *Igualmente*. The whole episode should take less than a nanosecond. You needn't think at all, and in fact the less you think, the better. That may not be an ideal rule for all verbal communication, but for learning comebacks it is bliss.

AFFIRMATIVE

For a perfectly adequate affirmative response you can always say *Sí*, of course. But for true fluency you should shop around for alternatives. How often, after all, do you answer with a simple yes in English? If someone asks if you want to go swimming, you are more likely to respond "Sure" or "All right" than "Yes." If someone says "I'll call you tomorrow," you may utter an "Okay" or "Good." "Can you give me a hand?" elicits a "Sure" or "No problem." "Nice weather we're having." "Really." "See you for dinner?" "Great." Likewise, stock phrases exist in Spanish for all manner of situations. Get a handle on a couple of them and you'll soon be saying yes in style.

CLARO (QUE SÍ)

Generally defined as "of course," we would more colloquially say "sure" in English. "Can you be here by four?" *Claro.* "Can you lend a hand with the dishes?" *Claro.* It is also commonly used as a sympathetic interjection for "obviously" or "naturally," and in this capacity it is often heard in one-sided phone conversations, with the listener repeating *claro* every so often to show he or she is still listening. Somewhat gaudier alternatives for *claro* include *desde luego* and *por supuesto.* ¿*Cómo no?* is very natural-sounding, but you will have to overcome your natural resistance to using a "no" phrase to say "yes." *Seguro* works fairly well as "sure," but is also used ironically, as "sure" is in English. To avoid doubt, use *claro* instead.

ESTÁ BIEN

This is the phrase of choice for avoiding "okay," which is used in Spanish and probably every other living language but is not native. Furthermore, some uses of "okay" are simply wrong if translated into Spanish. You would never say *Está O.K.* for "It's okay," for instance. So get used to saying *Está bien* instead. "All right" can also be rendered *Está bien.* In fact, *está bien* should be one of the commonest expressions to come out of your mouth when you speak Spanish. "I'm going home now." *Está bien.* "I'll call you later." *Está bien.* "I'll pick you up at eight." *Está bien.* "Let's sell everything and elope to Paraguay." *Está bien.* To sound slangier, you can say '*tá bien.*

CONSTE

This handy response comes from the verb *constar*, which is one of those untranslatable words that frustrate dictionary writers. Basically, the idea behind *conste* (from *que conste*, or "let the record show") is roughly "for the record"; as a comeback, it means "That's a confirmed fact" or "I'll hold you to that." Usually it is used in somewhat jocular fashion, as when a friend promises to visit you soon at your new home in Arizona. *Conste*, you would respond, wagging a friendly finger at your friend: "You've promised." Often it's followed by ¿*eh?* for emphasis. "I'll be home by eleven, Mom." *Conste, ¿eh?* ("Remember later that you said so" or "I'll be waiting up for you").

DE ACUERDO

Another good choice for the "all right" or "okay" group. It is usually reserved for cases where some definite accord has been reached, even if it's only an agreement to "see ya later." More formally, you can use *trato hecho* ("it's a deal") or just *hecho* ("done") in the same cases. "I'll pick you up at eight." *De acuerdo.* "Pick me up at eight." *Hecho.*

¿VERDAD?

A very simple remark but very common as well. It conveys the idea of "Ain't that the truth!" but works well for "Really," especially in response to questions that beg for an affirmative response. "This weather's lousy." *¿Verdad?* "Sure is nice to be here." *¿Verdad?* "That's a great movie." *¿Verdad?* It is often preceded by *sí: Sí, ¿verdad?*

NEGATIVE

Handy for requests made of you by friends, simple acquaintances, or even complete strangers, the negative phrase is everywhere useful. The intensity of a rejection, even without straying over to the side of obscenity, can range from the polite but firm to the impolite but firm. As with *sí* and the affirmative, you could just say *no* for your negatives. But read on and see what fun you'd be missing!

PARA NADA

The correct translation for "no way," as in "No way, José." "Wanna hear me play 'Feelings' on my kazoo?" *Para nada.*

EN ABSOLUTO

Watch out—the phrase means "absolutely not," not "absolutely." In fact, it means the same thing as *para nada*, but is more polite.

¡QUÉ ESPERANZAS!

Another fairly polite way of saying "Not on your life!" Literally, it means "What hope!" and suggests "You must be dreaming."

EN TUS SUEÑOS

A more impolite way of saying "You must be dreaming" or "Dream on!" "How about a kiss, sweetie pie?" *¡En tus sueños!* Add the appropriate qualifier at the end and you have a rude, power-packed rejection. *¡En tus sueños, imbécil!* = "Like hell, Dogbreath." Variants include *¡ni en sueños!* and *¡ni soñarlo!*

ESTÁS LOCO

This is the shortest way of saying "You're nuts," "You gotta be kidding," or "You must be out of your mind," but it's not always the

most natural-sounding. For that, use *Estás como loco* or the slangier
Estás como operado, which is like saying "You ought to have your
head examined." Remember to make the phrase agree in gender and
number with the object of your derision. *Están como locos* = "You
guys must be crazy."

NI LOCO

A very firm, very natural way of saying "No way." Literally,
you're saying "Not even if I were crazy (would I do such-and-such)."
"How about a quick game of Russian Roulette?" *¡Ni loco!* Remember to make gender and number agree: *ni loco, ni loca, ni locos,* or
ni locas.

YA BASTA

"Enough already!" or, in slangier situations, "Cut it out!" If
someone is relating a series of dubious anecdotes and ignoring all of
your newly learned expressions of disbelief, you may be able to shut
them up with a *¡Ya basta!* Said with a laugh, it means "No, don't go
on," "That's too much," or "Get outta here!"

ESO SÍ QUE NO

One you should learn just to impress your friends. It means—
are you ready?—"no." But why just say "no" when you can say *¡Eso sí
que no!* Actually, it's a little stronger than just plain no and comes
closer to "That's out of the question" or "Forget it."

FRUITS AND OTHER NONSENSE

Just for fun, you can substitute lots of irrelevant words for an
emphatic *¡No!* Two common ones are *¡Naranjas!* (sometimes *¡Naranjas de la China!*) and *¡Mangos!* Also used are *¡Narices!* and *¡Cuernos!*
The latter expression refers to (and is sometimes accompanied by) the
two-finger "hook-em-horns" gesture, which in turn can be traced back
to an indelicate reference to cuckoldry. Use it with caution.

SURPRISE

Surprises, by definition, catch you off guard. But that's no excuse to be tongue-tied as well. Here are some retorts that will enable
you to convey your surprise snappily.

¿EN SERIO?

This is probably the best translation for the ubiquitous English
question "Really?" and usually suggests that you genuinely believe

what you are hearing, though you might prefer not to. "Mary's had an accident." *¿En serio?* It needn't be traumatic news. "I think my watch has stopped." *¿En serio?*

¡N'OMBRE!

This universal slang phrase is an abbreviated form of *no hombre* but is pronounced very much like *nombre*. It is like *¿en serio?* but is slangier and indicates more surprise: "No way!" Said laconically, it's a simple negative, equating perhaps with "Nah."

¡IMAGÍNESE!

These exclamations mean "Imagine!" or "Imagine that!" but suggest stronger surprise: "Can you imagine that?" It's pretty formal and is a good phrase to throw around when formality is expected of you, as when your elders are describing shocking things that kids do these days: "And girls these days let the boys kiss them on the first date!" *¡Imagínese! abuela.* The familiar form is *¡Imagínate!*

¡QUÉ BARBARIDAD!

The phrase means "Goodness gracious!" or the like but is much more commonplace. "Good Lord!" or some other religious imprecation is often heard in English. It is used to respond to surprising and generally unpleasant news, such as a natural disaster or a problem in the extended family. It is not to be used when the surprising news is also good news. If you're told that your mother-in-law has just won a beauty contest, saying *¡Qué barbaridad!* might just earn you a fat lip. *¡Qué locura!* ("What madness!") is used in much the same way when the speaker is emphasizing the absurdity of the news as well.

ES EL COLMO

This can be a tough phrase to translate, but you'll recognize its use right away. It can mean "That's too much," "If that doesn't beat all," "That's going too far," and so on. It is used for "last straw" situations, as when you can't fathom why someone has finally done something utterly outrageous. "Did you hear about the Van Gogh freak who cut off his ear?" *¡No! ¡Es el colmo!* "That rude son of mine forgot to call me on my birthday!" *¡Es el colmo!*

Other interjections for surprise and shock include one-word responses that cover a fairly narrow range of meaning—from "Gosh" to "Omigosh," roughly. Two safe ones are *¡increíble!* and *¡caray!* Both of these can also be used with *Qué* to good effect: *¡Qué increíble!* and *¡Qué caray!* The first generally is in response to good news, the second to bad news. Other expressions are euphemistic but safe, including *¡Hijo de!* and *¡Hijo!* as well as (in Mexico) *¡Híjole!* They all mean "Son of a gun!" Common euphemisms for surprise in Mexico are *¡Chin!* and *¡Chihuahua!* The *Ca-* family of euphemisms is also a good source for mild, universally understood expressions of shock: *¡Caracoles! ¡Caramba! ¡Carachos! ¡Canarios! ¡Carape!* and so on.

DISBELIEF

If you are traveling through the Spanish-speaking world and are not yet accustomed to its idiosyncrasies, disbelief may well be one of your most common reactions. Oh, how you will long for some good expressions when your reservations are not respected, when the bus doesn't arrive after all, or when the town you want to visit apparently no longer exists! A good rule for visiting this magical kingdom is to suspend your disbelief, but when you don't succeed, you'll need to express it. Here's how.

NO PUEDE SER

Literally, "It can't be," even though of course it often can be and is. This is the ultimate expression of disbelief, the one that conveys "I am not experiencing this!" or "This is not really happening!" Good for when your breakfast bill tallies up to several thousand dollars.

NO ME DIGA

This covers the laconic "You don't say," as in English, but is also widely used for "Don't tell me that!" or "It can't be!" Slightly less desperate than *No puede ser*, it indicates a less significant break with reality. It can be used, for instance, when you arrive late to a concert and are told that this performance is sold out. In the familiar, it's *No me digas*.

¡A POCO!

Slangy and not universal. It usually suggests that you don't believe what you are hearing and can even be a curt cutoff of what you consider nonsense, like the English "Bull!" but without the feistiness. Maybe better English equivalents would be "You gotta be kidding!" or "Gimme a break!"

DÉJESE DE CUENTOS

This means "Cut the crap" but is somewhat more refined. "Come off it" might be closer. It does mean that you think you are being lied to—or at least being kidded with—so don't use it too loosely. A similar phrase is *No me venga con cuentos*. For a strong but perfectly decent way of saying "Like hell!" tell the neighborhood liar *¡Eso cuéntaselo a tu abuela!*—which means "Go tell your grandma."

¿CÓMO?

A simple but underrated form of expressing mild shock and disbelief. If the cabbie says it will cost you seventy-five dollars to get across town, you can very politely reply *¡Cómo!*—as in, "I'm going to pretend I didn't hear that, so let's try a new answer." Robert de Niro's character in *Taxi Driver*, had he been speaking Spanish, might have simply said *¡Cómo!* for "You talkin' to me?" To embellish this phrase, you can add a form of the verb *decir: ¡Cómo dijo!* or *¡Cómo dice!*

SEGURO

This means "sure," so it only works for disbelief if you ladle irony all over it. Since "sure" often gets this tone in English, that shouldn't be too hard to manage. The effect is like the English "Yeah, right." Other expressions used ironically to express disbelief are *claro, ¡en serio!* and *cómo no.* "Yes, Mr. Sánchez, your check is in the mail." *Cómo no.*

INDIFFERENCE

A lively and specialized vocabulary for indifference exists in Spanish, and it's well worth your while to learn a few of its forms. Regional differences are often pronounced, so do pay attention to what's being used around you and how people react to your usages. Keep in mind, too, that often the best way of expressing your total lack of interest is—again—with a phrase for surprise or shock and plenty of irony. *¡En serio!*—spoken as if you couldn't care less—works quite well for "I couldn't care less."

DA LO MISMO, DA IGUAL, ES LO MISMO, AND ¿QUÉ MÁS DA?

These four everyday phrases are used for polite indifference, as when you don't have a strong preference. They all mean "What's the difference?" or "It doesn't matter."

ME VALE GORRO, ME VALE SORBETE

A considerably slangier and ruder form of indifference, especially in Mexico, where you will often hear *Me vale* by itself. It roughly means "I couldn't give a damn." All of these *me vale* expressions are strong and can be considered substitutes for a rather rude expression discussed in Chapter 10. Don't worry about their literal meanings—as euphemisms, they are essentially meaningless.

ME IMPORTA UN BLEDO / COMINO / PEPINO

More universal than the *me vale* constructions and slightly tamer, it equals roughly "I couldn't care less." Literally, you are saying, "It is as important to me as a goosefoot plant/cumin seed/cucumber," respectively. In fact, add the minor foodstuff of your choice and you will probably be understood.

NO ME IMPORTA EN LO MÁS MíNIMO

Same idea using a less slangy construction. This is useful for when you're worried that eloquence may detract from the directness of your emotion.

¿Y QUÉ?

Meaning "So what?" this can sound quite rude, depending on your tone. In more friendly circumstances, it works as a slightly impatient "So what's the point?" *¿Y eso qué?* is a variant.

¿Y A Mí QUÉ?

This means "What's it to me?" Said with a snarl, it means "What the hell's that gotta do with me?" Said with a shrug, it's just a simple "I don't care."

¿Y?

All by itself, this word means "So?" Depending on the context, it can be an interested "So (what happened next)?" or an indifferent "So what?"

ASSORTED COMEBACKS

Here are several more comebacks that don't fit into any category but are useful in certain situations.

¿NO QUÉ NO?

A useful and cocky expression that means basically "I told you so." Coming back with tickets for the midnight train after being told that they were sold out, you might flash your prize and say *¿No qué no?* In certain circumstances, the phrase would be construed as "In your face!"

ES UN DECIR

This is a very handy expression that students of the language should try to learn. It means something like "It's just a way of speaking" but will help bail you out of any situation in which you think you're being misunderstood. "His Majesty would like to know if you just called the queen a cow." *No, es un decir nada más* ("Well, yes, but that wasn't what I meant" or "It's just a figure of speech").

O SEA

A very fine "crutch word" ("you know" or "um"), but also a useful response in its own right. Again, the student of Spanish should learn it early, since it is a formulaic way of saying "In other words" or "Sorry, I missed that." Someone explains to you a convoluted route you must take to reach the museum, starting with a right at the stoplight. You listen, get mixed up, miss the rest of it, and then say, *O sea, a la derecha en este semáforo . . . .* This generally gets the person to repeat the directions or clarify the point.

NO ES PARA TANTO

Translated, this would mean something like "Let's not get carried away here." Somehow, though, opportunities for it arise more often in speaking Spanish than the English equivalent would suggest. "You look pretty hot. You want a Coke?" *Sí.* "Want me to pour it over your head?" *No es para tanto.* In English you might say "I'm not *that* hot!" This is quite a useful phrase once you get the hang of it. "I liked that film." "If you want, we can sit through another showing." *No, no es para tanto.* Sometimes a good translation is "It's no big deal."

NI HABLAR

This common expression defies—or rather, embraces—categories. Depending on the context, it can convey "Don't mention it," "No way," "Oh well," and more. You're most likely to run across it when confronting an insurmountable obstacle. "The IRS has ruled that you can't count your trip to Bermuda as a business expense." *Ni hablar.*

NI MODO

This expression is heard primarily in Mexico instead of *ni hablar* when dealing with major obstacles or crisis situations. A single translation is hard to imagine, but a resigned "Oh well, what the hell" conveys some of the sentiment. So does "Tough luck!" "A generator blew and there'll be no electricity until July." *¡Ni modo!* "Mommy, I don't want to eat the broccoli." *Pues ni modo.* This is not a very sympathetic expression, especially if the problem is someone else's, so be careful how you use it.

INVECTIVE AND OBSCENITY   **10**

Familiarity breeds contempt, as a sage once noted, but without a little familiarity you can't breed anything. So it is, in a way, with learning to curse in a foreign language. On the one hand, offering pointers may give the impression that I am encouraging students to blaspheme, excoriate, maledict, and heap billingsgate on their fellow humans. On the other hand, it is a simple fact that many students of foreign languages will try their hand at four-lettered fricatives whether I offer my counsel or not. And the danger of a little familiarity, one fears, may be even greater than the danger of no familiarity at all. What is a teacher to do?

My imperfect solution is to set forth a short checklist of Spanish swear words, making clear that it serves equally well as a short course on how to sound rude, vulgar, and boorish. Most of these words and phrases, used at the wrong moment or in the wrong company, are definitely "fighting words," and fights—verbal or physical—in a foreign language, foreign country, or even foreign neighborhood are fights you are predestined to lose. So swear if you must, but swear intelligently. If in doubt about a word's strength or appropriateness, try it out first in the third person and on a neutral audience. For several of these words and phrases, in fact, your best bet is to forget that they can be used in the second person at all!

Two other hazards besides potential physical injury come into play when you indulge in the crasser forms of the King's Spanish. First, you will defile the image that some may have of you as a fine, upstanding man or woman—and not one of those reckless, godless, drug-crazed *norteamericanos* that every Latin American and Spaniard knows so well from U.S. television programs and movies. Foreign women are especially vulnerable to being "downgraded" or "depreciated" in this way in Latin cultures; it may not be fair, but it happens to be true.

Second, you risk sounding like a complete fool, as anyone who has heard a foreigner curse in English can imagine. I have seen U.S. schoolkids maliciously teach foreign classmates the wrong way to "cuss" only to reap pleasure from hearing Ivan or Pierre say, "I am so shit on myself I could piss dog farts!" So don't think you'll sound too much better cursing in beginner's Spanish. That out of the way, read on for some pointers in this most dangerous game. What follows is not meant as a comprehensive treatment but as a bare-bones primer. That said, I can assure you that if you follow the advice offered here, you will at least never sound as bad as Ivan or Pierre.

CABRÓN

A feisty fighting word. First, the etymology: a *cabrón* is a "he-goat" and, from there, "one with horns," "a cuckold," "one whose wife sleeps around." Its common use on the street, though, is usually to refer to an aggressive, unlikable, mean-and-ornery kind of person—exactly the sort of person whom you wouldn't want to call a *cabrón* face to face. (A mean and ornery woman would be called a *cabrona*—again, from a safe distance.) Among friends you may hear it, accompanied by a laugh, when one friend learns of a practical joke or dirty trick (*cabronada*) committed by another. If Juan is desperately waiting for María to call and José sneakily turns off the ringer on the phone, Juan might notice and say *¡cabrón!* In some parts of the Spanish-speaking world, *cabrón* can also be heard among tough-talking friends in an almost casual fashion, not unlike the way "motherfucker" is sometimes heard on the streets of the United States. Be very, very careful about imitating this quaint local custom: almost everywhere, saying *Oye cabrón* is like asking, "Hey, wanna knife me?" *Cabrón* is also widely used as an adjective for "difficult," generally with *estar*. *Está cabrón* would work nicely for "It's a bitch" when referring to a homework problem or a stubborn bolt. Like "It's a bitch," *cabrón* with *estar* can apply generally to any unpleasant extreme. "How about this heat?" *Está cabrón.*

CAGAR

The rude way to say "to shit" everywhere in the Spanish-speaking world. In some places it is ruder than in others, but nowhere will you use it to explain to your grandmother where you're going. For that, use simply *Voy al baño* or, to be witty, *Voy a donde nadie puede ir por mí* ("I'm going where no one can go in my place").

You may find that *cagar* is quite common in rude and figurative senses. *Me caga* is a crude way of saying "I hate" something. *Me caga el fútbol* = "I hate soccer." *Le caga ir al cine* = "He hates going to the movies." *Cagarse en* means "to shit on" and, figuratively, "not to give a shit for." *Me cago en tu opinión* = "I don't give a shit about your opinion." This phrase reaches fullest expression in the classic phrase of frustration and rage, *¡Me cago en Dios!* Save that one for real special occasions. *Cagar* is sometimes used transitively in the sense of "to screw (something) up." All of these usages should be considered grade-A vulgar, considerably stronger than "to shit" in English (see also *mierda*).

CARAJO

This is a useful expletive—universal, usually not too offensive, and plenty strong. In intensity, it is about on par with "goddam" in English. Thus *No oigo (veo) un carajo* = "I can't hear (see) a goddam thing." *Carajo* (literally, but locally, "prick") is often heard in certain fixed expressions, such as *¡Me importa un carajo!* ("I don't give a damn"). In this sense, it can also be used with *valer: ¡Me vale carajos (un carajo) tu opinión!* = "I couldn't give a goddam about your opinion!"

In Mexico, the *me vale* format is especially common for expressing intense indifference. By following it with meaningless euphemisms (*sorbete*, *gorra*, etc.), you approach "I don't give a damn." Add *madre* to it—i.e., *Me vale madre(s)*—and you have a crude, common, and colorful way in Mexico of saying you don't give a flying french-fry for anything. It is definitely obscene, but on the other hand you'll find it on T-shirts sold to tourists. By extension, in Mexico a *valemadrista* is someone who just couldn't care less about things and calls to mind a person halfway through a week-long binge. These can be fun expressions, but they are also quite offensive. Use them with care.

Another set *carajo* phrase is *Váyase al carajo*, which equates well with "Go to hell." Also very common for "Go to hell" is *Váyase al diablo*, literally "Go to the devil." In all of these constructions, if you know the person you are cursing, or if it's a young person, you would use *¡vete!* instead of *¡váyase! Mandar al carajo* is "to tell (someone) to go to hell" or "to tell (someone) to get lost." "Where's your kid brother?" *Lo mandé al carajo.*

Carajo or *carajos* can also be inserted into almost any question to give it a touch of rage and impatience. *¿Cuándo me van a atender?* ("When are you going to wait on me?") is what you ask after waiting five minutes. *¿Cuándo carajo(s) me van a atender?* is what you ask after waiting forty-five minutes. Likewise, *¿Qué carajo(s) estás haciendo* = "What the hell are you doing?" *¿Qué carajo(s) está pasando?* = "What the hell is going on?" To tone things down just a little bit, you can substitute *diablos* for *carajo* in most questions.

Finally, *¡Carajo!* or *¡Carajos!* by itself makes for a robust expletive. Euphemistic equivalents are endless: *caracoles, caramba, caray, cáscaras,* and so on.

CHINGAR

As Mexican as the margarita, this word has been studied and written about in considerable detail by some of Mexico's foremost scholars. Octavio Paz and Carlos Fuentes, for instance, dedicate sizable sections of *The Labyrinth of Solitude* and *The Death of Artemio Cruz,* respectively, to the psychosociological nature of the word in Mexican life. Compare an English text with a Spanish one, and you'll get an excellent overview of how these words are used in Mexico.

In general, the word equates remarkably well with forms of "to fuck," and all of its uses should be considered just as potent and perilous. *Chingue a su madre* is the classic Mexican curse: fists or bullets answer it, not other curses. An *hijo de la chingada* is about the nastiest thing you can call a person, and they're definitely fightin' words as well. *¡Vete a la chingada!* is the same as *¡Vete al carajo!* (see above), only more so. *¡Chingada madre!* is as strong but can be used as a generic expletive (that is, a word for a hammer-smashes-finger situation). If you must use it, make absolutely sure that no one around you even suspects that you're referring to them or their maternal ancestor. *¡Chingados!* (pronounced *chingaos* to rhyme with "house") is safer as an expletive, but just as strong. In fact, among the *chin-* alternatives, only *¡Chin!* can be considered an acceptable euphemism for this word; the others are too rude to count as euphemisms.

A rare few *chingar* usages and derivatives can almost be rated PG-13, including *chingar* ("to pester"). I've heard a twelve-year-old tell her father, *Ay papi, no me estés chingando.* That phrase and *No chingues* mean "Lay off!" or even just "Cut it out!" when used among good friends (see *joder*). A fun and useful word, meanwhile, is *chingaquedito,* meaning someone who pesters (*chinga*) in a sly, unobtrusive fashion (*quedito*). A *chingadera* is a rudish word for a "dirty trick," "nuisance," or "major annoyance." A common euphemism for *chingar* in Mexico is *fregar* (see *joder*), which can be extended to substitute for the naughty word in many of its various forms: *una fregadera* = "a nuisance."

COGER

Coger is, of course, a perfectly ordinary, acceptable, and decent verb meaning "to take" or "to grab." Unfortunately, it also has the meaning of "to fuck" in many areas, especially the Southern Cone countries and Mexico. More precisely, *coger* is a very crude way of saying "to have sex," but supports none of the figurative uses of "to fuck." (See *chingar* and *joder.*) The more poetic (and polite) way to say this, incidentally, is *hacer el amor* ("to make love"). You can, by the way, continue to use *coger* for "to take" in the countries mentioned above (Spaniards, for instance, do it all the time), but expect a lot of snickering and strange looks.

COJONES

Mostly heard in Spain, though universally understood, this word means "balls" in the sense of "testicles" and has many of the same figurative uses. *¡Qué cojones!* is "What balls!" Used by itself—*¡Cojones!*—it's just a generic expletive. In both usages this word ranks as one of the crudest in Spanish. It's a good word to avoid, especially given the existence of so many good euphemisms. Two common ones for the first usage are *¡Qué agallas!* (roughly "What guts!") and *¡Qué pantalones!* ("What pants!"). The second makes the association between "pants" and "manliness." In fact, if the woman is perceived as the one in charge in a relationship, it is said that *ella lleva los pantalones* ("she wears the pants").

In the physical realm, "balls" can be called—equally crudely—*huevos, pelotas,* or *bolas* in addition to *cojones.* The first and second are mostly American (i.e., of the Americas), and the third is quite rare. Polite alternatives are scarce, but then so are most polite references to this part of the anatomy. The proper word is *testículos,* but you can play cute and refer to the general zone as a man's *hombría,* or "manhood."

Huevos, in Mexico especially, is so widely understood to have a crude second meaning that people generally avoid using the word in the plural. You too should learn to say *huevo* instead of *huevos* whenever possible and to use the neutral *¿Hay huevo?* instead of the more risqué *¿Tiene huevos?* to ask a waiter or merchant if eggs are available. The word *blanquillos* ("little white ones") is also heard in Mexico, and though it seems unlikely that it has arisen as a "safe" alternative to *huevos*, you can use it that way if you wish. Also in Mexico you can refer folklorically to the testicles as *los aguacates* ("the avocados"), especially since *aguacate* comes from *ahuacatl*, the Nahuatl word for "testicles." Note that "Los Aguacates" is also the name of a traditional Mexican song, so be careful how you ask the band to play—i.e., *tocar*—it.

COÑO

A common interjection of the "Jesus H. Christ!" variety, but considerably cruder. It is sometimes used alone, but more often to introduce a comment. *¡Coño! ¡Qué jugada!* = "Christ, what a play!" This word is popular in Spain but only selectively so in the New World, so by using it where it's not common you may sound a little strange—like someone saying "Gor Blimey!" in a Texas roadhouse.

CULO

This is the crude but common word for "ass" in Spanish. In some countries it is cruder than in others. In Spain, *culo* is used freely and easily, extending even to the back end of a car, for instance. In Mexico, on the other hand, it is downright rude. You will certainly want to suss out the prevailing mood before unleashing a word like this. In the meantime, you can safely use *trasero* (roughly, "rear end") for most everyday anatomical references and *la parte trasera* for the rear end of cars. Other relatively polite words for the same corporal region include *las nalgas* ("buttocks"), *la popa* ("rear"), and *el pompi* or *las pompis*. The last three are somewhat infantile. If you want to have fun, refer to this region as *donde la espalda pierde su digno nombre* ("where the back loses its worthy name").

A related and quite offensive word, used mostly in the Americas, is *culero*, loosely ascribing homosexual tendencies to its target and most commonly heard in loud, lilting chants from the rowdies at soccer matches: *¡Cuuu-leeeeeeerooooooo!* The target here is usually the referee or a dirty player on the opposing team.

HIJO DE

Name-calling in Spanish often has less to do with insulting your opponent—a true macho doesn't care what you say about him—

than with insulting your opponent's mother. And the common way to do that, syntactically speaking, is to refer to your adversary as the son of something offensive. What with the expression "S.O.B." in English, the concept is not a hard one to grasp.

That said, it should be noted that the *hijo de* complex of insults includes some of the strongest epithets in Spanish. English's "sonnuva" selection is tame in comparison. In the most obvious case, a beginner might equate *hijo de puta* with "son of a bitch," reasoning that the structures are similar. Perhaps so, but the sentiments are a world apart. "Son of a bitch" hardly warrants a raised eyebrow these days, but *hijo de puta* is as strong as they come: "motherfucker" is probably the closest to it in intensity and offensiveness. *Es un hijo de puta* is quite simply the worst thing you can say of someone in most of the Spanish-speaking world. (See also *puta.*) Should you feel inclined to use this phrase, note carefully the correct pronunciation: in most countries, the *d* gets swallowed altogether and the phrase ends up sounding like *¡Hijo'e puta!* Incidentally, a fun word to describe the sort of actions you would expect from a *hijo de puta* is *hijoeputez,* a word so amusing-sounding that it almost avoids being obscene.

In Mexico, the form *hijo de la chingada* is sometimes preferred, but *hijo de puta* is universally used there as well. *¡Híjole!* is also common as an innocent and euphemistic interjection there. In various parts of Latin America, *hijo* is sometimes turned into *jijo*— pronounced "hee-ho"—for no particular reason. Either *jijo* or *hijo* can be used alone or with nothing but *de* to convey the anger of the full expression without having to employ vulgarities. Also popular as euphemisms are the harmless *hijo de su madre* and the regional, and fun, *hijo de su diez de mayo.* Keep in mind that phrases like *¡Jijo de!* can still be interpreted as an offense, even though it is quite general.

JODER

Outside of Mexico, this is the common vulgarism for "to fuck." Even in Mexico, most expressions using *joder* are readily understood, and some are used. Perhaps the commonest use of *joder* is by itself as an explitive: *¡Joder!* Also heard is *No me jodas,* meaning roughly "Don't fuck with me." *¡No jodas!*—like *¡No chingues!* (see *chingar)*—is less forceful, about like "Cut the shit!" or even "Bullshit!" This can be quite strong, but said lazily, it carries no more force than "Stop bugging me." For this concept you'll also hear the present-participle form: *No me estés jodiendo.* Again, strength depends largely on the tone. A euphemism for this usage in much of the Americas is *fregar,* as in *No me friegues* and *No me estés fregando.*

Joder in the past-participle form conveys a slightly different idea—closer to "fucked over" than "fucked with," though the difference is slight. *Los jodidos* of any country are the poor, downtrodden, miserable masses. A road in very bad shape might also be called *jodido*. Likewise, you and your friends would say *Estamos jodidos* if you ran out of gas fifty miles from town on a dirt road at night. Variations on this phrase will depend on the assessment of blame. If your group's poor planning skills were at fault, you might say *Nos jodimos* ("We fucked up"). If someone stole your gas to put you in that predicament, you could say *Nos jodieron* ("They fucked us over good!"). In Mexico, these forms of *joder* are used as a somewhat weaker substitute for *chingar*, and in general in Latin America *fregar* can again be substituted as a harmless euphemism: *¡Estamos fregados!* ("We're screwed").

LÍO

This word is neither rude nor obscene and, in a sense, doesn't belong here at all. But it is a useful word to group together a number of rude or rough-sounding expressions whose basic idea is "It's a mess." That would be *Es un lío* in polite Spanish; it could be many other things in less polite Spanish.

A lot of the "messy" words and phrases are regional. In Spain *un jaleo* may heard; in Mexico, *un relajo*. Neither of these is particularly strong. *Bronca* is safe and universal for "mess," "altercation," or "violent confrontation." Inversely, *No hay bronca* works well as a slangy "No problem" or "No sweat," and in slangy speech *La bronca es que* is a common sentence starter meaning "The problem is . . . ."

Ruder words that you are likely to hear in Mexico include *desmadre* (a "bloody mess" or worse), for which euphemists can substitute *despapaye*. In Mexico and some other countries, a very crude word is *pedo* ("fart"), meaning "big trouble" or "deep shit." (In other countries, *peo* is used instead of *pedo*.) The equally vulgar *No hay pedo* (roughly, "No problem, everything's cool") can be used—and often is—to back out of an ugly scene. In Mexico *pedo* also means "blind drunk" or "shit-faced."

MADRE

The mother is the paragon of the Latin family and is supposedly held sacred by the Latin male (especially). To show their deep respect for motherhood, Latin males (especially) have taken to inventing an entire vocabulary based on insulting other people's mothers. In

Mexican street slang, for example, *madre* shows up in just about every phrase, and almost invariably and paradoxically refers to the worst of everything. Some examples of what you might hear: *hasta la madre* = "wasted," "fed up," "drugged or drunk"; *dar en la madre* = "to beat the shit out of"; *romper la madre* or *partir la madre* = "to beat the shit out of"; *en la madre* = "in deep shit." The only exception to this linguistic paradox seems to be *a toda madre*, which means "great" (or, more correctly, "real fuckin' great"). Less vulgar alternatives include *a todo mecate* and *a todas margaritas*; the original expression is *a todo dar*.

Beyond *madre* the Mexicans have invented a host of crude words. A *desmadre*, for example, is a "total mess," and *desmadrar* means "to make a total mess of." *Madrazo*, besides being a common last name, is a crude word for a physical "blow" or even an "ass-kicking." The situation is such that the word *madre* is best avoided even in polite conversation in Mexico—use *mamá* instead. Finally, as on certain U.S. streets where you may hear "yo' mama" as a sort of all-purpose comeback, in Spanish *tu madre* can be handy. It is plugged into a sentence to rebuff a rude or inappropriate suggestion. For instance, *¡Hágase a un lado!* ("Move over!") can be answered with *¡Que se haga a un lado tu madre!* (literally, "Have your mother move over!"). *¡Termina rápido!* ("Hurry up and finish!") *¡Que termine rápido tu madre!* For those reluctant to delve into the subjunctive, *¡Tu madre!* by itself generally gets the point across. So does a simple *¡La tuya!*— which packs quite a useful, all-purpose punch and translates roughly as "Up yours!" For a watered-down version, *¡Tu abuela!* can be used instead. Sassy kids (like Mafalda, for instance) might use this. "Eat your soup, Mafalda." *¡Que la tome tu abuela!*

MALDICIÓN

As a mild expletive, *¡Maldición!* is equal to "Damn!" For "Damn you!" use *¡Maldito seas!* (or *¡Maldita seas!* for a woman). This works also for objects: *¡Maldito sea tu coche!* = "Damn your car!" For "damn" as an adjective, *maldito* is one of many words that fill the bill: *tu maldito coche* = "your damn car." *Mugre* is also in widespread use, though it is much more polite—akin roughly to "lousy" or "no-good." *Condenado* and *recondenado* are also heard, though less often. And in a few choice expressions, even *puta* is used as a modifier, chiefly in the phrases *¡Qué puta vida!* and *¡Qué puta suerte (la mía)!* Its euphemistic substitute in these expressions is *perra*. *¡Qué perra vida!* = "Life's a bitch."

In Mexico the word *pinche* serves this intermediary function as well. Although it's a good bit more vulgar than *maldito*, it is still exceedingly common. When the Mexican *bandido* cop in *Treasure of the Sierra Madre* says to Bogart, "Badges? We don't need no stinkin' badges!" what he would have said in Spanish for "stinkin'" is *pinches*. Literally, *pinche* is a noun referring to a lowly kitchen employee; the noun is still used, though now it can describe any low-level employee or "gopher." *Pinche gringo*, incidentally, is one of the typical remarks that sullen, gringo-hating Mexicans like to mutter under their breath as you walk by. Ignore it, or, if you're feeling especially feisty, say *Gringo sí, pinche tu abuela*. Better yet, buy the guy a beer.

MARICÓN

In a macho culture like the Latin one, there is no getting away from the epithets that attack an opponent's manhood. Most common, most unequivocal, and strongest is *maricón*, which is roughly equal to "faggot." Used by a woman against a man, it is a truly debilitating insult; that is, it can be a good way in certain public circumstances to get a man to leave you alone. Used by men, it is either a challenge equal to "coward" (or "pussy"), in which case it is a fighting word; or it is dismissive, as when the target of the insult really is effeminate—and thus not a worthy opponent for a "true" macho. Equally rude and offensive—though not as universal—are *puto* and *joto*. Somewhat less rude choices include *marica*, *mariquita*, *mariposón*, and *barbilindo*. They range in intensity roughly from "queer" to "queen." *Poco hombre* is a common expression for any "unmanly" man. Both it and *marica* mean little more than "wimp"—that is, without any allusion to sexual preference. In some parts of the macho's world, such epithets are appropriate for "unmanly" men who help with the dishes, allow women to go out by themselves, or show emotion when a woman leaves them.

MEAR

A vulgar word for urination and the equivalent of "to piss." The cutesy, children's way of describing urination is *hacer pis* or *hacer pipí*, which are essentially the same as "to go wee-wee." *Hacer aguas* is also heard. The only widespread and correct way of saying "to urinate" is *orinar*; note that it's spelled and pronounced with an *o*, not a *u*, at the start.

MIERDA

The universal vulgar word for "excrement" in Spanish is *mierda*, and you'll find that it is usually an accurate substitute for "shit." Some people consider *mierda* very offensive, while others use it quite freely. The kiddies' word is *caca*, as in *caca de perro* or *caca de vaca*. *Excremento* is the safe way out.

Overall, *mierda* is probably less frequently used in rude expressions than is "shit." Neither *caca de toro* nor *mierda de toro* would be understood as "bullshit" in its figurative sense, for instance. Nor is *mierda* used commonly as an expletive. About the only phrase in which it does take on a figurative meaning is *de mierda*, tacked on after a noun, to mean "worthless" or "piece of shit." *¡Coche de mierda!* = "Piece-of-shit car!" Likewise, *una mierda* by itself can mean "a piece of shit." *¡Este reloj es una mierda!* = "This watch is a piece of shit!" The epithet *comemierda* (literally, "shit-eater") is regionally favored (in Cuba, for instance) to describe just about anything or anyone disagreeable.

PENDEJO

This strong, wide-ranging insult literally means "pubic hair." Figuratively, it is almost universally used to mean "asshole" or "shithead," generally highlighting the target's stupidity more than his or her maliciousness. Thus a common phrase is *verle la cara de pendejo (a alguien)*, which means roughly "to note someone's stupidity in their face" or "to size them up as an easy mark." If a sidewalk merchant tells you a Coke costs four hundred dollars in local currency, you could rightfully ask *¿De qué me vió la cara?* ("What do you take me for?"). If you pay the money and don't realize it until later, how you feel about yourself is a pretty good summation of *pendejo*. By extension, a *pendejada* ("screwup") is any stupid behavior of the sort expected from a *pendejo*. Extended further, this helpful word can be stretched into *pendejez*, describing someone's general stupidity. "You paid four hundred dollars for a Coke?" *Fue un ataque de pendejez.* Polite substitutes for *pendejada* are *disparate* and *payasada*.

PUTA

Puta is a close fit for the English "whore," and possibly the most universal profane oath and expletive of all is *¡Puta madre!* or simply *¡Puta!* Shortening it further, to *¡Put!* or *¡'uta!* or even to just *¡'ut!* has the effect of cleaning it up a tiny bit for polite company. And as it can be trimmed down and thus sugarcoated, it can also be embellished for effect. Quality cursers can drag the curse on for umpteen syllables: *¡La puta que te parió!* ("The whore that bore you!") is an example; *La reputísima madre que te parió* a stronger, even longer one.

These phrases are fine as generic expletives, but as with other curses, be careful to make it clear that you are not referring to someone else present. If in doubt in the preceding examples, change the *te* to *me*, converting your oath against an unjust world to an oath against your own stupidity or clumsiness—and your own mother, incidentally. Note also that there is a thin line between a generic expletive and a foul insult, so be forewarned. *¡Puta madre!* is an unaimed expletive, but *¡Tu puta madre!* is a ballistic insult. You will want to be sure that both you and your audience are aware of the difference.

WHICH IS WHICH? **11**

For the foreigner, the path to fluency in Spanish is marked by constant dilemmas. *Ser* or *estar*? Imperfect or preterit? Subjunctive or indicative? Do you want the word on the left or the word on the right? Do you want to keep the word you have, or do you want to trade it for the word behind Curtain Number One? Or do you want to swap it all for the word Linda is bringing down the aisle in a lovely gift-wrapped box?

For foreigners learning English, one of the greatest bugaboos is the tendency for one English word to have three or four (or a dozen) different meanings. The problem is worse with verbs, which team up with prepositions in a million-odd ways to produce new meanings altogether. As an exasperated Mexican friend once noted, "What can you expect from a language where first you chop a tree *down* and then you chop the same tree *up*?"

The converse of these difficulties are your difficulties, as a native English speaker, in learning Spanish. Every single English word, it seems, requires a bundle of totally different foreign words to describe it. And worse, you're expected to learn them all!

In this chapter, we look at some of the English words that don't have a single Spanish equivalent. Instead, you must pause in your palaver and search for the correct Spanish word. And while no book can present and resolve all possible word-choice dilemmas, this chapter can help you sort through the choices so you will know which ones you need to learn.

BACK

The body part, as you probably know already, is *la espalda*. But what about all those other uses of "back?" For these, you'll need to study *tras*, *atrás*, and *detrás*, plus *de regreso* and *de vuelta* and, last but far from least, *fondo* (or *al fondo*).

Generally, to express "in back of" or "behind," *atrás* and *detrás* are the words you'll use most. *Tras*, for all intents and purposes, is just like *detrás* and can be safely discarded for the time being. As for the difference between *atrás* and *detrás*, native speakers will tell you they distinguish between these two words "by which one sounds right." That is true, but of little help to you, the student. So we must turn to rules, though they are far from perfect, to clarify the situation.

Here's the main rule to remember: use *detrás de* instead of *atrás de*, and you'll usually be right. In fact, it is hard to think of a case where *atrás de* would be correct and *detrás de* wrong. So you are free to forget about *atrás de* altogether. Or almost. One exception is in reference to someone coming behind or after someone else. Here, *detrás de* suggests "in pursuit of"; *atrás de* just means "back there somewhere" or even "later." *¿Dónde está tu mamá? Viene atrás de mí.* "Where's your mom?" "She's coming behind me (later)." Change *atrás de mí* to *detrás de mí* and you have "She's coming after me"—in hot pursuit.

The underlying intuitive difference between *atrás* and *detrás* is hard to pin down. In most cases, *detrás* suggests a spatial relationship, or one thing "behind" another or being blocked by another. *Atrás* is much vaguer, meaning "in back," "back there somewhere" or "behind (the speaker)." You might say, for instance, that there is a mountain *detrás de mi casa*. But if someone inside the house asks where the mountain is, you might say *allá atrás*.

In fact, if we accept *detrás de* as (almost) always the correct choice, then we could invent a second, equally imperfect rule to cover *atrás*: when you don't need the *de*, use *atrás*. That is, when standing alone as an adverb, *atrás* is correct and sufficient. This usually covers backward motion, as in *va hacia atrás* or *va para atrás*. In keeping with its vague "backness," *atrás* is usually the word of choice in figurative expressions. *Se está echando para atrás* = "He's backing out." *No mires atrás* = "Don't look back."

For other uses of "back," *de regreso* and *de vuelta* both mean "back" in the sense of "returned." Both are used with *estar*. *Está de vuelta después de su viaje* = "He's back now after his trip." Of course, *regresar* and *volver* convey the same thing.

Fondo, or *al fondo*, is one of the handiest words for "back"

and one you should try to learn. *El fondo*, as a noun, refers to the
"back" of a bus, movie theater, or building (as well as the "bottom"
of a glass, swimming pool, and so forth). You'll hear *al fondo* for "to
the back" or "all the way in the back." Ask the bus driver or theater
usher if there are any seats and the answer may be *Sí, al fondo*. *Atrás*,
especially with cars, can be used this way as well. It means something
like "in the back" as opposed to "at the very back," which is *al fondo*.
Al fondo is extremely common when giving directions, particularly
indoors. Ask where the bathroom is in a restaurant and the reply may
be, for instance, *Al fondo a la derecha* ("All the way back on your
right").

BECOME

This is perhaps the gold-medal winner for troublesomeness
in the English-to-Spanish olympics, especially when "to become" includes the sense of "to get." As a rule, *ponerse* is the handiest word for
"to become," but you should learn at least some of the others. *Ponerse*
in general is for fleeting states of mind or conditions, as in *ponerse fu-
rioso* ("to get/become furious"), *ponerse viejo* ("to get/become old"),
ponerse nervioso ("to get/become nervous"), and so on.

For longer-term, usually nonreversible conditions, *hacerse* is
often the verb you want. *Me hice rico* = "I became (got) rich"; *El pe-
nique se está haciendo inútil* = "The penny is becoming useless"; *El
nuevo baile se está haciendo popular* ("The new dance is becoming
popular"). The distinction is subtle, sometimes to the point of near invisibility. Thus one can also *hacerse viejo*, but it suggests "becoming
an old person" or "becoming elderly," whereas *ponerse viejo* hints at
"starting to feel (or look) old."

Volverse, another word for "to become," is perhaps best translated as "to turn into." *Se ha vuelto una verdadera molestia* = "He's
become (turned into) a real nuisance." It involves a more sudden and
unexpected change than *hacerse*, though it shares with that word a
change into a more or less lasting state. *Se volvió rico*, for instance,
can also be used to say "He got rich," but it gives the impression of
overnight wealth—winning the lottery, perhaps, or inheriting a for-
tune—and also carries an intimation of criticism, as if the change were
undeserved as well as unexpected. *Volverse* is also the only phrase to
be used for "to go crazy" in the permanent sense: *volverse loco*.

Both *transformarse* and *convertirse* can also be rendered
"turned into," but usually in connection with a more thoroughgoing,
physical change. *El agua se transforma en vapor* = "Water becomes
(turns into) steam." *Clark Kent se convierte en Superman* = "Clark
Kent becomes (turns into) Superman." Sometimes these phrases can

cover more figurative conversions: *Se ha convertido en un buen escritor* = "He's become a good writer." *Llegar a ser*, meanwhile, works well as "to turn out to be," as in *La fórmula llegó a ser muy útil* = "The formula turned out to be very useful." This phrase also covers "to become" in the sense of "worked his (or her) way up to." *Después de muchos esfuerzos, llegó a ser médico.* = "After a lot of hard work, he became a doctor." In many cases, an easier construction can be made with the verb *resultar*, which also means "to turn out." *Este libro resultó ser muy interesante.* = "This book turned out to be very interesting."

A very common but often overlooked way of saying "to become" in Spanish is through the use of reflexive verbs, especially those that are little more than an *en-* or *a-* prefix attached to an adjective or noun: *acalorarse* ("to get/become hot"), *enfriarse* ("to get/become cold"), *entristecerse* ("to get/become sad"), *acercarse* ("to get/become close"), and so on. Sometimes no prefix is needed with the adjective, as in *mojarse* ("to get/become wet") and *cansarse* ("to get/become tired"). Pay attention to which nouns and adjectives can be made into verbs and how, and you'll be well on your way to conquering the "get/become" problem.

BURN

In English, this is a fairly simple if destructive process; in Spanish it's a little more complex. *Arder* refers to the actual act of burning; think of it as "on fire" or "burning up." Thus houses and candles *arden*, and so do fever victims: *Estoy ardiendo en calentura.* Out of context, *Estoy ardiendo* can sound like *double entendre*—"I'm on fire, baby, sweep me off my feet." Figuratively, *arder* comes into play in the expression *está que arde*, meaning someone is "burning mad" or a situation is "boiling over."

Incendiar, another choice for "to burn," is usually used for things that should not be burning: forests, buildings, the lawn, the lawn furniture, and so on. Think of it as "to set on fire." Even in the case of *pasión incendiaria*, the implication is that the fire has gotten out of hand and may end up being destructive.

Quemar also translates as "to burn," but generally brings to mind (in the reflexive *quemarse*) "to burn up" or "to burn down," (another case of contradictory prepositions in English saying almost exactly the same thing). If you go away for the weekend and come back to find your toolshed in ashes, a neighbor might explain simply, *Se quemó. Quema* in its nonreflexive form is the usual way to convey the transitive "to burn (something)." *Estás quemando el bistec* = "You're burning the steak." (If you were to use *incendiar* here, you would be saying, "You're setting fire to the steak.") The general idea behind *quemar* is "to consume (or damage) by fire." It is the correct verb for when one thing "burns" another: the sun *quema* your skin, the stove *quema* your fingers, and so on. The painful and unappealing marks left on your skin to mark these mishaps are called *quemaduras* ("burns"). To say "I burned myself," whether in the sun or the kitchen, you would say *Me quemé.*

CORNER

Ninety-five percent of the time, just use *esquina* for "corner." For that matter, use it for "intersection" too, although *intersección* is increasingly heard these days. For a "crossroads," or intersection of highways, use either *entronque, encrucijada,* or *cruce de caminos.* Dictionaries will give *rincón* for "corner" as well, but it generally refers to an inside corner where two walls meet—the corner of a room, in other words. By extension, it is used to mean a "nook" or "cranny," and is a favorite word to assign to cocktail lounges, piano bars, and the like.

DATE

Here you'll have to slow down and analyze what exactly you're trying to say. Do you mean "the date," as in July 13, 1984? Then the Spanish word you want is *fecha.* If you mean "date" as in "appointment," you have a couple of words to choose from. A "date" of the sort that thrills teens (and, let's be frank, some postteens as well) is almost universally a *cita.* A *cita* is also what you have with a doctor or lawyer, however—in other words, an "appointment." That is, in Spanish you can have a *cita* with your doctor without upsetting your spouse. A *compromiso* is also an "appointment," usually an unspecified one. It can almost mean simply "something to do" and implies an obligation to be present at a certain time—but no more. Thus, to escape from a dreary luncheon, you can excuse yourself with *Perdón, tengo un compromiso.* All you're really saying is "Sorry, gotta go."

FAIL

The best all-purpose word for "to fail" is *fracasar,* though one 1952 edition of a heavyweight Spanish-English dictionary I consulted defines it as "to crumble, to break into pieces: applied commonly to ships." A ship that crumbles into bits would certainly meet my definition of "failure," but *fracasar* in common usage covers much more ground than that. *Fallar* is also used for many general senses of "to fail," though it seems a little kinder and less permanent than *fracasar*. *Falló en su intento* suggests "He did not succeed"; *Fracasó en su intento* hints "He was a total flop." Often you'll hear *fallar* in the form *estar fallando* to mean "not to be working well," "to be on the blink," in reference to some appliance or gizmo. When someone or something "fails" you in the sense of not living up to your expectations, either *fallar, defraudar,* or *decepcionar* can be used. To "fail" an exam or a course, *reprobar* is much used in the Americas, while *suspender* is more frequent in Spain. Thus *un suspenso* on your exam in Madrid is beyond suspense: it's an F. In Mexico City receiving an *F* would be expressed as *reprobar el examen* or *ser reprobado por el profesor*.

FRONT

This word opens an unruly can of worms on its journey into Spanish. The basic problem is the excess of believable cognates, which then have to be sorted through. For instance, you can say there is a fountain *al frente de la casa, enfrente de la casa, frente a la casa,* or *de frente a la casa,* and you won't necessarily be saying the same thing. What's the difference?

Al frente de is usually the expression for the English "in front of." It means "at (in) the front part of (something)." In the earlier example, a fountain that is *al frente de la casa* is on the property at the front of the house. Next come a host of prepositional expressions that, in many circumstances, mean "in front of" but generally only in the sense of "facing." *Enfrente de* is one of these expressions, and it is better regarded as a trickster (see Chapter 3). Think of it as a synonym for "facing" or "across the way." A fountain that is *enfrente de la casa* is likely to be across the street from the house. *Frente a* means much the same and should be viewed as just as unreliable as *enfrente de* in most cases. Sometimes the act of "facing" is implicit. *Lo tienes frente a los ojos* = "You have it in front of your eyes"—that is, "staring you in the face." *De frente a,* finally, states very clearly that something is "face to face," literally "with its front facing (something)." *Estoy parada de frente al sol* = "I'm standing facing the sun."

Perhaps the safest word of all for "in front of" is *delante,* usually followed by *de*. Generally, whenever you can use "ahead" or "ahead of," you should probably be using *delante* or *delante de*. But it also covers a wide range of "in front of" situations. The fountain can be *delante de la casa,* for instance. *Bob se sienta delante de mí en la clase* = "Bob sits ahead of me in class."

The classroom example may prove, well, instructive. Ana's seat is in the third row; Bob sits *delante de ella.* Pedro sits in the front row, *delante de Bob* and *al frente de la fila* ("at the front of the row") and *frente a la maestra* ("in front of—i.e., facing—the teacher); when Ana gets up to read her book report, she goes *al frente del salón* and stands facing the class, or *de frente a la clase.* Ana's sister is in the classroom across the hall, or *enfrente del salón de Ana.*

Finally, whereas *atrás* is "in back" (see "Back"), *adelante* is usually "up front"—in the front seat of a car, for instance. To refer to "the front" or "the front part" of something, *el frente* can usually be used. *El frente de la tienda está sucio* = "The front of the store is dirty." *La frente,* in the feminine, refers exclusively to "the forehead."

FUNNY

Does it make you laugh or wonder? That's the first question you'll need to ask (and answer). If it's the former, you can choose from *chistoso, gracioso,* and *cómico.* If the latter, stick to *extraño* and *raro.* Pick your favorite and use it; they are virtually interchangeable. Anything having to do with "fun," incidentally, should be carefully distinguished from things that are "funny," since what's fun isn't always funny. "Fun" needs either the adjective *divertido* or the noun *diversión* to describe it.

HAPPEN

"To happen" can almost always be covered by some form of *pasar* in Spanish. Other counterparts exist—including *acontecer, ocurrir, suceder,* and *acaecer*—but there's really no need to learn them other than to recognize them when you hear them. You will have to learn some of their noun forms, however, since *pasar* doesn't have one. *Acontecimiento, hecho,* and *suceso* are three of the most frequently encountered words for "happening," "occurrence," and "event." *Evento* will be understood—and is gradually being incorporated in this sense—but technically it means something that happened by chance or with no advance planning.

HERE

Spanish is funny. Even when you know you're "here," you have to know which "here" to use. Two words, *acá* and *aquí,* cover the situation. Which is which? Textbooks generally promote the idea that *acá* is the correct word for verbs of motion, as in *Ven acá* ("Come here"), while *aquí* is the word of choice for stationary presence in a given place, as in *Estoy aquí* ("I'm here"). After hearing one person on the street shout *Estoy acá*, though, you might wonder why grammarians even bother with these distinctions.

The comparative forms of *acá* come into play when giving guidance to, say, someone backing a truck down an alley. *Más acá* means "A little more this way," *No tan acá* means "Not so much this way," and *¡Ya!* means "Just right, hold it." *¡Praaac!* ("Crunch!") means you won't be asked to help truck drivers back down alleys anymore.

Finally, a very common use of "here" in English is to say "Here you are" or "Here you go" when giving someone something (for example, paying the cab driver the fare). In Spanish you can say pretty much the same thing with *aquí: Aquí está* and *Aquí tiene* both work, as does *Tome* ("Take"). A somewhat archaic expression that still creeps into written Spanish is *He aquí*, and some dictionaries will tell you that it means "Here is . . . ." Actually, it's closer to "Behold!" Before trying it out on the cabbie, try to imagine yourself saying "Behold, the ten pesos!" in English. Then go back to *Aquí tiene*.

HOT, WARM

Native English speakers aspiring to fluency in Spanish should be aware of the latter language's hierarchy of "heat" adjectives. Apart from the several words representing various degrees of heat, different words are used depending on the object in question. A soup fresh off the fire, for instance, will drop in temperature from *hirviendo* ("boiling hot" or "scalding") to *caliente* ("hot") to *calientita* ("pretty hot") to *tibia* ("lukewarm") to *templada* (not hot but not cold either). A cold beverage goes from *helada* to *fría, fresca, al tiempo* ("room temperature"), *tibia*, and *caliente*. For weather, you can describe the day in order of ascending temperature: *helado, frío, fresco, templado, calientito, caliente*, and *caluroso*. A good word for warm days is *cálido*, often in the sense of "unseasonably (or pleasantly) warm." As expressive alternatives for *caluroso* you can say *Hace un calor bárbaro* (or *tremendo, bochornoso, sofocante*) or simply *Hace un calorón*.

"Hot" in its many figurative senses in English can be a dangerous concept to convey in Spanish. *Caliente* in reference to other people, especially of the opposite sex, is risky. Think of *caliente* as "in heat" rather than "hot-looking," and you'll get the general idea. As for the common novice mistake of saying *Estoy caliente* instead of

Tengo calor ("I'm hot"), those of you who have used it know the consequences: usually belly laughs all around, sometimes an unwanted offer.

HURRY

Several choices present themselves for the concept of "to hurry," and mostly it's a matter of choosing one and using it. There are some differences, though. Your choices are (the envelope, please): *tener prisa, apurarse,* and *darse prisa.* The first means "to be in a hurry," and *Tengo prisa* is a basic Neurotic-Speak expression. *Apurarse* is less common except in the phrase *¡Apúrate!* (or *¡Apúrese!*), meaning "Hurry up!" and then only in the Americas; *apresurarse* replaces *apurarse* east of the Atlantic. The adjective *apurado* is often heard, but implies more "harried" or "frantic" than just "in a hurry." *Darse prisa* is sort of like "to make oneself hurry" or "to get a move on," and *¡Date prisa!* is practically interchangeable with *¡Apúrate!* for urging someone to get the lead out. When you're in such a hurry that you can't even stop to say "Hurry up," appropriate grunts include *¡Ya! ¡Aprisa! ¡Deprisa!* and in Mexico *¡Ándale!* and *¡Órale!*

LOOK

"To look" in English covers a lot of ground. "To look for" is not the same as "to look at," for instance, and "to look good" is a different concept from "to look like." As usual, one English verb can combine with a score of prepositions to produce dozens of distinct meanings—each of which in Spanish may require a different verb. The most common Spanish words for the concept "to look" are *buscar* ("to look for") and *mirar* ("to look at").

"To look" by itself is *verse,* a verb you should learn to use. *Te ves bien* = "You look good." *Se ve horrible* = "It (or he or she) looks horrible." *¿Cómo me veo?* = "How do I look?" And so on.

"To look like"—with the meaning "to resemble" or "to remind one of"—is either *parecer* or *parecerse a. Ese señor se parece a mi padre* = "That man looks like my father." When "to look like" means "to look as if," *parecer* by itself is enough. *Parece que va a llover* = "It looks like (as if it is going to) rain."

MISS

Your husband goes away on a bus and you miss him. He misses the bus, so you don't miss him. On his way to the bus, another bus just misses him, causing him to miss the bus and you almost to miss him very much. Still with me? There's obviously a lot of missing going on in this world. And in Spanish, you must take care to differentiate what you do to your husband and what the bus does.

Let's deal first with the verb that expresses what you feel when any loved one goes away. This sense of "to miss" in the Spanish of the Americas is handled by *extrañar*. In Spain, you'll hear *echar de menos*. As in English, you can "miss" not only a person but your bed, your favorite brand of candy bar, or any once-regular activity, like your nightly mud bath. All are covered by *extrañar* and *echar de menos*.

Now let's look at "to miss" in the context of missing a bus, a plane, a party, a movie, a lecture, and so on. In Spanish, this idea is handled by *perder*, which of course is also the word for "to lose." *Perdimos el tren* = "We missed the train." If you miss something that you were expected to attend, you would use *faltar a*, as in *Falté a la clase de español* ("I missed the Spanish class"). Think of it as "to miss" in the sense of "to be absent from." When something is "missing" or "absent," *faltar* is also the word of choice. *Faltan once dólares de mi cartera* = "Eleven dollars is missing from my wallet."

Then there is "to miss" in the sense of the close call—"The bus barely missed the parked truck"—which is a fairly tricky concept to translate into Spanish. Some dictionaries might have you use *errar*, *no acertar*, or *no dar en el blanco*, but these imply that the bus was trying deliberately to hit the truck—and may even have gone back for a second shot. These are all useful expressions, but they are best saved for when your jump shot goes astray or when you guess something wrong. To convey the idea of the bus "missing" the truck, you would have to resort to *pasar rozando* ("to graze") or *pasar cerca* ("to go by close"). To get the point across even more clearly, you would need to trade in "miss" for "almost hit." *Un autobus por poco* (or *casi*) *atropella a mi marido* = "A bus just missed (running over) my husband."

NEXT

At some point in your progress as a student, you will realize that *próximo* is not the only word for "next." Soon afterward, you will realize that it's often not even a very good word for "next." What are the other words, and when are they used? For starters, you're safe with *próximo* when "next" means some indefinite "next time." In fact *próxima vez* ("next time") is one of its commonest uses. But *próximo* does not work for "the next day," which is *el día siguiente* (or *al día siguiente*). It works again for "next week" (*la próxima semana*), and fairly well for "next year" (*el próximo año*), but you are probably more likely to hear *la semana que entra* (or *entrante*) and *el año que viene.* Somewhere someone has probably thought up an explanation for these deviations; ignore it and just learn the phrases.

Another slight deviation to be alert for is the use of *otro* for "next," which you will run across constantly. *Al otro día* can mean "the next day," for instance. More common is *la otra* for "the next" street, stoplight, or corner when being given directions. *Está en la otra calle* = "It's on the next street over." What tends to confuse beginners is that the noun is often implied, not stated. *Dé vuelta no en ésta sino en la otra* means "Don't turn here (at this corner) but at the next one."

For "next to" in a physical sense, *próximo* is flat-out wrong; *junto a* or *al lado de* is correct. *La tienda está al lado de su casa* or *La tienda está junto a su casa* = "The store is next to his house." Note that as an adverb of place, *junto* does not change with the gender of the subject. "The girl next door" is either *la muchacha de junto* or *la muchacha de al lado.* Colloquially and quite commonly you will hear *pegado* (literally, "stuck to") for "right next door."

OFFICE

Such an easy concept—and such a wealth of Spanish words to cover it. Let's start with—and discard—*oficio*, which applies only to "office" in the symbolic, conceptual sense: "the office of vice president." For a room where someone works, several words could fit, depending on what you want to say. The most generic term for "office" is *oficina*, and this can be used safely about 90 percent of the time. Getting pickier, we can distinguish between the larger office under the boss's control and the actual office where he or she works, which could be called his or her *privada* ("private office"). Doctors and dentists have special offices called *consultas* or *consultorios.* Lawyers dwell in *bufetes*, which works for both the physical office and the "firm." A *despacho* is a workplace, usually nongovernmental, that is often involved in accounting or administration, though lawyers can labor in *despachos* as well. A *taller* is a "workshop" where manual labor is done. *Taller mecánico* means "worskhop" or "garage" and has nothing to do with the height of the mechanic who works there.

OLD, OLDER

The main problem with this concept is the word *viejo*, which you should probably be taught from early on not to use in reference to people.

The other problem is the concept of "older," which in English can refer to a two-year-old in comparison with a one-year-old. In Spanish, *viejo* means "old" in the very specific sense (for humans) of having been on the planet for more than fifty or sixty years. *Más viejo*, naturally, means "older," in the sense of having been among us for sixty-plus years. Therefore, when referring to your "older brother," you can't say he's your *hermano más viejo* unless he is, officially, a potential Gray Panther. He is your *hermano mayor*—your "greater brother," in age if in nothing else. A very common way of phrasing this idea is with *grande*. *¿Tienes hermanos más grandes?* = "Do you have older siblings?" A "grown-up," in fact, can safely be translated as *una persona grande*—"a big person."

I say "safely" because, as always when talking about age, there are numerous ways to stick your foot in your mouth. Almost all of them have to do with the word *viejo*, which, as noted, you would do well to forget except in reference to buildings and such. With senior citizens, the tendency in all cultures is to avoid calling them "old"—thus terms like "senior citizens." There's nothing wrong with being old—most of us take special precautions to become old ourselves—but nobody seems to like being reminded that they've achieved this status. So in Spanish you say things like *Mi abuela ya es muy grande, Es una persona ya grande* or *Es una persona mayor* instead of saying *Mi abuela es vieja*. Other words given for "old" by the dictionaries are also borderline rude except when talking about, say, pyramids. These include *anciano* and *antiguo*, especially.

Mi viejo and *mi vieja*, meanwhile, come in for frequent colloquial use. They can mean "the old man" (or father) and "the old lady" (or mother), but more commonly they refer slangily to one's "guy" (husband, boyfriend, or lover) or "gal" (wife, girlfriend, or lover). *Viejo* (without the *mi*) is also used slangily in many countries for "buddy" or "man," regardless of the age of the person addressed. *Vieja* is not used this way ever, though, since *una vieja* is a rude way of referring to a woman, similar to "a broad" or even "a bitch."

ORDER

In this case, your choice is the same word but with different genders: *la orden* and *el orden*. Which is which? Well, if you're traveling through Spanish-speaking areas, you should first learn the word for "an order" of the sort that you submit to a waiter or waitress at a restaurant. It is *la orden*, the feminine form, and you should invent some mnemonic gimmick to make this stick. *El orden*, the masculine form, means "the order" of things—that is, their organization or sequence.

Ordenar as a verb, to mean "to order (in a restaurant)," is being used increasingly in Latin America, but the proper word for this is *pedir*. *Ordenar* really only means "to put one's things in order." "To order (someone about)" would be *mandar*. A final note on "order": "in order to" should be handled with *para*, never with an expression using *orden*.

PIECE

This is a tricky one, and even most Spanish speakers won't be able to explain the subtle distinctions—though they will invariably and instinctively use the correct form. First of all, banish *pieza* from your mind for all but a few usages, usually having to do with a "part" of a machine or car. Think of it as a self-contained "piece," and not so much as an arbitrarily determined or broken-off "fragment" of some larger whole.

For fragments, the two most common words are *trozo* and *pedazo*. Sometimes, these two are interchangeable—with a "stretch" of highway, for instance, either *trozo* or *pedazo* will work (though *tramo* would be an even better word here)—and other times they're not. The difference seems to reside in whether the piece in question is a plainly three-dimensional chunk (*trozo*) or not (*pedazo*), whether the piece in question is useful in itself (*trozo*) or not (*pedazo*), whether it's an indistinct division between part and whole (*trozo*) or a fairly clear one (*pedazo*), and so on. An object breaks into *pedazos*, and you normally would ask for a *trozo* of something at the dinner table.

In this last setting, however, bear in mind that many comestibles come in *rebanadas* ("slices"), and that this is the preferred word for "pieces" of bread, cake, pizza, and so on. A cute word for a "little piece," "smidgeon," or "tad" is *nadita*—"a little nothing." The word *tajada* is also used widely to mean "piece" or "slice," but in many areas it also carries the connotation of a "cut" or "percentage" of an illegal or dirty business.

PLAN

As a noun, "plan" equals *plan* pretty consistently, but keep in mind the difference between *plan* and *plano* (a building's "floorplan" or "design," a town "map"). To be in a certain *plan* is a colloquial way of saying to be "in a phase," to be "on a kick." *Estoy en mi plan limpiador* = "I'm in my cleaning mood." For the verb "to plan" it is almost always better to forget about *planear* and use *pensar* instead, unless you are consciously planning a scheme or a strategy. *Pensamos irnos mañana* = "We're planning to leave tomorrow."

QUIET

In general, *quieto* translates better as "still"—as in "keep still"—than as "quiet." So what's the right word for "quiet?" That depends on what you're using it to say. "Keep quiet" is *Cállate* (for a single noisemaker) or *Cállense* (for a band of rowdy tykes). But be careful with your tone: *Cállate* can convey the rudeness of an abrupt "Shut up!" and in fact can be difficult to say without sounding rude. With friends, a clever way around this problem is to address them in formal tones: *Cállese usted.* Paradoxically, this more formal construction tones down the harshness of *Cállate* quite a bit. The formal construction is also commonly used on children, much as a parent might say "John Joseph Doe, you quiet down" instead of "Be quiet, Johnny." Where all else fails, "Shhhh" translates quite well as *Shhhh.*

Callado as an adjective means "hushed" or "not answering," as in how a stadium crowd reacts when the visiting team scores a touchdown. *Callar,* the verb, can be used to convey "speechless." *Lo callaron* = "They left him speechless." (This could also be rendered *Se quedó sin palabras,* or "He was left speechless.") A person who is "quiet" by nature could be called *una persona callada* or *una persona de pocas palabras.*

Many times, "quiet" in English is used to describe serenity, calmness, peacefulness, and ease: "Let's just have a quiet night at home, dear." For these cases, *tranquilo* is the correct choice. It also covers "quiet" places. *Busquemos un lugar tranquilo para platicar* = "Let's look for a quiet place to talk."

SAVE

Once you learn that *salvar* is rarely the word you want for "to save," it becomes tempting to use *ahorrar* all the time. And it does work for many usages: "to save time" (*ahorrar tiempo*), "to save money" (*ahorrar dinero*), "to save (making) a trip" (*ahorrar un viaje*), and so on. Still, it's not always the smoothest translation of these and similar common English idioms. For "to save a trip," for instance, *evitarse* ("to avoid") could be used comfortably. *Me evité un viaje a la tienda cuando llegó con azúcar* = "I saved (myself) a trip to the store when she (or he) showed up with sugar."

Another common use of "to save" in English is in the sense of "to set something aside," and in these cases *ahorrar* should be avoided. Instead, use *guardar*. *Guárdame un trozo para más tarde* = "Save me a piece for later." *Guardar* is also the correct verb for "saving" ticket stubs, receipts, and other items, and can often be translated "to hold on to." *Salvar* is also a perfectly good word for "to save," of course, but only in the very specific sense of "to rescue." "Lifesavers," both the candy and the flotation device, are *salvavidas*.

SHORT

Ask yourself: "short" as in "not tall" or "short" as in "not long"? In English, we lump these concepts together: "A short man took a short trip." In Spanish, you have to distinguish between the two: *Un hombre bajo hizo un viaje corto. Breve* can generally be substituted for *corto*, never for *bajo*.

SIGN

As you travel through the Spanish-speaking world, you may find yourself asking directions and, in the course of doing so, asking if there are "signs" marking the way. After a period of traveling there, of course, you'll realize the quaint innocence of this question in many places, but in the beginning at least you will need a word for "signs." What shall it be? The best all-purpose word for "road sign" is *letrero*, and that's what you would generally ask for: *¿Hay letreros?* The word *rótulo* is also used (in some countries more than others), but generally this word refers to the sign over a shop.

What about *signo*, you wonder? For the most part, ignore it—outside of math and grammar it gets little use. You will find it in stock expressions like *signo de interrogación* ("question mark"), *signo de admiración* ("exclamation point"), *signo negativo* ("negative sign"), *signo (de) menos* ("minus sign"), and so forth. A more all-purpose word for "sign" in the sense of an intangible "signal" or "indication" is *señal*. *Es una buena señal* = "It's a good sign."

Other words that you may want to incorporate as you gain fluency are *huella* ("sign" in the sense of "trace" or 'clue"), *seña* (a hand "signal" or "gesture," including but not limited to obscene ones), *indicio* (safe for "indication"), *muestra* ("sign" in the sense of "evidence of something"), *marca* ("mark"), and so on. There's much overlap in the use of these words, and for the most part you're safe—if not excessively precise—with just *letrero* and *señal*. "To sign," of course, is *firmar*, and *una firma* is "a signature."

SKIP

In spoken English, "to skip" is used more than you might at first think. You can skip breakfast, skip to school, skip school, skip a grade in school, skip ahead in math or, if you don't like math, skip it altogether. Still, many dictionaries and textbooks neglect "skip" as, well, not very dignified English. In Spanish, most figurative uses of "to skip" have a good equivalent in the reflexive *saltarse*, which—like "to skip"—is much used in daily speech. *Me salté el desayuno* = "I skipped breakfast." *Se ha saltado un renglón* = "He's skipped a line." "Skipping school" would call for some other expression, of which many local variants exist—*irse de pinta* in Mexico, for instance.

THERE

As in the case of "here" (see above), the several words that are used for "there" differ only slightly from each other. *Ahí*, the linguists say, means "there" when "there" is "over there"—near the person being addressed. *Allí* is "over there" when this is not near either the speaker or the listener, but is generally within sight. *Allá* is "way over there"—that is, far away, out of sight, yonder. As in the case of *acá* and *aquí*, the linguists overlook the fact that most Spanish speakers tend to use the three "theres" almost interchangeably.

Still, in certain expressions there is a correct "there" to use. One of these is *más allá*, which means "beyond" or "past." When you tell the cab driver where you live, for instance, you might say *Vivo más allá del parque* ("I live past the park"). When he stops at the start of your street and looks back at you, you might say *Más allá* ("Farther on"). Don't confuse *más allá* with *el más allá* ("The Great Beyond"), though you might think that, from the way the cabbie is driving, that is his ultimate destination.

Another note on *allá*: it is often used as a kind of shorthand way of referring to a foreign country. A visitor to Mexico, for instance, might be a little befuddled the first time he or she hears, completely out of the blue, a question like *¿Y tienen tequila allá?* ("Do they have tequila there?"). On the other hand, *allá* is a handy substitute for stuffy-sounding expressions like "where I come from "or "in my country." Where the context is clear, it works in a way as "back home." *Allá tengo esposa y tres hijos* = "Back home I've got a wife and three kids."

Finally, remember that in Spanish "there" is usually left out of the traditional phone query, "Is So-and-so there?" Instead, you simply ask *¿Está Fulano?* If you must get the "there" into your question, you

can ask *¿Está por ahí Fulano?*—though this can come off sounding
fairly informal.

WORKER

What should you call your co-workers? That may depend on
your mood, but in Spanish it also depends on what kind of work they
do. *Obrero* may seem to work well as "worker," but it refers almost
exclusively to "laborers" doing manual work. Within this grouping,
there are *albañiles* ("construction workers"), *labradores* (usually,
"field hands"), and *jornaleros* ("day laborers"). *Trabajador* is the generic term for "worker," though it too connotes some actual, sweat-
producing labor. For "white-collar workers" or "office workers" (i.e.,
the sweat-free positions), *empleado* and *oficinista* are close fits. Note
that *empleado* means more than just "employee" and is by itself a
fairly respectable job description, often suggesting a job in the public
sector. In fact, many government forms offer *empleado* as an occupational category all by itself.

12 SAY IT RIGHT

Some everyday concepts in Spanish just seem to resist translation. As a result, many students of Spanish never seem to learn to say them right. Perhaps common usage doesn't conform to the bilingual dictionary's definition, or maybe there's just not a good dictionary translation to be found. Regardless, you'll need to express these concepts, and the sooner you learn how to say them, the better. Here is a selection of the commonest hang-ups for students of Spanish.

CHOICE

The problem here is really quite simple. In English, you "choose" between "choices," but in Spanish you can't *escoger* between *escogibles* or *escogisiones* because these awkward, horrible-sounding behemoths don't really exist. *Escogimiento* does exist, but if you use it, you're liable to be hit. Instead, use *opciones* and *selecciones* when you want to translate, but keep your eyes and mind open for alternative constructions. "What's your choice?" would be expressed as *¿Qué escoges?* "There's no choice" would be *No hay de otra* or *No hay remedio*. "Good choice" = *Buena selección* and "What are my choices?" = *¿Cuáles son mis opciones?*

While we're on the subject, "choosy" is another concept that confounds many students of Spanish—especially when you add in "fussy" and "picky." In Spanish you have to leave the universe of "choice" altogether to express this concept. One of the most common (if least expected) ways of expressing it is with *especial* ("special").

Ella es muy especial para la comida = "She's a very picky eater."
More formally, *exigente* ("demanding") works well, and in some parts
you may hear *fastidioso* for someone who is annoyingly fussy. (Note
however that *fastidioso* does not mean "fastidious" so much as "an-
noying" or "bothersome," though it may be taking on the English
meaning more and more. See Appendix B.) In Mexico a slangy word
for "annoyingly picky" is *sangrón*. *Es muy sangrona para la comida.*
Likewise, *No seas tan sangrón* = "Don't be so picky."

ENOUGH

Most students of Spanish learn early on that "enough" is *bastante*, pure and simple. So it will come as something of a surprise to
discover that "enough" is not *bastante*—or rarely. Some dictionaries
try to gloss over this problem, giving you a variety of forms—from
¡basta! to even *bastantemente*—to let you wriggle out of a jam. In
fact, *bastante* in the sense of "enough" almost never works as well as
suficiente, which you should carve into your memory as the correct
word for "enough."

This is not to say that *bastante* is not a useful word; it is,
and immensely so. But it is much closer to "plenty" than "enough,"
as a few examples make clear. When the waiter is serving you brus-
sel sprouts and you think that six is enough, you naturally would say,
"That's enough, thank you." In Spanish, this would be *Es suficiente,
gracias. Es bastante, gracias* sounds almost like a complaint—"Whew!
That's plenty." A waiter, on hearing it, might even offer to take some
of your sprouts back. *Ya basta* will get your point across, but it comes
off sounding like a rude "Enough already!" *Tengo suficiente dinero*
means "I have enough money" (to buy gas, or food, or whatever),
whereas *Tengo bastante dinero* sounds like a bit of a boast: "I've got
plenty of money."

A good verb to keep handy for situations involving money, especially, is *alcanzar*, meaning "to reach" but also "to be enough." It is
a very common word, and you will probably hear *¿Te alcanza para una
Coca?* more often than *¿Tienes lo suficiente para una Coca?* Similarly,
"I don't have enough" is usually just *No me alcanza*. Note that *alcanzar* requires inverting subject and object. In English, you have the
money; in Spanish, the money reaches for you. *Alcanzar* is also probably the best way to translate "to afford," a notorious bugaboo in translators' circles. "Can you afford new shoes?" would be *¿Te alcanza para
nuevos zapatos?*

Bastante is very common as a modifier of adjectives, much as
"plenty" is in colloquial English. *Es bastante guapo* = "He's plenty

handsome" (and not "He's handsome enough," which sounds like a backhanded compliment). *Es bastante listo con las computadoras* = "He's real clever with computers" (and not "He's clever enough"). For "clever enough" and "handsome enough," you have to dig down deep for *suficientemente*, as in the phrase *Es lo suficientemente listo*.

Of all the typical usages of "enough," only "Enough already!" wouldn't be disposed of better by some form of *suficiente* and would in fact be rendered *¡Basta!*

FEAR

Here is a classic minefield for the foreign speaker of Spanish. Not only are there many alternatives to choose from, but most of them depart from our customary perspective in English. *Asustar, dar susto, temer, temor, pavor, espantar, dar miedo, tener miedo*—all of these are used, and it's quite a trick to learn exactly how.

To start with, keep in mind that "fear" in Spanish is something that you "have" or "give." Thus, you aren't "afraid" but "have fear." And you don't "scare," you "give fear." With this in mind, lie down on the couch over there and proceed to analyze your fears. Fear, in Spanish, can be broken down roughly as follows. A *temor* is a very specific fear, almost more like a deep-seated, haunting feeling; *temer* is the verb that goes with this type of fear. Thus *Temo que algo haya pasado* = "I'm afraid something has happened." *Mi temor es que escapen los animales* = "My fear is that the animals may escape." *Temer* is also used in polite expressions, just as "fear" is in English: "I fear we may have arrived at a bad moment" would be expressed as *Temo haber llegado en un mal momento* or *Temo que hayamos llegado en un mal momento*. Note that all subordinate clauses built off of *temer* and *temor* require the subjunctive, because fear of what may happen or what may be happening is naturally the province of the subjunctive.

Miedo, meanwhile, is your run-of-the-mill sort of fear. You "have this fear" of the dark, of scorpions, of large fellows who drool, and of public speaking. Of these fears you would say, *Me dan miedo* or *Tengo miedo de ellos*. Perfectly natural. These things always "give you" this fear, regardless of the circumstances.

A *susto* is more sudden than a "fear." Properly speaking, it is a "scare," even a "shock." *¡Qué susto me diste!* ("What a scare you gave me!") you tell your roommate, whom you found hiding in the closet with a wolf mask on. This type of fear even gets its own verb: *asustar* ("to scare"), which means exactly the same as *dar susto*. Here, though, you have to be careful about your English, since "to scare" is commonly used for both sudden fears and for fears which you always have, regardless of the circumstances. "Bears scare me" would normally be *Tengo miedo de los osos* in Spanish. You might hear *Los osos me asustan*, especially from kids, but it suggests that certain bears are in the habit of sneaking up behind you and yelling "Boo!" in your ear.

When "to scare" means "to scare away," *espantar* is used instead of *asustar*. Thus an *espantapájaros*—literally a "scare-away-birds"—is a "scarecrow." *Espanto* in Latin America is also a common word for "spooks" or "ghosts"; the "haunted house" at the amusement park is in many countries called *La Casa de los Espantos*.

Another problem is the word "scary." Some authors cite "scary" as one of those words that simply doesn't have a Spanish translation. (And two Spanish-English dictionaries I have at hand simply mistranslate "scary" as *miedoso* and *pusilánime*—both of which mean "cowardly.") I remember one student of Spanish describing a film he had seen as *espantosa*, thinking it meant "scary" or "frightening." Instead, it usually means "frightfully bad" or "dreadful," far from the speaker's intent. Possibly the safest way to convey "scary" is with *miedo*. "It's a scary movie" = *Es una película de miedo* or *Es una película que da miedo* (or *una película de horror* in the specific case of *Friday the 13th*–style horror flicks). You might also hear *tétrico* for "scary," though it tends more to "spooky" or even "eerie." Still, it can be the perfect word to describe a lonely alley late at night. *Aterrador* is like "scary" but considerably scarier; "terrifying" hits the mark.

Two other words round out our study of fears. They are *pavor* and *pánico*, the second being a slangy addition to the list. *Pavor* is an intense, almost phobic fear, mingled with equal parts dread and loathing. *Me dan pavor las tarántulas* = "I'm terrified of tarantulas." Like *miedo*, *pavor* is a long-term, constant fear, not a sudden shock like *susto*. Colloquially, you may hear *me da pánico* to mean much the same as *me da pavor*, and *me da terror* fits this mold as well. *Me da horror* is also used to mean "It disgusts me" or "It grosses me out." Along these lines, you'll sometimes hear *Me da cosa*, a slangy phrase that could be rendered "It gives me the creeps." *Ese señor me da cosa* = "That man gives me the creeps."

GUESS

This word crops up a lot more in spoken English than you might at first think. And until you break the habit of translating your thoughts, you'll need a good selection of phrases for it. "To guess" often can be handled by *adivinar*. *Adivina quién es* = "Guess who it is." *¡Adivina qué!* = "Guess what!"

But in English "guess" is stretched well past its original intent in many colloquial instances. Obviously, we aren't actually guessing at our own actions when we say, "I guess I'll be going now." For "guess" in this sense, you would need to resort in Spanish to some similar qualifier. *Suponer* works fine: *Supongo que ya me voy.* In some other examples, *imaginarse* might be called for. *¿Vas a ir esta noche? Me imagino que sí.* = "Are you going tonight?" "I guess so."

Two other verbs—*atinar* and *acertar*—also come into play here. Both mean, more or less, "to guess right." *Le atinó a mi nombre* = "He guessed my name." *A ver si le aciertas al ganador* = "Let's see if you can guess the winner." Both of these words are commonly heard in Spanish, and you would do well to learn to recognize them. *¿De qué país eres? Adivina. Pues, de Canadá. ¡Atinaste!* = "What country are you from?" "Guess." "Canada?" "You got it!" Many times, when we would be tempted to use *adivinar*, we should probably use *atinar* or *acertar*. "Let me guess" could be rendered either literally, *Déjame adivinar*, or more naturally, *A ver si le atino* ("Let's see if I can guess it").

HALF

Learning about "half" and "middle" in Spanish is essentially a matter of learning one word—*medio*—and how to use it. Only when "half" is a noun does another word—*mitad*—come into play. At all other times, *medio* or a related form covers "half" and "middle." Examples: *la mitad de la pizza* = "half of the pizza" but *media pizza* = "half a pizza"; *una pizza medio cocida* (or *una pizza cocida a medias*) = "a half-cooked pizza."

Students of Spanish mostly err in this case when they overuse *mitad*. Note how much easier and smoother it is to say *media botella de vino* instead of *la mitad de una botella de vino.* Both mean "half a bottle of wine." *Mitad* is much used but fairly specifically, and especially where no noun is present. *Dáme la mitad* = "Give me half." *Irse a mitades* is a slangy phrase for "to split the cost of something" or "half-and-half." *Si compramos una pizza, nos vamos a mitades* = "If we buy a pizza, we each pay half."

The adverb *medio* is extremely common as a modifier of adjectives. It equates with "kind of" in English in the sense of "kind of ugly," "kind of happy," "kind of drunk": *medio feo, medio feliz, medio borracho.* Since it's an adverb, it never changes genders. For example, *Ella está medio borracha* and *La pizza está medio cocida.*

A couple of *medio*-related phrases are *a mediados de, en medio de*, and *a medias.* The first one means "around the middle of" and is almost always used with time constructions: *a mediados de diciembre, a mediados del mes*, and the like. *En medio de* is "in the middle of" in the physical or figurative sense: *en medio de la calle* = "in the middle of the street"; *en medio de un gran lío* = "in the middle of a big mess." *A medias* is an adverb describing how something is done, and its best translation is "half-way" or just "half." *¡Hiciste la tarea? La hice a medias.* = "Did you do the homework?" "I kinda half did it." Note that this is not the same as *Hice la mitad*, which means "I did half of it." You often hear *a medias* to describe a poorly done job; in this sense, it equates with "half-assed." *¡Esos albañiles lo hicieron a medias!* = "Those construction workers did a half-assed job!"

HOW

This innocent-looking word earns special mention for the widespread but incorrect use of *cómo* to translate common questions like "How do you like it?" Even almost-fluent foreigners, especially those whose native tongue is English, make this mistake. *Cómo* should never be used this way. *¿Qué tal?* can often be used instead. *¿Qué tal estuvo la película?* = "How was the movie?" Shorter and sweeter: *¿Qué tal la sopa?* = "How's the soup?" You can also construct "How did you like" questions with *parecer* (*¿Qué te pareció . . . ?*) and *gustar* (*¿Te gustó . . . ?*). But *¿Cómo te gustó . . . ?* is always an absolute no-no.

MAYBE

At least once in each of his films, the Mexican comic Capulín would answer someone's urgent request for information with a thoughtful, unhelpful *No lo sé, puede ser, a lo mejor, tal vez, ¿quién sabe?*—in other words, "Maybe." There's one other common translation that Capulín left out, and that's *quizás* or *quizá*. Now you too are equipped to be noncommittal and unhelpful. Use any one of these phrases to say "maybe" in good Spanish.

But wait, you say breathlessly, isn't there any way to differentiate among these many alternatives? *No lo sé, puede ser, a lo mejor, tal vez, ¿quién sabe . . . ?* But seriously, you should be careful about overusing *quizás* and neglecting *a lo mejor*, which in many countries is the common conversational way of saying "maybe." *¿Vienes esta noche? A lo mejor.* = "Are you coming tonight?" "Maybe." *Tal vez* is also extremely common and all-purpose. *Quizás*, on the other hand, somehow sounds loftier and more grandiose. *Puede ser que, puede que, a lo mejor, tal vez*, and *quizás* can all be used to start sentences.

All but *a lo mejor* are usually followed by the subjunctive to highlight the uncertainty being expressed. *Tal vez esté enojado* = "Maybe he's mad." *A lo mejor no quiere* = "Maybe he doesn't want to." On the streets, finally, it is increasingly common to hear *chance* for "maybe," but don't tell your teacher I told you. *¿Vienes esta noche? Chance.* The words you want to avoid are *probablemente* and *posiblemente*, especially the former. Both are perfectly legitimate Spanish words, but they're not as common as their English cognates. Were they as common, Capulín would have thrown them in for good measure.

MOTIVE

Life being what it is, there will come times when you slip up, trip up, or flub up. It can't be helped. You're walking down the street in, say, Santiago, happy as a lark, when your hand knocks into the ice cream cone of a six-year-old girl and sends the cone scattering on the pavement. The passersby eye you with suspicion. The six-year-old eyes you with disbelief, then with unbridled hatred, and then starts to bawl. You look around at the crowd assembling on all sides. Think quick: what can you say to them?

In English, you might breezily announce "Sorry, I didn't mean to" or "It was an accident." You might even add, "It wasn't on purpose." In Spanish, your simplest, most universal excuse—and one you should have at the tip of your tongue at all times—is *Fue sin querer* (literally, "It was without wanting"). *Sin querer* can also be added on to any verb to mean "accidentally" or "not on purpose." *Lo pateé sin querer* = "I kicked it by accident." *Sin querer borré tu nombre de la lista* = "I accidentally erased your name from the list." To vary your vocabulary (if you flub up a lot, for instance), you can use *sin pensar*, *por distracción*, or *involuntariamente*. Of course, if you can pronounce that last one, you probably don't have to worry about flubs.

When you want to say something was "on purpose," *a propósito* (or in some places *de propósito*) works well. But don't overlook *con querer*, the opposite of *sin querer* and every bit as common and as handy. *Lo hice con querer* = "I did it on purpose." *Adrede*, which means the same thing, is less common, but you will hear it. Save *deliberadamente* for effect.

Be careful with *accidente* and its derivatives. Although both *por accidente* and *accidentalmente* are used widely, they sound a bit forced, and neither gets the heavy work assigned to its English cognate. *Fue un accidente* will get you away from the maddened crowd and the six-year-old. But *Fue sin querer* will do the job more smoothly, without overdramatizing the incident.

OBLIGATION

Here's one you simply must learn. You have to. Really, you should. You'd better, anyhow. That is, you ought to.

The difference in degrees of obligation are a subtle issue that you will master only after many years of listening to Spanish being spoken. As in English, there are many ways to convey the notion, but there is no simple way to explain which is the correct choice for any given sentence.

Perhaps the most useful way to classify the "musts" is by the strength of the obligation they imply. Intuitively, you can sense the different strengths in English: "You must go" is greater than "You have to go," which is stronger than "You'd better go," which is a tad more forceful than "You ought to go," which is up a notch from "You should go." In Spanish, a parallel ranking, in order of decreasing obligation, might go something like this: *Tienes que ir, Más te vale ir, Has de ir, Hay que ir, Mejor vas, Debes/deberías ir*. Of these, you can safely discard *Has de ir*, which has a scolding schoolmarmish quality about it. *Hay que* plus a verb, meanwhile, is very common but is limited to impersonal situations. You cannot say *Hay que ir tú*, for instance; you would have to say *Tienes que ir tú*. *Mejor vas* and *Más te vale ir* are both good translations of "You'd better go," with the second implying "or else . . . ."

Deber with an infinitive is "should," and whether you use the present indicative (*debes*), the conditional (*deberías*), or even the past subjunctive (*debieras*) seems to be largely a matter of personal preference. For all intents and purposes, *Debes ir mañana, Deberías ir mañana*, and *Debieras ir mañana* are equivalents.

Adding a *de* to *deber* creates another construction that is hard to find a consistent English equivalent for. It is used when the speaker has some sign or evidence that something "is supposed to" be or "should" be. An example will help here. *No debe de haber llegado* means "He (or she) must not have arrived yet" and would be used when the speaker is looking around an untouched room or notices that all the lights are turned off, for instance. That said, many Spanish-speakers will use *No debe haber llegado*, without the *de*, to say the same thing, and in some countries *debe de* seems to replace a simple *debe* in many cases. Note though that by changing the verb to the past, you change the meaning significantly. *No debió haber llegado* would be saying "He shouldn't have arrived"—that is, the person did in fact arrive but against the speaker's better judgment.

For events in the past, stick to a past form of *deber* with a past participle for most constructions. *Debías* (or *debiste*) *haber ido* = "You should have gone." If you instead use the preterit plus the infinitive—*debiste ir*—you are stressing more the obligation than the missed opportunity. *Debías haber ido a la fiesta* suggests you missed a good time at the party; *Debiste haber ido a la fiesta* suggests the same, only a fraction stronger, and hinting maybe at "I told you so"; *Debiste ir a la fiesta* means it was your duty to go—the party was in your honor, for instance. The fourth combination—imperfect plus infinitive, or *debías ir*—is not used, so forget about it. Perhaps the best construction for past obligations—that is, your "should haves"—is also the simplest: *hubiera* plus the past participle. *(Te) hubieras ido* = You should have gone. *Hubiéramos llamado* = We should have called.

A final note on words of obligation deals with the word *obligar* itself. In Spanish, this word is much more widely used than "to obligate" is in English. In fact, in many cases where in English we use "to make" or "to force," in Spanish you should be thinking *obligar*. *La policía nos obligó a salir* = "The police forced us to leave." *El diablo me obligó a hacerlo* = "The devil made me do it." One way to remember to use *obligar* is to remind yourself that *forzar* is relatively rarely used. It's a perfectly legitimate word, of course, but until you're accustomed to using *obligar*, you're better off forgetting that *forzar* exists.

USUALLY

The basis of the confusion here is the word *usualmente*, which does exist but which you should treat as if it didn't. Dictionaries tend to give it as the translation for "usually," but in actual practice you could go a month or a year without hearing a native Spanish speaker use it. It is easy to remember, and technically it's accurate, but it sounds stiff and strange. You decide.

If you decide to avoid *usualmente* (smart choice!), you will be left with the slight problem of substitutes. Never fear; they abound. *Generalmente* is safe, but a mouthful; *normalmente* is easier and just as good. *Por lo general* is also a good choice. A verbal construction that works very well involves the irregular verb *soler. Suele pasar a las seis* = "It usually comes by at six."

While we're discussing the frequency of things, note that if you're still translating from the English, you'll find your brain feeding you lines like "most of the time" and expecting you to translate them. This leads to hideous constructions like *la mayoría del tiempo*, as in

La mayoría del tiempo sólo bebo agua ("Most of the time I just drink water"). In Spanish, this sounds as if you have made a scientific study rather than an off-the-cuff remark. In general, forget about translating "most of the time" and all other "most of" expressions—"most of the people," "most of my life," "most of the class"—and look for ways around them. The use of *casi* ("almost") often provides a way out: *casi siempre* = "most of the time"; *casi todos* = "most of the people"; *casi toda la clase* = "most of the class."

WASTE

The tendency here, once again, is to translate our English thoughts too literally into Spanish. The proper word for "to waste" in Spanish is *desperdiciar*—a real mouthful that, once you learn it, you are justified in wanting to use as often as possible. Unfortunately, for most expressions requiring "waste" in English, *desperdiciar* is not the word. Generally speaking, simple old *perder* ("to lose") is. Thus "to waste time" is *perder el tiempo* and "to waste an opportunity" is *perder una oportunidad*. The use of *perder* carries over to the nouns: *una pérdida de tiempo* = "a waste of time." *Malgastar* can also be "to waste," but perhaps translates better as "to misspend." Some dictionaries list *echar a perder* as a translation for "to waste," but correctly this phrase means "to ruin," as in *Echaste a perder el juego* ("You ruined the game"). Its reflexive form, *echarse a perder*, means "to go to waste" or "to spoil," generally in reference to perishable foodstuffs. With people, it also means "to spoil." *Estás echando a perder al niño* = "You're spoiling the boy."

13   SPANISH ROOTS

Until now, we have been treating "Spanish" as a single unit, a monolith unchanging over time, an easily dissected collection of words, phrases, syntax, and morphology. It makes sense to approach it this way, of course. The book that presents the entire history of Spanish, while trying to make modern Spanish intelligible to foreign speakers, would be a much, much longer book than this. I'm glad I don't have to write that book, and I hope you never have to read it.

But a little history is useful and, for some students, fascinating. For the history of a language is also the history of the people who spoke it, the voyages they took, the castles and forts they built, the wars they waged, and the ideas they attacked and defended. In the case of Spanish, it is the family history of more than 300 million modern-day Spanish speakers. But it is also the history of Europe, of the New World, of Western civilization, of the entire planet.

You may not have much need for an understanding of the linguistic differences between today's Spanish and what was spoken in the kingdom of Castile a millennium ago. But it somehow adds to the thrill of speaking Spanish to know that the language we speak today is pulsing with the life of centuries. The language in its present form is but a point on a continuum in the evolution of Spanish; by learning it, and learning about the worlds that gave birth to it, we join the process in a small but exciting way.

Spanish, of course, came from Latin, as did French, Italian, Portuguese, Romanian, and several other less widespread European languages. In fact, a good way to grasp the origins of Spanish is to examine where, why, and how it branched off from Latin. And for that, we have to step back in time more than 3,000 years.

A thousand years before the birth of Christ, the Iberian Peninsula—what today is Spain and Portugal—was already home to distinct tribes and incipient civilizations. At the mouth of the Guadalquivir River, the Phoenicians founded the city of Tharsis, or Tartessus, which became known for its wealth and commerce, according to Old Testament reports. In the tenth century B.C., according to the Book of Kings, King Solomon's navy went every three years to Tharsis "and brought from thence gold and silver, and elephants' teeth, and apes, and peacocks." Four centuries later the Hebrew prophet Ezechiel talked of the "merchants of Tharsis," who apparently conducted a busy trade with Phoenecia (modern-day Syria) at the other extreme of the Mediterranean.

The Greek historian Herodotus, in the fifth century B.C., refers to the inhabitants of "Iberia," located presumably near the mouth of the Iber (Ebro) River in southern Spain. The Greeks also established colonies in southern Spain, and by the third century the Carthaginians (from what today is Tunisia) began to conquer the entire Iberian peninsula. Their capital was Cartagena—"New Carthage." Not until 201 B.C., with the conclusion of the Second Punic War and Rome's victory over Hannibal's Carthaginian forces, did Spain start to fall under Roman rule. That date also marks the formal arrival of Latin in Iberia—the arrival, that is, of the antecedent of the Spanish language.

The Iberians, as we call them today, had a relatively advanced culture that peaked in about the fourth century B.C., or right before the Carthaginian invasion. A few examples of Iberian coins and sculpture survive to this day, and the remnants of their written language still largely defy translation. Tharsis also boasted of a written language dating back, they said, some 6,000 years! The extant examples of this language are totally unlike ancient Iberian but just as indecipherable. Their only common trait is that both seem to have originated in Africa.

Spain's early history (and, indeed, much of its later history) is a function of its location between the European and African continents. If the Iberians and others came from North Africa, then other tribes, including the Celts and Ligurs, came from the European heartland. In fact, the Celts, who began settling the northwest of the peninsula in about the eighth century B.C., began mixing with the Iberians, creating a "Celtiberian" culture in north-central Spain.

Of the pre-Roman groups, only the Basques have survived as a separate ethnic group, and only the Basque language has reached modern times more or less intact. The state of scholarship on the Basque language reflects the mystery surrounding pre-Roman Iberia as a whole. Scholars who struggle to locate the origins of a now extinct Iberian or Turdetan language must also recognize that they are unable even to trace the origins of Basque, which alone among existing European languages is from non–Indo-European roots. Where, then, did Basque come from? Once it was thought the Iberians simply became the modern-day Basques, but recent scholarship has poked holes in that theory. Now scholars surmise that Basque may have come from Caucasian, a language spoken in modern-day Georgia between the Black and Caspian seas. Or, others say, perhaps it is from a Hamitic source, like certain Sudanic languages, with which it has similarities. Then again, it may be from Coptic, an Afro-Asiatic language of Egyptian stock still used today in the liturgy of the Coptic Church. One modern scholar has even suggested that Basque is but another Romance (i.e., Latin-based) language!

THE FATE OF LATIN IN IBERIA

The combined effect of Iberia's pre-Roman cultures and languages on the birth of Spanish is small but significant. Words taken from Celtic, from Basque, and even from Iberian still linger in the language. From Celtic, early forms of such common words as *cerveza, caballo, carro, camisa*, and *camino* were born. Celtic place-names on the Iberian Peninsula include Segovia, Evora, Coimbra, and Coruña, although all of these names have undergone considerable changes from the original Celtic words. Basque has contributed a handful of words, most of them uncommon, to Spanish, with *izquierda* being probably the most used.

Other everyday Spanish words that can trace their lineage to Iberia before the arrival of the Romans are *barro, conejo, gordo, muñeca, perro*, and *sapo*. Certain suffixes are also viewed by today's scholars as typically "Iberian" in origin (though not necessarily from the Iberians themselves). These include *-rro, -rra, -ago, -ero, -iego*, and *-asco*. The ending *-ez* also dates from pre-Roman times and can still be found in names like Sánchez, López, Ramírez, González, Rodríguez, Velázquez, Pérez, and so on.

Even some changes in "spelling" between Latin and Spanish have been blamed on the residual impact of pre-Roman languages. The conversion of the Latin *f* to a now silent *h* in Spanish has been explained as part of the legacy of these languages and can serve to begin our study of Spanish's slow but steady departure from its Latin roots. The Spanish words *hijo, hacer, hoja, hundir*, and *humo*, for example, come from the Latin roots *fīliŭs, făcĕre, fŏlĭa, fŭndĕre*, and *fūmus*. In these cases, French and Italian remained truer to their Latin roots with *fils/figlio, faire/fare, feuille/foglia, enfoncer/affondare*, and *fumée/fumo*. Though now we look on these variants as "spelling changes," at the time they were changes in the spoken language, which lexicographers only later would get around to assigning a spelling to. Mostly, though, the pre-Roman languages, written and otherwise, bowed to Latin and had vanished by the year 100 A.D., only three centuries after the Romans' arrival. And Rome's relatively unmolested control of the Iberian peninsula was to last another three centuries, giving Latin a firm foothold there that may never be shaken loose.

Latin, of course, was far from a "pure" language itself, and Latin speakers borrowed freely from other languages, especially Greek, to supplement their native tongue. And Vulgar Latin—spoken on the streets of Rome and by the soldiers in the invading Roman legions— was a far cry from the literary Latin that has come down to us in Roman and other texts. Latin speakers' willingness to improvise probably accounts for the ready reception of Iberian, Celtic, and Basque words and morphology. The result was that by the third century the language being spoken popularly was an even less pure, less "literary" Latin.

Except for a handful of appearances of "common folk" in Roman comedies, few written examples of Vulgar Latin have survived to the present. Scholars, though, have been able to recreate it based on how Latin looked a few hundred years later. The "sloppiness" of its vocabulary and some of its forms also prompted linguists of the time to write tracts condemning developments in spoken Latin. One of these was written in the third century by a man named Probus, whose work shed considerable light on how Latin was changing. Probus also became somewhat famous among later scholars because nearly every one of the "errors" and examples of bad grammar that he railed against was subsequently incorporated—Probus be damned— into medieval Latin.

Students of languages amuse themselves by watching words change. In this era of Latin, there was amusement enough to go around. New words were absorbed and old words took on new meanings. *Laborare*, a perfectly functional Latin word for "to work," was gradually replaced by *tripliare*, referring to a three-sticked instrument of torture or punishment used on recalcitrant slaves. Thus as work became more tortuous, a new word was needed to emphasize the unpleasantness of the experience. And so a word was "born" into popular usage, eventually turning into the modern word *trabajar*, "to work."

Other common words have similarly intricate histories and show in passing how Spanish began to emerge from shared Latin roots. The Latin word for "grandmother," for instance, was *avia*; in France the word was abandoned in favor of a Germanicized *grand-mère*; in Italian, *nonna*, evidently a Late Latin derivative from child's talk (and the source for the word "nun"), was adopted; only Spanish was to hold on to the original Latin, and then only after "sweetening" the word by attaching the diminutive suffix *-ola*. From there *aviola* became *abuela*, the modern Spanish word for "grandmother." Knowing this history makes it curious to hear the form *abuelita*, which has begun to replace *abuela* in many parts of the Spanish-speaking world—and for the same reasons that *aviola* replaced *avia*. The word, twice diminished, can hardly get any sweeter!

Some words, in use in the protected worlds of the church or the law, survived this period of change intact. Sometimes these "original" Latin words continued to exist in these closed confines while on the streets new words were being coined from the Classical Latin roots. Sometimes, too, society's more cultured elements returned to the Latin to express themselves, refusing thereby to "lower" themselves to the level of Vulgar Latin. This reintroduction of "cultisms" would continue for centuries after Vulgar Latin had evolved into Spanish (or, strictly speaking, Castilian). As a result "Classical Latin" and "Vulgar Latin" words survive side by side in Spanish today: *frío* and *frígido, oreja* and *aurícula, delgado* and *delicado, entero* and *íntegro,* and so on.

GERMANIC SPANISH

At this point, around the year 400 A.D., Spain and its language seemed destined for a fairly uneventful development. Latin would continue to be used, and abused, and the language that would evolve would be but a regional, distorted, and "vulgar" version of the Classical Latin of Cicero and Caesar.

It almost worked out this way, but not quite. In the year 409 A.D., the Vandals (the original ones, for whom all later vandals are named) crossed the Pyrenees into Spain. The Vandals were a Germanic people, and their invasion of Spain was to be the first of a wave of Germanic invasions. The Vandals themselves only lasted twenty years on the peninsula. Hot on their trail—and fresh from sacking Rome in 410—the Germanic Visigoths reached Spain only a few years later. Their arrival, in fact, pushed the Vandals clean off the continent. The Vandals crossed into North Africa in 429, conquered Carthage ten years later, and sacked Rome themselves in 455. The Visigoths, for their part, completed their conquest of Spain under their king, Euric (466–484), and placed their capital in Toledo. Their stay was to last a little longer than the Vandals'—some three hundred years, in fact.

The Visigoths' language was, of course, a Germanic one, which meant that it shared an ancient Indo-European heritage—but little else—with Latin. Still, the linguistic shock of the Germanic conquest was considerably less than might have been expected. First, the Visigoths already spoke Latin and were themselves quite "Romanized" as a result of being based for a full century in Toulouse before sacking Rome and spreading into Spain. Second, the Visigoths kept to themselves ethnically, especially at first, swearing off mixed marriages. And third, the Germanic languages had been filtering into Latin since at least the first century A.D., which explains why many of the Romance languages have parallel Germanic constructions.

Still, the Visigoths did leave their mark linguistically in proper names, place-names, and in words associated with what they did best: fighting. The word *guerra* ("war") is of Germanic origin, as are *orgullo* ("pride"), *riqueza* ("riches"), *robar* ("to rob"), *ganar* ("to win"), and *bandido* ("bandit"). Of the place-names attributed to Germanic influence, Andalusia is probably the best known; it is but the Arabized form of Vándalus, referring to the Vandals. And the proper names Alvaro, Rodrigo, and Fernando are "Hispanicized" versions of the Visigothic names Allwars, Hrothriks, and Frithnanth.

The lasting significance of the Visigoths on Spain, however, had more to do with politics than with linguistics. Their conquest of Hispania, for instance, effectively severed its ties with Rome for nearly three centuries, leaving the Latin on the peninsula to develop in isolation and thus stray further from the Latin being spoken elsewhere. By conquering most of the many disparate tribes on the peninsula, the Visigothic lords also accomplished the first unification of Hispania, giving birth to a larger political entity that later groups would struggle to recreate.

ARABIC SPANISH

The three-century domination of Hispania by the Visigoths ended in the year 711, when Arab forces (or Moors, as the Arab/Berber Moslems on the peninsula were called) routed the Visigoth force. Within seven years the Moslems, whose founder and prophet Mohammed had died only eighty years before, had conquered virtually the entire peninsula. The Visigoths stayed on under Moorish rule, enjoying the tolerance of the new rulers. Science, art, and philosophy flourished under the Moors, who promoted (or at least presided over) a bilingual culture in which the Romanized groups became progressively more Moorish and the Moors increasingly Romanized. The first group is known as the Mozarabs (in Arabic, "would-be Arabs"), the second, as the Mudejars ("those who have been allowed to stay"—after the reconquest began, primarily). Hispania under Arab rule became a hotbed of scientific activity, leading Europe in this sense and attracting some of the best minds from around the continent.

The bicultural aspect of Moorish Spain loses none of its power to astound more than a millennium later. Arab scholars wrote treatises in Latin; Christians baptized their children with Arab names. Christian scholars, writing in Arabic, expounded on the fine points of their religion. In Moslem Cordoba, churches, mosques, and synagogues could be found in close proximity and operating openly.

The language, of course, opened its arms to embrace such diversity. The legacy is a Vulgar Latin full of "Arabisms"—more than 4,000 in all have survived in Spanish to our day. Many of these words were to pass through Spanish (or more commonly, through French) into English. A short list of the more indispensable ones barely scratches the surface: *azul* ("blue"), *escarlata* ("scarlet"), *limón* ("lime"), *naranja* ("orange"), *adobe* ("adobe"), *talco* ("talcum powder"), *azar* ("hazard," "chance"), *aceite* ("oil"), *cero* ("zero"), *cifra* ("cipher," "figure"), *ajedrez* ("chess"), *cenit* ("zenith"), *nadir* ("nadir"), *jazmín* ("jasmine"), *azúcar* ("sugar"), *azafrán* ("saffran"), *zanahoria* ("carrot"), *aduana* ("customhouse"), *tarifa* ("tariff"), and *arroz* ("rice").

Ojalá, which translates to English roughly as "I hope," is but a Hispanicized version of the Arabic expression *wa-sa Alláh* (or *in sha'allah*), meaning "may Allah wish it."

Another vast group of Spanish words of Arab origin are those beginning with *al-*, which is simply the definite article "the" in Arabic. This list also includes a number of words well known to English speakers, such as *algoritmo, álgebra, alquimia* ("alchemy"), *alcohol, alcoba* ("alcove"), and *almanaque* ("almanac"). With a little imagination a few other *al-* Spanish words from Arab roots will look familiar to us as well: *alcanfor* ("camphor"), *algodón* ("cotton"), and *almirante* ("admiral"). Some *al-* words you will need to learn in Spanish, if you haven't already, include *alfiler* ("pin"), *almacén* ("warehouse"), *almohada* ("pillow"), *alcalde* ("mayor"), *alfombra* ("rug"), and *almorzar* ("to eat lunch").

Many of these "Arab" words are really just Arabized Latin and Greek words; others are words that Arabic took from Persia, China, India, and Sumatra. But all of them entered Spanish (and some entered French and Italian as well) through Arabic, and the vast majority of them entered during the period of Moorish rule on the Iberian Peninsula. During this time the Moors also contributed mightily to Spanish place-names, such that some of the places we consider most "Spanish" are, in fact, Arab toponyms: Caceres, Gibraltar, Guadalquivir, and Guadalajara, for instance. Many others are Arabized forms of Latin names: Sevilla from Hispalia, for example, and Zaragoza from Caesaraugusta.

The kingdom of the Moors was to last almost 370 years in Toledo, some 500 years in Cordoba and Andalusia, and an astonishing 770 years or more in Granada. When the Moriscos, or "leftover" Span-

ish Moors were forcibly expelled from Spain in the seventeenth century—more than 300,000 were "sent back" to Africa between 1609
and 1614—the "Arabs" had been in Spain three times as long as the
"English" have been in America.

CASTILIAN SPANISH

The stage is now set, in our lightning recapitulation of Iberian
history, for the "reconquest" of Spain by Romanized Christian forces.
But to understand well what was to happen to Spain and Spanish in
later centuries, we should pause here and look at what else was going
on in Spain while the Moors held control of the bulk of the peninsula.

Beyond the mountains to the north and northeast, groups that
had managed to remain free of the Moorish yoke settled into small
kingdoms. To the northwest, the kingdom of Leon considered itself the
direct descendant of the Visigoth reign; to the northeast, the largely
Basque-speaking Navarre kingdom extended well into France; south of
Navarre, a tiny kingdom called Aragon, speaking a Vulgar Latin much
like that of Leon, took hold under Navarre's protection and began an
independent expansion; Catalonia (Cataluña), to the east, was basically
part of France this whole time; Portugal set itself off as a kingdom and
eventually broke away altogether in the twelfth century; in Moorish
Spain itself, finally, the Christian Mozarabs continued to live in a vari-
ably bicultural and bilingual setting. Their language—the Mozarabic/
Visigothic/Vulgar Latin of southern Spain—evolved relatively little in
comparison with the tongues being spoken in the northern part of the
peninsula.

Lastly, a tiny kingdom carved out a niche for itself in the unin-
viting borderlands between Leon to the northwest, Moorish Spain to
the south, and Aragon to the northeast. This kingdom, called Castile,
was made up of a feisty, stubbornly independent people who fought
encroachment on all sides and with ever-increasing success. They re-
sisted the Visigothic trappings and laws of Leon but refused to completely "Arabize" themselves either. Their language was coarse—unlike the relatively uniform dialects of Vulgar Latin being spoken on all
sides. In both Aragon and Leon, on either side of Castile, people said
muller; in Castile they said *muger*; in modern-day Spanish we say
mujer. In both Aragon and Leon people said *ferir*, *fieto*, and *uello*; in
Castile these words were *herir*, *hecho*, and *ojo*. In short, from the
standpoint of the rest of the peninsula's residents, the Castilians had
a strong and bizarre accent. And, thanks to political developments, in
a few short centuries almost all of Spain would have it as well.

From as early as about 1000 A.D., manuscripts from Castilian

monasteries show translations—in the form of margin notes or glosses—
from the Latin to the Vulgar Latin in use at that time. These translations are taken by many scholars to represent the first written record
of Castilian, and thus to mark the birth of the Spanish language some
1,000 years ago.

The Castilians were to become the "reconquerors" par excel-
lence of the Iberian Peninsula. In 1029 the kingdom fell under Navarran control almost by default, and Ferdinand, the son of the Navarran
king, inherited it and declared himself Ferdinand I, king of Castile. His
neighbors in Leon didn't think much of Castile having a king and tried
to take the wind out of Ferdinand's sails, only to be defeated themselves in 1037. Ferdinand I thus became the king of Castile and Leon
and went on to annex a chunk of Navarre at the expense of his brother,
who had inherited it and whom Ferdinand murdered.

Castile thus became a regional power, and though the union
did not stay in place permanently, Castile was strong enough now
to begin expanding southward, into Moorish country. The advance
of Castile was like that of a wedge splitting the peninsula in two.
In 1085, Castile took Segovia, Avila, and Toledo and two years later
moved its capital to the last of these.

THE SPREAD OF CASTILIAN

The advance of the language was slower than the military and
political thrust. A century and a half after Castile's "reconquest" of Toledo, for example, Arabic was still being used for official documents
there. Castilian forms and pronunciations were being used in the "New
Castile" based in Toledo, but simultaneously many Mozarabic words
were infiltrating Castilian. Overall, Castilian was an open and innova-
tive language, absorbing influences as its speakers advanced politically
and geographically.

Not until the reign of Ferdinand III (1217–1252) was the use
of Castilian imposed on New Castile. It was also Ferdinand III who re-
newed the spread of Castile's power, "liberating" Caceres to the west
(1227), Valencia to the east (1238), and Cordoba (1236) and Seville
(1248) to the south. By the end of his reign, Moorish Spain was backed
into one kingdom—Granada—and for his trouble and for his efficiency,
Ferdinand III was to be granted sainthood. Granada was defeated 250
years later (its liberation and the unification of Spain was the big news
on the peninsula in 1492) by Isabel. Isabel, queen of Castile, had a de-
cade earlier married Ferdinand V, king of Aragon, thereby joining those
two kingdoms and setting the stage for Spain's final unification.

Castile's conquest of Spain, except for Granada, was essentially completed by the mid-thirteenth century. Consolidation came

next, and in the case especially of the language, the man for the task
was Ferdinand III's son, Alfonso X, a.k.a. "The Learned" (1252–1284).
Alfonso was a studious sort, not given to military escapades and not
very successful in those he did attempt. Instead, he surrounded himself
with sages, scientists, poets, and historians, and set up his court at Toledo as a patron of scholarship. Though Alfonso took pains to assure
the harmonic mingling of Spain's special "triple heritage," made up of
Christian, Hebrew, and Arabic learning, he adopted Castilian as the official language of the court and the kingdom, replacing Latin.

The importance of the decision also resided in Alfonso's work
(with the help of his hired scholars) in unifying criteria for his new language. Thus for Castilian to have any meaning as a language, someone
had to decide which form of a word—the Mozarabic, the Old Castilian,
the Aragon, the Leon—was to be adopted thereafter for incorporation
into New or "Toledan" Castilian. His choices naturally became the official ones, not so much by decree as by consent—and by the fact that
the court commissioned much of the literature and published most of
the peninsula's written texts. The growth of Castilian literature, promoted by Alfonso, marked the definitive emergence of the Spanish
language.

In certain essential respects, the Spanish written in 1200 and
1300 is much the same as the Spanish of today and can be read with
relatively little difficulty by modern Spanish speakers. *Cantar del mio
Cid*, dating back to about 1200 but not written down until 1350 or so,
is quite intelligible to any modern Spanish-speaking person; Chaucer's
Canterbury Tales, on the other hand, was written close to 1400 but
is usually "translated" for present-day English speakers. Certainly by
1500, except for the influx of foreign words, the shape and structure of
Spanish was pretty well carved in stone.

In fact, foreign influences had never stopped. From roughly
1100 to 1300, a vast number of French words entered through the
north of Spain, brought by religious "tourists" on pilgrimage to Santiago de Compostela in Galicia. The route they took across the north
of Spain, through Navarre, Castile, and Leon, was littered with Gallicisms, some of which survived the intervening centuries and persist in
modern Spanish. These include numerous -*aje* words (*mensaje, home-
naje, coraje, viaje, salvaje*) and other terms related to the traveling life:
mesón, jornada, jardín, and *ligero*. The 1400s, in contrast, were years
of great Italian influence, as Spanish scholars strove to catch up with—
or even keep up with—the advances of Renaissance Italy. The incorporation of Italianisms was an ongoing process, lasting several centuries,
that counted among its harvest such everyday words as *marchar, mil-
lón, banca, balcón, diseño, modelo, capricho, novela, cortejar, charlar,
manejar, pedante, grotesco, piloto, soldado*, and *alerta*.

The close of the 1400s was typified by that dramatic year

1492, which saw the expulsion of Spain's Jewish population (the dispersed Sephardic Jews), the discovery of America, and the fall of Granada and reunification of Spain. In this year as well Nebrija published his *Gramática de la lengua castellana*, which was an attempt to standardize Spanish and the first published grammar in any modern language. In short, while Spain was extending its reach geographically, it was slowly closing itself off to "outside," non-Christian intellectual influences. These years were to witness the start of the Spanish Inquisition as well, although its influence was not fully felt in Spanish culture until the late 1500s.

INTERNATIONAL SPANISH

The 1500s began with Spain asserting itself internationally. The conquest and colonization of America took place in these years, and newly unified Spain was assured a prominent place in Europe. Castilian was by the 1530s the language spoken throughout unified Spain. Spain was ruled from 1516 to 1556 by Charles V (Carlos I of Spain, known in the Spanish-speaking world as Carlos Quinto). Born in Ghent, in present-day Belgium, Carlos didn't set foot on Spanish soil until he was eighteen years old, but he is still considered one of history's great defenders of the Spanish language. By 1550, Italian gentlemen took pains to learn Spanish, which for the next one hundred years would reign as Europe's preeminent language. Around 1660, for example, anybody who was anybody at the court of Brussels spoke Spanish.

The reign of Carlos's son, Felipe II, ran from 1556 to 1598 and marked the high point for the Inquisition and Spain's xenophobia. It also marked the low point in many other respects. Felipe II was a repressive, autocratic, and intolerant king even by sixteenth-century standards, and the religious zeal that characterized his rule earned Spain a reputation for backwardness and barbarism that it has never overcome in some parts of Europe. Paradoxically, Spain's Siglo de Oro, or Golden Age, began in earnest under Felipe. It was a century that saw the emergence of such cultural greats as Cervantes, Góngora, Lope de Vega, and Quevedo.

The exploration and conquest of America had a lasting effect not just on Spain but on its language. Spanish became filled with "Americanisms," many of which it then passed on to other European languages. The names of fruits, animals, and American products came into Spanish from the Carib, Nahuatl, Quechua, and other indigenous tongues (see Chapter 14). From the ongoing exploration and slave trade in Africa came words from that continent into Spanish, with *banana, conga, bongó,* and *samba* among the ones that have survived to the present.

Spain's importance geopolitically in these years translated into what we now view as an excess of pride and arrogance. The same attitude that permitted the mass expulsion of 300,000 Arabs from Spain in the period 1609–1614 appears in the language as well. It was in the early years of the 1600s, for instance, when a new form of respect, *usted,* was invented. Until that time, Spanish speakers had used *vos,* the second-person plural, in respectful forms of address. This construction shares the logic of the "royal we" in English, by which royals refer to themselves in the plural. At some point their vassals must have figured that if the king or queen considered himself or herself to be a plural, it was not the vassal's duty to inform the monarch otherwise. And thus plural forms of address like *vos* (*vous* in French, *voi* in Italian) were born. For certain Spanish lords of the seventeenth century, though, *vos* had become too widely used, and a new form of address was "needed" to distinguish those who genuinely merited adulation. The form proposed and adopted, in a matter of decades, was *vuestra merced* ("your grace"), which in just twenty years of popular use was chopped down in size to a more manageable *usted.*

By the 1700s, the effects of centuries of intellectual isolation and repression were clearly showing. The Siglo de Oro was long gone, and nothing even close to its output was accomplished through the 1700s. Instead, the eighteenth century was a good one for lexicographers and grammarians, as creative energy and talent was channeled away from more risqué endeavors. For example, in the years 1756, 1759, 1762, and 1764, respectively, the Inquisition banned in Spain and its possessions the works of Montesquieu, Diderot, Voltaire, and Rousseau. The Royal Academy of the Language, meanwhile, was founded in 1713, and spent the century publishing reference works—the equivalent of decrees—on grammar, spelling, and literature. These had the effect of establishing official spellings for Spanish words (much as Noah Webster did for American English half a century later), and although Spanish has certainly changed since this period, its changes have been minor ones.

French influence heightened in the 1700s, and in fact by century's end Spain found itself controlled outright by Napoleon. By far the largest number of Gallicisms entered the language during this period, a collection of words that includes, for starters, *asamblea, burócrata, controlar, finanzas, pantalón, chaqueta,* and *equipaje* (another *-aje* word). French phrases and constructions were imported in this era as well; for example, the expression *hacer el amor* in the sense of "to court" or "to woo" became popular. (Its other, more modern sense is attributed to the influence of American English.) One wonders how

many more French words would have entered in this period if Montesquieu, Diderot, Voltaire, and Rousseau had not been blacklisted!

Napoleon's misadventures in Europe gave Spain's colonies the
opportunity to slip away in the early 1800s, but the effect of this on
the language was minimal. American Spanish was already firmly established, a product and stepchild of the Andalusian Spanish spoken by
many early settlers. Thus the practice of *seseo*, or pronouncing *c* and *z*
as *s* (*meses* rhymes with *veces*), is universal in America and dominant
in Andalusia, but uncommon in the rest of Spain. In some parts of the
New World, expressions that died out at home (in Spain) were kept
alive. Other expressions were born in the colonies and made their
home there, never to infiltrate Castilian Spanish. The result, today, is
an American Spanish that is considered a distinct (though by no means
uniform) dialect, one easily understood by Spaniards if not "approved"
at all times by their official institutions—particularly the archconser-
vative, arch-Castilian Royal Academy of the Language.

CONSERVING SPANISH

Conservativeness in language is a practice that tends to make
its practitioners look silly a few centuries or even a few decades later.
Resistance to change is almost invariably a losing battle. In the case of
Spanish, scholars and students of the language understandably seek to
preserve as much as possible the legacy of one thousand years of written tradition. They want speakers of the language one hundred and five
hundred years from now to be able to read and enjoy Cervantes, García
Lorca, and Neruda in the original—not in "translations to modern
Spanish." And that, most would agree, is a goal worth looking a little
silly for.

The defense of Spanish in our time has largely become a stand
against the influx ("contamination," some would say) of English words,
a reflection of the fact that English, for the better part of the twentieth
century, has been the dominant language internationally (as Spanish
was from 1550 to 1670, more or less). That defense, and its trials and
tribulations, is the subject of Chapter 14.

This defense of Spanish, like all defenses that seek to protect a
language from its speakers, has little chance of final success. That said,
it is even less likely that an upstart language like English—useful in
commerce and science, trendy in popular entertainment—will ever
supplant Spanish when it is time to talk of the stars, of the gods, and
of love. For these concepts, for words of passion and glory, power and
drama, Spanish need look no further than its own vibrant history.

THE BIG MIX   **14**

Spanish, as we have seen, is in a way a melting pot of linguistic influences. All languages are. And few would deny that Spanish has benefited from its contacts with other languages. Without its prehistoric Iberian, Celtic, and Basque influences, without the influx of Germanic terms during the reign of the Visigoths, without the thousands of Moorish words imported from Arabic, without the Italianisms of the Renaissance and the Gallicisms of recent centuries, Spanish would simply not be Spanish as we know it and speak it today. It would be Modern Latin.

In the twentieth century, English is the language that has most influenced Spanish (and about every other world language, for that matter). U.S. commercial, political, and cultural dominance has in the field of languages resulted in the steady infiltration of English words into Spanish. What is thought up on Madison Avenue, put on screen in Hollywood, or schemed in Washington almost inevitably turns up, in one form or another, in spoken Spanish. And though the tendency to adopt Anglicisms is often presented as an acutely Latin American phenomenon, any visitor to Spain or reader of Spanish magazines will see that English has insinuated its way deep into the heart of Castile as well.

As an English speaker learning Spanish, you are present on the front line of this phenomenon. And the military metaphor is not out of place. For there is a battle going on between perfectly adequate Spanish words and aggressive English invaders. It is a battle that causes lexicographers to lament and purists' blood to boil.

Avoiding Anglicisms in your Spanish is generally synonymous

with being a careful and respectful speaker of the language. As a beginning speaker (or even a lazy advanced speaker!), you will find yourself tempted to use English words as a shortcut or a crutch. At other times, unknowingly, you may give Spanish words a meaning that their cognates have in English—but not in Spanish. Finally, even as a near-fluent speaker you will have to guard against using English constructions and translating English phrases "incorrectly." Often these are borderline judgments, as when choosing between *peor es nada* and *mejor que nada* for "better than nothing," or *un día de estos* and *uno de estos días* for "one of these days." It is the difference, in other words, between being correct and being more correct. Proceed attentively, and let your ear be your guide.

These adjustments take time and attentiveness. And some English loanwords you may find useful or even necessary to your style of speech, especially when everyone around you is using them. For the most part, though, it is probably better for the "contamination" of Spanish to occur at its own rhythm, without your contribution.

Scholars have long debated the reasons for the adoption of foreign words, but the only clear reasons are the obvious ones. When something is invented or introduced to a culture, for instance, it often comes with a word—or an entire nomenclature—attached. Computers are a good example: *software*, *hardware*, and *mouse* are all "Spanish" words now. Similarly, when the word *toronja* was adapted from the Arabic, *burócrata* from the French, and *canoa* from the Arawakan, it was because the products or concepts they described were new to the Spanish-speaking world.

The adoption of foreign loanwords is not always so simple a matter. In the fifteenth century, for instance, the Spaniards found themselves in need of a word to describe "mustache," it not having occurred to a Spaniard until that time that such a thing could exist without the rest of the beard. At first, the Germanism *bigote* found favor (itself a word that some claim came via Norman French from the English expression "by God," presumably for what the English said when they first saw a Norman wearing one). A century later, the Italianism *mostacho* (originally from the Medieval Greek *moustaki*) became the rage. Eventually, the Germanism won out, though *mostacho* lives on in Spanish as an infrequent archaism.

As the pace of inventions has accelerated in recent decades, the need for new words to describe them has grown. But usually there are numerous options for fulfilling this need. As the use of motorcars spread, for example, the construction of special roads to accommodate them began in earnest. In English, one of the words given to these roads was "highway." In Spanish, new words were needed as well. Which word would be used? Had the sway of English been as powerful then,

Spanish speakers might have undertaken the direct importation of
"highway," as in the Spanished *jaigüey* or some similar monstros-
ity. A generation earlier "highball" had been imported and rewritten
as *jaibol*. Fortunately, perhaps, that didn't occur. Another possibility
might have been to translate the meaning of the English word into
Spanish, again presuming English was influencing the selection. This
would have produced a phrase like *camino alto* for the English word.
But this didn't happen either. A third choice would have been to invest
an existing word or words with the new meaning. This in fact did happen with two words—*carretera* and *calzada*—both of which predate
highways but are now used in modern Spanish to describe them. Other
words came and went. As late as the 1950s, for instance, bilingual
dictionaries gave *camino real* as a translation for "highway," but this
phrase has since plummeted from common use. Lastly, an altogether
new word, or "neologism," could be coined to handle the novel concept of a high-speed road. *Autopista* was just such an invention.

Often the importation of a concept can result in a combination
of linguistic responses, or even different responses in different places.
One word may be coined in Mexico, for instance, while another is
coined in Puerto Rico, a third is invested with the new meaning in
Chile, and the English word imported lock, stock, and barrel in Spain.
A 1974 study of Latin American students in the United States explored
this process and found, among other things, that the concept "sneak-
ers" had led to seven different words in eighteen different countries:
*tenis, zapatos de tenis, zapatillas, champion, zapatillas de goma, za-
patos de caucho*, and *zapatos de lona*. Other "imported" concepts had
as many as nineteen different Spanish names! Dictionaries—and in
particular the dictionary of the Royal Spanish Academy—are reluctant
to include a word until it has shown some staying power. As a result,
speakers of the language are left with no guidance in the meantime and
must invent, invest, adopt, or adapt as they can.

Practical necessity, moreover, is but one of the many mothers
of the invention of new words and the importation of foreign ones.
More often than many like to admit, foreign words are imported because using them makes the speaker or writer seem more suave, chic,
and debonair. Foreign words have a certain je ne sais quoi that can
make them simply irresistible. We use them not because English or
Spanish doesn't have the words we need, but because we are a little
bored with the words we have. We feel the urge to break out of the
angst and the Sturm und Drang of our daily drudgery, so voilà, we import "new" words—ad nauseum. In short, we like to show off.

Sometimes, too, we use foreign words because we want specifically to convey a sense of the exotic. Advertisers are especially
guilty of this, but they are not the only ones—and they can't always

be blamed. Would you sooner choose Boca Raton or Mouse Mouth for a Florida honeymoon? Need something dramatic to tell your daughter and son-in-law as they head off for their week in Mouse Mouth? How about "Bon voyage!" instead of "Have a good trip"? What is more explicit than "blitz" to describe eleven grown men attacking a quarterback? And after a nice, refreshing shower, would you rather sprinkle yourself with eau de toilette or toilet water?

In Spanish, too, words are imported left and right, and the state of world superpowers dictates that many of those words are English ones, for the time being. Someday, to paraphrase Kurt Vonnegut, Chinese linguists and historians might find the phenomenon quite interesting.

ANGLICISMS

The Anglicisms that enter Spanish do so via different paths. Some enter exactly as they are written and spoken in English and remain that way. Others are modified to meet Spanish rules of grammar, pronunciation, and spelling. Some are misappropriated or misspelled. Some are introduced and then acquire new meanings.

Though there is great variation, imported words tend to follow a fairly predictable pattern. Imports in Spanish-speaking countries often start as the province of the educated middle and upper classes, who generally speak a little (or a lot of) English and know how to spell it. After a word is imported as a foreign term, it must withstand the test of time. If there is a need for the word, real or perceived, it may survive and spread into the general public. There it is twisted and shaped until it slides more comfortably off the tongue and is written as it sounds to each ear, half a dozen different ways, until a uniform spelling is settled on or imposed. Then, much later, it may be approved by the gatekeepers of the Spanish language at the Royal Academy. And then again, it may not.

In English-speaking or bilingual areas, the importation of words seems to be almost a haphazard process: anyone can play, and most do. It is these areas—the borderlands between Mexico and the United States, the streets of New York, the barrios of Los Angeles— where hundreds if not thousands of Anglicisms are bred. The words that emerge from these cultural and linguistic cauldrons are often the ones that seem most grating and most unnecessary to language purists. As the two languages mingle freely, terms like *edible* (instead of *comestible*) and *marqueta* (for "market") begin to appear as a result of the, well, mélange.

These *pochismos*, as the border loanwords are called in Mex-

ico, are hard to feel neutral about. On the one hand, it is difficult to
stand in the way of a language's inevitable and inscrutable evolution.
Linguists have found that the incorporation of loanwords follows a system, and argue that the invention or adaptation of English words by
immigrants is in many cases a defensible response to the trying conditions of immigration. Concepts that are common in the dominant culture but unfamiliar to the minority culture frequently require new
words to express them. The loanword-loaded Spanish of the border
areas, moreover, has become an integral part of the bilingual and bicultural identity of many of its speakers.

On the other hand, it is hard to justify pronouncing any English word that pops up with a Spanish accent and calling it Spanish.
Most people try to avoid the extremes and decide for themselves which
words are acceptable to them. A quick study of Appendix A—an anno-
tated list of many of the more frequent imports—will help you draw
your own line.

An English word's transition into Spanish isn't always a
smooth one. In fact, there's many a slip twixt English and Anglicism.
The word *crack*, for instance, appears on the financial pages in the
Spanish-speaking world to refer to a stock market "crash." Similarly,
in Mexico a car's "brake lights" are called *luces de stop*, or "stoplights," which of course are a different thing altogether. "Hitchhiking,"
a practice almost certainly introduced to Spanish-speaking countries,
generally goes by the name of *autostop*, though it is not known by that
term in any English-speaking country.

Other cases of the "wrong" word being imported include *lift-
ing* ("facelift"); *clip* ("paper clip"); *smoking* ("tuxedo" but presumably
an abbreviated form of "smoking jacket"); *dancing* (usually a "dancing club," not the act of dancing itself); and *happy* (almost invariably
"drunk" or "tipsy" in Spanish slang).

Nor does the importation process seem to pay too close attention to word morphology and gender. "Punch" became *ponche* but the
similar *ponchar* comes from "to puncture." Spelling presents problems
as well. Aware of the penchant of Spanish speakers to place an *e* before English words beginning with *st* (*estrés, estéreo, estéik*, Rolling
Estones, etc.), some word-importers overcorrect and write "establishment" as *stablishment*.

What happens to the spelling once a word is in the public
domain is the stuff of orthographers' nightmares. Would you have
guessed, for instance, that *estíur, bisté, friquearse*, and *náilon* are your
old friends "steward," "beefsteak," "to freak out" and "nylon?" How
about *uachimán* ("watchman") and *yes* ("jazz")?

Ironically, using these foreign words is not at all frowned upon
in most Spanish-speaking circles, just as using "chic," "debonair," and

"suave" is considered perfectly acceptable if slightly snooty English. Overall, different rules can apply for verbs, which require greater inventiveness and Spanish endings to adopt "correctly." Few verbs, in fact, overcome the initial years of sounding downright frightful.

BARBARISMS

Perhaps it just reflects an elitist attitude, but English words are usually not stigmatized until they reach the level of popular use—and misuse. When *lunch* becomes *lonche* and every corner boasts a *lonchería*, then some of the charm of using a foreign word wears off. *Shopping* is used by Spanish speakers who can afford to take shopping trips to the United States; pronounced *chopping* or written *chópin*, it becomes a "vulgar" usage. Thus you can sound cosmopolitan talking about tonight's *speaker* at the club; call him or her an *espíquer*, though, and you're liable to have your club membership revoked.

The distinction between cultured imports and vulgar imports is mostly a specious one. Is *stand* somehow "good Spanish" and *estand* "bad Spanish"? Is *hamburger* fair and *hamburguesa* foul? You can be your own judge. Is it acceptable to refer to your car's *clutch* but vulgar to call it a *cloch?* Can you talk uprightly about *containers* but should you bow your head in shame when you utter *contenedores?* Is *rin* worse than *rim*, *sóquet* worse than *socket*, and *zíper* worse than *zipper?* Is using *nipple* crass only when you pronounce it "knee-play" and write it *niple?* These, for the most part, are the "barbarisms" that you will be warned away from using by more careful speakers of the language. And as a rule, these warnings are well taken. You won't impress anyone with your command of English—you will only disappoint with your laziness in not learning the correct Spanish word.

Other barbarisms are a subtler prey, requiring far greater alertness than is needed to avoid saying *breakecito*. As English contaminates Spanish in border areas and, indeed, around the world, odd phrasings and meanings begin to emerge from otherwise innocent-looking, fully legitimate Spanish words. Phrases like *vacunar la carpeta* appear, trying to mean "to vacuum the carpet" but in "real" Spanish meaning "to vaccinate the folder." "Groceries" becomes *groserías*, which in fact means "rude remarks" or "offenses." The nice new neighborhood on the outskirts of town is called a *suburbio*, though that's what the slummy part of town was called a generation ago. And on and on.

Most English-influenced barbarisms are considerably less astonishing than these, and Appendix B lists a number of them for your perusal. Some are so subtle that it is really a judgment call whether the English is influencing or not. For instance, *admitir* has as one of its accepted meanings "to accept, to consider provisionally an explanation, thesis, etc. as good or true." But is it correct to say, as newspaper headlines throughout the Spanish-speaking world do, that *el criminal admite su culpa* ("the criminal admits his guilt")? Technically, probably not, but you'll find it just the same.

If you think that this is but a semantic splitting of hairs, consider the word *remover*, which has as its second accepted meaning "to take away an inconvenience or an obstacle." Still, its first and by far most common usage in Spanish is "to move about, to stir, to jiggle." If the person using *remover* is a doctor speaking to a nurse about the catheter sticking out of your arm, you may not think it nitpicking at all to explore the subtleties of this verb.

For many Spanish words, the culprit in their increasing confusion with English cognates may be the news media—specifically the wire services, whose translated news reports are sent to newspapers, radio stations, and television networks worldwide. When translating vast amounts of text a night, as wire-service translators based in New York or Miami must do, it is easy to accept an easy, ready-made translation instead of a more complicated one. Thus "to remove" becomes *remover* instead of the more correct *quitar*; "admits his guilt" becomes *admite su culpa* instead of the more precise *reconoce su culpa*; and so on. These hairline infractions then travel the globe and reach into people's living rooms at night and across their breakfast tables in the morning. Their influence is incalculable.

Other scholars blame the movie industry—and especially the movie-dubbing industry—for distorting Spanish grammar. When an actor in a close-up says "I am waiting for him," for instance, the temptation is to translate it *Estoy esperando por él* to match the lip movements. This is bad Spanish, but that may be the price we pay for good dubbing.

REVERSE *POCHISMOS*

English has not always been the world's dominant language. For most of the last three centuries, France held that position, and before that—for much of the sixteenth and seventeenth centuries—Spanish was the language that worldy men and women went out of their way to learn. Those years of dominance have left their mark in the Spanish we speak today. For just as border and other forms of Spanish are being infiltrated by Anglicisms and English influences, so were Hispanisms and Spanish influences a "problem" for English and French in centuries past.

The centuries of Spanish sway span much of the European exploration of the Americas, and it is no surprise to find that many of the Europeans' discoveries bear Spanish names. Even when the original name was Taino or Arawakan, it passed through a Spanish filter before reaching French, English, and the rest of the Old World's languages. Thus foods ("maize," "tomato," "chile"), animals ("peccary," "llama," "jaguar," "iguana"), and other concepts ("canoe," "cacique," "hammock," "hurricane," "cigarette," "cannibal") reached English from native languages via Spanish. (The word "potato," as a former U.S. vice president would be happy to hear, has been misspelled from the start: it originated as a confusion between the Quechua *papa* and the Arawakan *batata*, becoming thereby the Spanish *patata* and the English "potato.")

Spanish influence turns up unexpectedly in our everyday speech. "Tuna" comes from the Spanish, as do two of the three classic ice cream flavors ("chocolate" and "vanilla"). We have Spanish to thank for "mosquito" and "cockroach," as well as for "amigo" (of course) and "comrade." The Spaniards' dedication to settling the New World gave us landholding terms like "ranch," "hacienda," and "estancia." Early settlers' obsession with racial distinctions gave English "mulatto," "creole," "mestizo," "negro," and "sambo." "Coconuts" are so called because the first Europeans to see them—Spanish or Portuguese sailors—saw scary faces in the stained husks, and thus called them *cocos*, or "bogeymen."

Many Spanish words entered English through the U.S. Southwest, which of course used to be the Mexican Northwest. Topographical terms such as "canyon," "barranca," "arroyo," "mesa," and "cuesta" reached English this way. So did ranching terms like "chaps," "stampede," "buckaroo," and "rodeo." The wildlife of the Southwest boasts many Spanish names: "coyote," "armadillo," "chuckwalla," "chaparral," "saguaro," "yucca," "pinyon," "locoweed," and so on. The states of the Southwest themselves point back to a Spanish-language heritage: Arizona, California, Colorado, and Nevada (plus Florida and Montana, of course).

From the Southwest and the Old West come some of English's more colorful Spanish loanwords, a few of which lost more than a little of their "Spanishness" in the translation. Still, no western would be complete without some "desperado" "lassoing" a "bronco" (from *desesperado, lazo,* and *bronco*). "Lariat" is but the Spanish *la reata,* just as "alligator" is a lumping of *el lagarto*. If you were a bad guy in those parts, you could end up in the "calaboose" or the "hoosegow," which originated as *calabozo* and *juzgado,* respectively. When we call something a "cinch," furthermore, we are recalling the Spanish *cincha,* which was the sure and steady "saddle-girth" used by southwestern horsemen. The bad guys, incidentally, wore black "sombreros," whereas the good guys could be counted on to show up in white "ten-gallon" (from *tan galán*, or "so gallant") hats. When they did show up, they "mosied" down Main Street, while the bad guys went "vamoose" (both from *vamos*). After all, these were some tough hombres!

Some words are of more dubious Spanish origin. "Hoosier" and "hoodlum" are words whose beginnings are lost to history, but which some scholars speculate had Spanish origins. "Loafer" (and thus "to loaf") may come from *gallofero*, an old word for "vagabond," and "pa-looka" may come from *peluca*, equally archaic for "severe reproof." My own personal favorite folk etymology is for "cocktail," perhaps in part because it's a word that is now considered an Anglicism in Spanish. According to one published version, King Axolotl VIII of Aztec-era Mexico had a daughter named Xochitl, who invented the cocktail and had it named after her. Xochitl gradually became Coctel, and the rest is history—or nearly so.

The process of linguistic infiltration continues in modern times, of course. With North Americans' more recent "discovery" of Mexican food, words like "taco," "burrito," "tortilla," and "frijoles" have entered everyday English. Spanish names play a prominent role in recent automotive history; Mustang, Barracuda, Vega, Granada, Mata-dor, Pinto, and Fiesta are some well-known examples. And "macho" is just as much English as Spanish these days, though the phrase "macho women," using the masculine form, must sound odd to Spanish speak-ers. Just as when words travel from English to Spanish, some that have gone from Spanish to English have had a rough trip. You may hear "mano a mano" in English these days, for instance, but the usual meaning as-signed to it is "man to man," not "hand to hand." Appendix C lists other words that Spanish has contributed to English over the years. Many other such words exist, and more still are being imported and exported, across borders and within them, even as we speak.

As we speak, indeed.

SPANISH'S ANGLICISMS AND BARBARISMS

What follows is an exhausting (but by no means exhaustive) list of Anglicisms in use in modern Spanish. As a sample listing, this list should enable the reader to get a feel for the process by which some English words are incorporated into Spanish. Some of the examples given are quite rare in actual use, but are included for didactic purposes or just for fun. Other examples are to be found in the text, and another two to three thousand, or perhaps double or triple that, are to be found on the streets of Lima, Los Angeles, Madrid, and Managua.

Many native Spanish speakers use English words to show their worldiness and—why not say it?—to show off a bit. For much the same reason, many native English speakers use French, Latin, German, Greek, and even Spanish (see Appendix C) terms. But you, as a native English speaker, will wow absolutely no one by using English terms in your Spanish. To the contrary: you will impress by your command of correct Spanish. Spanish is a living, ever-evolving language. But let's allow the Spanish speakers be the ones to change it, ¿no?

Words are listed by their English source word, with accents added when used. When the English spelling rarely or never appears as such in Spanish, the common Spanish form follows in parentheses. Thus "basketball" will sometimes be found written that way in Spanish, but "baseball" never appears with its English spelling.

ALIBI This Latin term is an unnecessary import since *coartada* (another Latin word) already exists in Spanish.

ALLIGATOR One of the most ridiculous barbarisms to enter Spanish, since the word is itself a barbarism imported incorrectly from

Spanish into English: *el lagarto*, or "the alligator," became "alligator."
Fortunately, it is a rare loanword.

ANCESTOR   (*ancestro*) Borrowed from either French or English.
It is not accepted yet by Spain's Royal Academy, although *ancestral*
has been approved; *antepasado* is the correct word for *ancestro*.

ANTIQUE SHOP   To attract the tourists?

APPOINTMENT   (*apointement*) Simply silly. Stick to *cita*.

ATTORNEY   I'm impressed. And you?

AUDITÓRIUM   This barbarism is probably from English, but
since it's technically a Latin word, some scholars tolerate it in Spanish. Used for both "audience" (*auditorio*) and for the building or hall
itself (*sala*).

AVERAGE   Unnecessary import; *promedio* works fine.

BABY   This word is starting to appear more frequently in the
Spanish-speaking world (perhaps because of car signs that say "Baby on
Board" and pop songs crooned to one's "baby"). You may be told that
bebé is the correct Spanish word, but it is in fact a Gallicism of not
much greater vintage or approval. Try *nene* instead.

BACK   The verb *backear* is a border loanword or *pochismo*.
Especially common around cars, presumably since *échate en reversa*
takes too long to say.

BACON   In Spain they use this, though they don't have permission from the Academy. *Tocino*, anyone?

BANK NOTE   Banker talk considered too important to translate. Rare.

BAR   Considered classier than *cantina* and more mainstream.
An establishment that calls itself a *ladies bar* is even open to that
other half of the population.

BASEBALL   (*béisbol*) Still awaiting approval by the Academy.
What else it might be called is beyond me.

BASKETBALL   Usually *basquetbol*, though the English form
still appears at times. The correct (i.e., invented) term for this sport is
baloncesto. Note, however, that you must call the ball itself *un balón
de baloncesto* or *un balón de basquet*, never *un basquetbol*. Note also
that one of the dangers of allowing *basquetbol* is that you start to hear
basqueta being used instead of *canasta*!

BAZOOKA   Usually written *bazuca*; the shot from one is a
bazucazo.

BEEF   (*bife, bifstec, bistec, biftec, bisté*) All ways of saying
carne de res or *filete de res*. *Bife* is especially common in Argentina,
but one of the above forms will probably be on the menu in whatever
part of the Spanish-speaking world you visit. You may even hear *un
bisté de puerco*, which is quite a mouthful. *Bife* and *bistec* have both
been declared kosher by the Academy. (See also *steak*.)

BIG BANG   Some scientists have suggested calling this theory of the explosion of the universe *el gran ¡pum!*, but for reasons I cannot fathom it hasn't caught on.

BIKINI   Also spelled *biquini*. Neither is recognized by the Academy.

BINGO   Anglicism.

BLOCK   Used for "pad" (of paper). Possibly a Gallicism, as "block" doesn't have this meaning in English. *Bloc* is the most commonly used form; *bloque* is the linguists' attempt to "Spanishize" it. (See also *bloquear* in Appendix B.)

BLUES   The same in any language.

BLUFF   Whether as *blof, blofeador, blofear, blofero,* or *blufar,* this is a widespread import. *Bluff* and *blof* are most common, but none meets with the approval of the Academy. They are used as in English, except as nouns they can be applied to people as well: *Ese tipo es puro bluf* = "That guy's a fraud" (or "an imposter" or even "a disappointment"). *Fanfarrón* (noun) and *fanfarronear* (verb) are more traditional Spanish words meaning much the same thing as "bluff."

BOOM   In the business sense of "boom years" or a 'financial boom." *Auge* is the correct Spanish word.

BOWL   (*bol*) Much used in most of the Spanish-speaking world for "soup bowls" and larger receptacles.

BOYCOTT   Variants are *boicot, boicoteo, boicotear, boycotar.* A word of Irish origin now accepted by the Academy and widely used. (Consider it a fair trade for "embargo," which English imported from Spanish.) The uses spelled *boi-* are the official ones.

BOX   A sports import that includes *boxear, boxeador,* and *boxeo* ("to box," "boxer," and "boxing," respectively). The Spanished *boxeo* is to be preferred to *box*. In a slightly related vein, *box spring* is widely used as well, as is *boxers* ("boxer shorts").

BOY SCOUT   Various attempts have been made to find a Spanish translation for this imported concept, but none has caught on. Some of them are *exploradores, escultistas,* and *excursionistas.* "Girl scouts," interestingly, has not been widely imported.

BRAKE   Also appears as *breik, brek, breke,* or *breque*—border talk for what stops your car. Strangely, all of these words exist to avoid saying *freno*. (See also *break*.)

BRANDY   If this and *whiskey* count as Anglicisms, then "tequila" and "mezcal" are "Hispanisms."

BREAK   Popular in U.S. Spanish, especially in the sense of "give me a break." *Dame un break* or *dame un breakecito* are the phrases you are most likely to hear. The borrowing is not surprising, since *oportunidad* doesn't cut it and *chance* (see below) is also an Anglicism. In the sense of a "break" from work, though, *descanso* is a better word.

BROTHER   In street slang you may hear *brodi, bróder, broíta* and so on.

BUDGET   Some claim it's a Gallicism, but it seems more likely to have entered Spanish with a host of other financial Anglicisms. It needn't have, since *presupuesto* was already here.

BULLDOZER   Why not?

BUNCH   (*bonche*) A border *pochismo* that is gradually working its way south and into mainstream Spanish. Not there yet, however.

BUNGALOW   Actually comes from Hindi via English. Widespread wherever tourists are found. It will need an accent (*búngalow*) at least if it stays in Spanish.

BÚSHEL   Gradually disappearing, even in English. Never widespread in Spanish.

BUSINESS   An inevitable import, since in much of the world the business of English is business. Often used in street slang (spelled *bísnes*) in the sense of "to give someone the business."

BYE   Widespread but not official. But then neither is *ciao* (or *chao*), imported from Italian and also widespread.

CADDY   All's fair in science and sports.

CAKE   Pronounced as in English but often spelled *queque*, particularly in South America. *Torta, bizcocho*, or *pastel*, depending on the region, would be more traditional Spanish.

CÁMEL   The color.

CAMPING   A common Anglicism to describe what is essentially an imported concept. Some prefer the Spanishized *campismo*. The verb in all places is *acampar*, and in many instances it can and probably should be used instead of *camping*.

CASSETTE   The spelling may be Spanishized someday, but otherwise this word is here to stay. *Cinta* is the nearest Spanish term for "tape" but usually refers to the reel-to-reel type.

CATCH   (*cachar*) This word is traveling south at a frightful pace and replacing *atrapar* and *coger* (where it's not a dirty word). This word sounds so Spanish (in fact, the word *cachar*, with another meaning, existed long ago in the language) that it is almost certain to stick.

CLIP   Means "paper clip." *Clip para papel* would be understood but is redundant.

CLOSE-UP   Filmmakers' talk. Not pretty, not approved, but not surprising.

CLOWN   Used in Spain especially (sometimes as *clon*), where *payaso* apparently isn't precise enough.

CLUB   Well-established Anglicism. Works for a garden club or a country club (*club de golf* or *club campestre*).

CLUTCH   The common word for the car part in some countries. Sometimes as *cloch*.

COACH   Usually spelled *couch*, the term refers to the team leader in sports. (See also *manager*.)

COCKTAIL   (*cóctel*) Recently approved by the Academy. See Chapter 14.

COMPACT   Used for both cars and disks, though *compacto* exists and is widely used as well.

CONTAINER   (*contenedor*) This Spanishized term is widespread. *Recipiente* covers most of the same ground, but the use of containerized cargo in world commerce has brought about the birth of this neologism based on the age-old Spanish word *contener*.

COOLER   This word is creeping into Spanish in the sense of a container that keeps things cold—your Igloo or Thermos, in other words. Others prefer *hielera*, not least because *cooler* sounds a lot like a certain Spanish obscenity.

COOLIE   Despite objections to *cooler* (see above), the word *culi* has been approved by the Academy to refer to an "indigenous servant." Though it may be linguistically correct, it almost certainly isn't politically so; in any case, it is but a rare or locally used word.

CORNFLAKES   *Hojuelas de maíz* just hasn't caught on.

COTTAGE   This looks like a Gallicism but is in fact an Anglicism. (See also *bungalow*.)

COUNTRY CLUB   Hard to say whether this is better or worse than *club de golf*. (See also *club*.)

COVER   Used in the sense of "cover charge" in bars and nightclubs and for "cover versions" of songs.

COWBOY   Part of U.S. folklore that has been exported, although a true cowboy would be called a *vaquero* (or a *gaucho*).

CRACK   Also written *crac, krac, krach, krack*, or *craqueo*. A strange import referring to a business or stock market "crash." This word apparently merged with the onomatopoetic *crac*, which probably already existed in Spanish, to form these variants. Of them, *crac* is the most common. Also refers to the drug, just for the record.

CRACKING   Refers specifically to a chemical decomposition process employed in the petrochemical industry. This term and the verb *craquear* are approved by the Academy only for this technical use.

CRAMP   (*crampa*) Of either French or English origin. Use *calambre*.

CRAWL   Approved as *crol*, referring to the swimming style.

CROONER   Transmogrified into *crúner*, this word should be an offensive *pochismo* but for some reason it has appeal. *Baladista* already existed, but somehow that just doesn't capture the essence of the Latin lounge-singer.

CHAMPION   Meaning *campeón*, perhaps from the influence of boxing. Not at all necessary, of course, but vintage slang.

CHANCE   Written *chance* or *chanza* (as a result of confusion with an existing word), this word is very common in regional slang for what we might use "break" for in English. *Dame chance* = "Gimme a break." (See *break*.) *Chance* is also common slang for "maybe."

CHECK   (*cheque*) A ubiquitous Anglicism from the banking world (with U.K. English spelling but Spanish pronunciation). The verbs *checar* and *chequear* are also probably Anglicisms; although unapproved, they are extremely common, especially in American Spanish. They mean much the same as in English and substitute for *revisar*, *averiguar*, *comprobar*, and so on. A *chequeo* is generally a medical "checkup."

CHRISTMAS   Just to show off. *Navidad* is adequate.

DANCING   Usually refers to a "dancing club" more than to the act itself.

DANDY   An old import from a time when dandies populated English and European society. Perhaps more common in Spanish than in English these days.

DERRICK   From the oil industry. (See *cracking*.)

DETECTIVE   Usually refers to a private (not police) detective. It probably entered via Hollywood and has since been approved by the Academy.

DOCK   Port towns the world over pick up foreign words for local use. This one is unnecessary, however, as *muelle* says the same thing just as well.

DRIVE   A computer term. Strangely, "hard drive" tends to be translated as *disco duro*, but "drive A" will be called *drive A*. The verb *drive* is used only in borderspeak, where you may even see or hear *draivear*.

DUMMY   Used but not approved in both journalism (a layout imitation or guide) and libraries (to label stands). Sometimes it shows up as *domi* or *domio*.

DUMPING   The commercial practice of selling products under cost in a foreign market. In widespread use in the business world.

EXPRESS   Other forms are *exprés* and *expreso*. Considered an Anglicism and used (but not approved) for trains, buses, rapid-mail services, and coffee.

FAN   In English, we might call one of these an "aficionado," so I suppose there's no reason we can't let Spanish speakers call theirs *fans*.

FASHIONABLE   What in English would be "très chic."

FEELING   A strange and regionally used import, usually referring to something that's missing. A painting or project that lacks that "something special" could be said to *faltar feeling*.

FERRY   The proper word is *transbordador*, but it is uncommon. I've never seen a Spanishized spelling, but it's probably on its way. *Ferryboat* is also sometimes used.

FIFTY-FIFTY   Slang for splitting something "half and half." Use *mitad-y-mitad*.

FILM   Not something for your camera (although that usage is probably due to arrive any day) but in the sense of what in American English is called a "movie." A snobby, unnecessary import, but the Academy approved it anyhow, while changing its official spelling to *filme*.

FLAMINGO   This is an English misappropriation of the Portuguese "flamengo" that has started slipping back into Spanish. The correct name of this bird is *flamenco*, like the music.

FLASH   Used widely for "camera flash," this word also has spawned the verb *flashear*, meaning "to flash," "to blink on and off." A *flashazo*, at least in Mexico, is a blinding flash of light.

FLASHBACK   More filmmakers' talk.

FLIRT   Meaning almost the same as in English but with more sexual overtones. Maybe "tease," used in a fairly vulgar sense, would be closer to the mark. Amazingly, it has been approved by the Academy as *flirteo* and *flirtear*, the verb. *Coquetear* and derivatives are the closest Spanish equivalents, equating perfectly with "flirt" (and "coquette").

FLOPPY   Computer talk. *Disco flexible* may win out in the end.

FÓLDER   Widespread for the folder of the manila type.

FOLKLORE   Also *folklórico* and *folklorista*. The meaning is the same as in English, with the added irony that the most traditional, autochthonous, and indigenous groups often use this Anglicism to describe their style, beliefs, and way of life.

FOOTBALL   (*fútbol* or *fut*) The neologism *balompié* was invented to replace this Anglicism, but only bored sportswriters use it. Remember that *fútbol* means "soccer," and *fútbol soccer* is sometimes used when there's a doubt. For North American–style football, you have to specify *fútbol americano*.

FOX-TROT   A musical term—one of dozens—imported into Spanish (or exchanged for *salsa, merengue, tango, rumba, cha-cha-cha*, etc.).

FREAK   Youths both north and south of the border are starting to use words like *friquearse* for "to freak out" and *friqueado* for "freaked-out." Academy beware.

FREEZER   Used in some American Spanish instead of *congelador*.

FRIGIDAIRE   Used in some parts for *refrigerador*.

FUMBLE   As an example of what happens when you open the door to sports Anglicisms, consider the following three verbs: *fomblear, tacklear,* and *driblear*. Repent now!

GANGSTER A term brought to the Spanish-speaking world by Hollywood. It has stayed, though the Academy hasn't approved it.

GARAGE May well have entered from French, at least originally. The alternate spelling is *garaje*.

GAY Now entering Spanish in its modern sense of "homosexual." Interestingly, the adjective *gayo* already existed in Spanish, meaning "happy" or "showy," and was probably an earlier import that didn't prosper.

GÉNTLEMAN Actually, *gentilhombre* exists in Spanish, but *caballero* is the common and correct word.

GHETTO Widely known and used, almost always in reference to ghettoes in the United States. Other spellings: *gueto, gheto, getto, geto*. The word presumably entered Spanish originally from Italian, in reference to Jewish sections of European cities.

GIN AND TONIC On second thought, make that a margarita.

GOLF Probably destined to stay, since *golfo* is already the Spanish word for "gulf."

GONG Like the kind on *The Gong Show*. The Academy wants Spanish speakers to say and spell it *gongo*, but no one does, yet.

GRILL Used widely and in much the same way as *bar* (see above) is. *Parrilla* is the more appropriate word.

GROG A drink containing rum, sugar water, and lime. An old (if not very widespread) Anglicism that comes originally from Admiral Edward "Old Grog" Vernon (1684–1757), who fed the mixture to his sailors.

GROOM Used for the person who grooms horses, not for "bridegroom."

HALL The correct equivalent is *pasillo*, but *hall* is generally used to refer to the vestibule or antechamber encountered immediately upon entering a building.

HAMBURGER (*hamburguesa*) On second thought, though, we'll have tacos.

HANDICAP This term is spreading from horseracing lingo into other enterprises; it is not used for disabled people, however.

HAPPY In some countries, the expression *andar happy* means "to be tipsy," "to be feeling no pain."

HARDWARE Used in the sense of computer equipment, but not for your local hardware store, which is a *ferretería* most places and a *tlalpalería* in Mexico. Terms like *software* and *mouse* are also appearing in Spanish.

HEAVY METAL Another musical term of recent importation. Often just called *heavy*.

HIGH This word creeps into Spanish in a number of usages. In some places Spanish speakers refer to the *high-life* and in others, simply to *la high*, meaning the same. A *jaibol* is our old friend "high-ball," and in some countries *el colegio high* is "high school."

HIPPIE   A U.S. export from a bygone era; the type is known if not always loved throughout the Spanish-speaking world.

HIT   Also *jit*, used in baseball. It never quite sounds as good as *un imparable* ("an unstoppable") or *un indiscutible* ("an unarguable"), though.

HOBBY   Also written *joby* or *jobi*. This import is widespread among Spanish speakers, although *pasatiempo, afición,* and *manía* seem to cover the same idea pretty well.

HOME RUN   Written as *jonrón* in some parts, this is but one more example of baseballese. The correct term is *un cuadrangular.*

HOTCAKE   "Pancake" in most places.

HOT DOG   Everywhere the same.

ICEBERG   Pronounced roughly as in English, this is the only commonly used Spanish word for this phenomenon. *Témpano* (or *témpano de hielo*) is sometimes substituted, but technically this means "ice floe."

INTERVIEW   Common especially in Spain, where it is often written *interviú*. An *entrevista* is exactly the same thing.

JAZZ   This word has even entered the common parlance of some places as *yes*!

JEANS   Other regional words work, but people everywhere know what this word refers to.

JERSEY   Pronounced "hair-say," this import refers to a sweater and is one of a handful of English words for clothes that have been adopted into Spanish. The pronunciation "jair-see" is also sometimes heard, usually in reference to New Jersey.

JOCKEY   This is the only common Spanish word for the small people who ride racehorses. Pronounced "yo-kay."

JOGGING   Close to becoming a Spanish word if a substitute isn't found fast.

JOINT   In the sense of a marijuana cigarette.

JUMPER   Girls' clothing (usually a sleeveless dress).

JUNGLE   (*jungla*) Originally a Hindi word meaning "waste-land." Spanish has borrowed this word from English and uses it (albeit rarely) for "rain forest." *Selva* remains the common word for this, though.

JÚNIOR   Probably an Anglicism; in any case, it is a foreign way to refer to a son bearing the same name as his father. The typical Spanish way would be to distinguish *padre* and *hijo*—i.e. Juan Pérez padre and Juan Pérez hijo. As a formal title, it is not needed in Spanish-speaking countries where two last names are used, since a son would presumably not share both of his father's *apellidos*. In Mexico, *un júnior* is "an obnoxious rich kid."

KHAKI   Spelled many different ways; only *caqui* is approved.

KLEENEX   As in English, this brand name has done well and become a generic term that is widely used in Spanish-speaking countries.

KNOCKOUT   Often spelled *nocaut* on the sports pages, this word is restricted to boxing.

LEADER   (*líder*) With its official Spanish spelling, many Spanish speakers don't realize this word is an import.

LOBBY   What a more traditional Spanish speaker might call *un hall* (see above).

LOCKOUT   An anti-union tactic that evidently knows no borders.

LONG-PLAY   A common word for that increasingly uncommon object, the phonograph record. Usually, as in English, just called an LP, which is often written *elepé*.

LOOK   Used in the sense of "the fall look" or "the Paris look," this word is probably imported from the fashion industry. An individual can also have a "look"; if a friend shows up dressed in firecracker-red leotards, she might ask ¿*Te gusta mi look?*

LUNCH   Also written *lonch* or *lonche*. As often happens, this word is grudgingly accepted as a noun but vehemently railed against as a verb (*lonchear* or *lonchar*). It generally refers to a late-morning snack or light meal, not the large midday meal (*la comida*).

LYNCH   (*linchar*) This Anglicism has been around so long that few think of it as a "foreign" word. (It owes its name to one Charles Lynch, an eighteenth-century Virginia judge.)

MANAGER   Another boxer's special, enshrined forever in the typical post-bout declaration *Todo se lo debo a mi manager* ("I owe it all to my manager").

MARATHON   (*maratón*) It's a little hard to call this quintessentially Greek word an Anglicism, but most Spanish dictionaries don't include it yet. It is widely used, however.

MARKET   (*marqueta*) Borderspeak. Some argue that a border *marqueta* isn't quite the same as a *mercado* and thus warrants a new word.

MARKETING   An imported concept in its modern, quasi-scientific sense, this practice has produced a number of neologisms in Spanish, including *mercadeo* and *mercadotecnía*. Some simply call it *marketing*.

MASKING   As good a word as any for "masking tape." (See also *scotch*.)

MASSACRE   (*masacre*) Probably entered Spanish through the French originally, though I suspect its persistence is due to the translated news services. "Massacre" can be easily handled by *matanza*, but the verb "to massacre" presents translators with a problem, which some solve by resorting to *masacrar*.

MATCH   A tennis and soccer term, it is also written *metcha* and *matche*.

MEETING   (*mitin* or *mítin*) Like *líder* (from "leader"), this is so common a word in political circles that many don't realize it's an import. It usually refers to a large-scale public rally rather than a private gathering.

MOHAIR   This English word can trace its origins back to the Arabic, but the Spanish word is simply the English one.

MUFFLER   (*mofles*) Frequently seen on signs south of the border.

MUSIC HALL   Also spelled *musicól*, but otherwise there's no difference between the English word and the "Spanish" one.

NICE   A word that has made it into Spanish, sometimes as *nais*. Often used snobbily to refer to the "beautiful people" or ironically to refer to the nouveaux riches who think of themselves as beautiful people. Strangely, the nearest Spanish word to "nice" etymologically is *necio* ("stupid," "stubborn"), both originating from a Latin word meaning "ignorant."

NURSE   Used in Spain to refer to a "nanny," especially a foreign one.

NYLON   Take your pick from *nylon*, *náilon*, or *nilón*—an example of what havoc can be wreaked while the Academy is making up its mind.

OFFSET   The printing technique.

OVERALL   (*overol*) Another piece of clothing that had no ready Spanish word to describe it.

PAMPHLET   (*panfleto*) Usually refers to a political tract or manifesto issued in pamphlet form. One who does such things is known as a *panfletista*.

PANCAKE   (*panqué*) This widespread Spanish word may come from the English, despite its French appearance. It doesn't refer to a "pancake," however, but to a muffinlike or loaflike bread. (See also *hotcake*.)

PANTS   Certain forms, such as *pants*, *pantis*, and *pantimedias* hint at an English origin, although *pantalón* is a perfectly legitimate Spanish word. The first generally refers to sweatpants; the second to women's underwear (or "panties"); and the last to pantyhose. In any case, both the English and Spanish words come from Italian via French.

PARK   (*parkear* or *parquear*) A pet peeve of almost every Spanish scholar, these verbs are almost universally derided as one of the world's worst *pochismos*. (Strangely, though, *aparcar* is considered all right because it comes from the French!) In U.S. and border Spanish you are likely to hear *parking* for "parking lot," whereas in Spain the equally dubious *aparcamiento* is widely used. The correct words, according to those fussy prescriptive grammarians, are *estacionar* and *estacionamiento*.

PENTHOUSE Many apartment buildings (as indicated on elevators) have a *pentjaus*, as it is sometimes written. No good Spanish equivalent exists.

PICKUP This common Anglicism is widely used for what would more correctly be called *una camioneta*. Note that the word is feminine: *la pickup*.

PICKLES Some would have you call them *pepinillos agrios*, while others will tell you that they are *legumbres encurtidas*. Increasingly, and not surprisingly, they are just called *pickles*.

PICNIC If the Academy adopts this word, will it be spelled *piquenique*? One can only hope. *Día de campo* covers the same concept as "picnic," but Spanish is not the only language that has felt the need to adopt the English word.

PIE This means "foot" in Spanish, of course, but that doesn't stop many Spanish speakers from using it, as in *pie de manzana* ("apple pie"). The spelling *pay* is also found.

PLAYOFF You may find this in the sports pages, often as *pléiof*.

PÓKER Also spelled *póquer*, it refers to the card game.

PONY (*poney*) This word is used everywhere Spanish is spoken to refer to a kid-size horse.

PÓSTER Of the sort that hangs on the wall. Perhaps there's a proper word for this in Spanish, but I've never heard it used. *Cartel* comes close, but without being as specific.

PULLMAN If this isn't foreign enough for you, call it a *slíping-car*. (See *sleeping*.)

PULLOVER One of several words for cold-weather wear (*jersey, suéter*) that make one wonder what the Spaniards of generations past wore for cold weather—and what they called it.

PUNCH (*ponche*) This alcoholic concoction has found a home in Spanish. A *ponchera* is a "punchbowl." In *béisbol* a *ponche* is also a "strikeout," and the verb *ponchar* can mean "to strike out" (in both the transitive and intransitive sense). (See also *puncture*.)

PUNCTURE (*ponchar*) In some countries this verb means "to puncture." (See also *punch*.)

PUNK Another English contribution to the world that refers to this music and lifestyle (blue mohawk haircuts, etc.), a feature of magazines and news shows worldwide.

PUSH   This borrowing turns up in the expression *púshele* along the border. Warning: do not try to use expressions like this at home.

PUZZLE   Pronounced "poose-lay" and used in Spain, this is called a *rompecabezas* ("headbuster") in most places.

RÁID   Of the police-knocking-down-doors sort. (See also *ride*.)

RÉCORD   Not approved by the Academy but everywhere in the sports pages (and increasingly elsewhere) to refer to new world "records." *Marca* is a good word for this, too, but it's losing ground fast.

RELAX   Used in slang as a noun and an adjective but virtually never as a verb—its main use in English. As a noun *relax* refers to a state of mind, almost a place: *Estoy en el puro relax*. As an adjective, it means "relaxing" or "cool" (or "groovy," for that matter). *¿Qué tal la fiesta? Está muy relax*. In Spain, the classified ads have a section entitled "Relax" that mostly advertises prostitution.

RESORT   Tourism has given us this word, which is going to be a toughie for the Academy to Spanishize. (*Resorte* means "spring," of the sort in your old-fashioned watch.)

RIDE   This word is spreading fast in the sense of a ride in a car. The correct words—*vuelta* and *paseo*, for instance—suggest someone deliberately taking you for a "ride," in the country perhaps. A *ráit* (slang) means you're just hopping in back to save bus fare. In Mexico the word for this is *aventón*, but the Academy and dictionaries don't recognize it, either.

RING   Where *un match de box* is held.

ROASTBEEF   (*rosbif*) See *beef, steak*.

ROCK, ROCK AND ROLL   The Academy is probably in no hurry to approve this one, so I might as well tell you that it is already being Spanishized as *rocanrol*.

ROUND   Boxing term.

SANDWICH   Believe it or not, you can find this written *sángüichi* or *sánguche* in some places (Argentina, for instance). *Sandwich* is used everywhere in the Spanish-speaking (and non-Spanish-speaking) world and is fast replacing *torta* and *emparedado*—and not just linguistically.

SCOTCH   A widespread word for Scotch tape; often written and pronounced *escotch, escoch*.

SELF-SERVICE   We tend to forget that a store where you serve yourself off the shelves is a fairly new concept in much of the world and thus needs a word to describe it. *Self-service* does that, as does *autoservicio*.

SÉTTER   The dog. Many breeds of dog have English names, though others are translated (*pastor alemán* = "german shepherd"). A cocker spaniel is called a *cócker spaniel*, which is a bit strange when you consider that the word "spaniel" comes from the Old French word *espaignol*, meaning "Spanish!"

SEXY   No comment.

SHAMPOO   English speakers may be surprised to find this word written *champú* in Spanish, but then Hindi speakers are probably a bit surprised to find their word *champo* written as "shampoo" in English.

SHOCK   Used either for the state of shock or for an electric shock. (Some say that *chocar* and *chocante* were taken from the English "shock" and "shocking," but others see a common onomatopoetic origin.)

SHOP   Sometimes Spanishized as *chop*, this refers to what you do at the mall. *Chopear*, the verb, is one of borderspeak's uglier contributions to Spanish. *Shopping*, lifted straight from English, is also used, especially south of the border to refer to "shopping sprees" north of it.

SHORTS   So un-Spanish is it traditionally for adults to wear shorts that the word they have for this piece of clothing is lifted from the English. You could call them *pantalones cortos*, but most people will look at you quizzically and say, *¿O sea, shorts?* ("You mean shorts?").

SHOW   This word appears on every marquee and television variety program. Purists prefer *espectáculo*.

SKETCH   Conserves an older meaning of "sketch," what we would nowadays call a "skit."

SKI   Rapidly adapted as *esquí* and *esquiar*.

SLEEPING   In some places a train's "sleeping-car" (also *slíping-car*), in others a "sleeping bag." (See also *pullman*.)

SLOGAN   Commonly used for a political or publicity slogan. Many Spanish words cover the same ground, among them *lema*, but *slogan* and *eslogan* are winning out.

SMOG   You can't read a newspaper in most Latin American capital cities without seeing a story about the *esmog*. In fact, in certain capitals you may not even be able to see the newspaper because of the *esmog!*

SMOKING   From "smoking jacket"; in present usage it means "tuxedo."

SNOB   Very widespread. If you are a true snob, you pronounce it *snob* and not *esnob*, like the plebians do. Usually used as a predicate adjective rather than as a noun: *Es muy snob* instead of *Es un snob*.

SNORKEL   Not the sort of word that has a ready, Latin-based equivalent. Expect to hear *esnorklear* on the tropical beaches of the Spanish-speaking world.

SPEAKER Quite commonly heard, especially in Spain, for the orator at a public gathering or on the radio. Also refers to a congressional leader ("speaker of the house"), and is gradually coming into use for stereo speakers as well. Spellings vary wildly: *speaker, espeaker, espíker, espíquer,* and so on.

SPEECH What a *speaker* gives.

SPLEEN A Spanish word—*bazo*—exists, but this term, more than most other medical ones, tends to appear in Spanish, as *spleen, splin,* and even *esplín.* The common use in Spanish—for instance in a famous Piazzola tango—is not medical but metaphorical or poetic, meaning "tedium" or "despondency."

SPORT Now used almost exclusively for clothing, except in the combined forms *sportsman* and *sportswoman,* which are generally written *sportman* and *sportwoman* these days.

SPRAY Aerosols are on their way out, but they are still called *spray* in many places. Usually pronounced to rhyme with "high."

STAFF Words exist in Spanish for this simple concept, but many office workers and managers refer complacently to the *staff,* and it's tempting to do the same.

STAND This word is common for the little booths set up at trade shows and other events, probably because Spanish speakers visit many trade shows in English-speaking countries. A more correct Spanish word for these is *puesto.*

STÁNDARD Used widely in the sense of "international norm." Such phrases as *tamaño stándard* are typical of its use. It also refers to stick-shift cars, which are called *stándard* or *estándar.*

STEAK Spelled *steak, stéik,* or *estéik.* (See also *beef.*)

STEWARD This word has been written *stíuar* and may end up as *estíuar,* at which point its English origins will be lost to the average observer.

STOCK Stores everywhere count up their *stock* or have things in *stock.*

STOP In Spain the stopsigns say "STOP." Possibly got its start in universal telegram language, in which a "stop" was needed to sign off. In Mexico brake lights are called *luces de stop,* though "stoplights" means something else in English.

STRESS Too many foreign expressions at one sitting can contribute mightily to *estrés,* as the term is sometimes written. Wouldn't you rather that English contributed words for "peace," "love," and "understanding"?

STRIKE Only as a baseball term. The English spelling has held up so far, strangely.

SWEATER Now officially approved as *suéter,* you may still see it with the English spelling. There may be a Spanish word for this garment, but nobody I know uses it. My dictionary gives the following definition: *jersey.*

SWITCH   Usually written as *swiche* or *suich;* used in the electrical sense.

SWING   The music, predictably, but also the baseball term "swing." Used interchangeably in some places with *abanicar* ("to fan") when it's "a swing and a miss."

SYRUP   (*sirop* or *siró*) *Sirop* is the French spelling, and this barbarism probably has French roots. *Jarabe* is the proper word. Incidentally, maple syrup is generally called *jarabe de maple,* though a *maple* is an Anglicism as well. Stranger still, the Canadian maple leaf is known in Mexico as *la flor de maple,* though it is technically an *hoja,* not a *flor.*

TEST   Well-established, usually for the self-tests that popular magazines offer their readers.

THINNER   As in "paint thinner." Written *tíner,* among other spellings.

TICKET   Possibly a word adopted to help people deal with English tourists, it is now widespread even for laundry chits and the like. There are many Spanish alternatives, including *boleto, billete, papeleta,* and *resguardo.*

TIMER   No good Spanish word seems to exist for this concept, and the English term is making inroads. A clothes dryer or microwave oven without one is almost unheard of.

TIP   Not used for a gratuity (that's a *propina*) but for a piece of advice or helpful information: *¡Gracias por el tip!*

TOAST   Used sometimes instead of *brindis* for the after-dinner, glasses-raised, bottoms-up procedure.

TRAILER   Means "tractor-trailer" or "eighteen-wheeler." A *trailero* is common borderspeak for "truckdriver."

TROLLEYBUS   Where trolleys are still found, they are usually called the *trole* or *trolebús.*

TRUCK   Borderspeak also gives us *troca* (or *troc*), though it needn't have. Usually refers to a pickup. (See also *pickup.*)

TRUST TRUST, TRUSTE   , and *trusti* have limited use for "trustee" arrangements with banks.

VOUCHER   Sometimes spelled *báucher,* the word is largely synonymous with *ticket.*

W.C.   In addition to *W.C., water, watercló,* and *waterclos* are all vintage ways of saying "the john." Now used only locally. More widespread terms are *sanitario, retrete, inodoro,* and *baño.*

WALKIE-TALKIE   Every politician worth his salt must have at least three bodyguards carrying *walkie-talkies.*

WALKMAN   Should a Sonyism count as an Anglicism?

WATCH   (*wacho*) This is what a *reloj* is called on and near the border. Even more widespread is *wáchalo* for "keep an eye on it."

WATCHMAN   Usually written *guachimán* or *uachimán*.

WEEKEND   Properly, *fin de semana*. Not as widespread as it might be, perhaps because the five-day work week is still a dream for many employees in the Spanish-speaking world.

WHISKEY   See *brandy*.

YACHT   Now written *yate* in most places. *Yachting* is also sometimes used.

YANKEE   The Anglicism of choice for those who rail against the system and the *American way of life*, as it's known in Spanish. Written (and approved) as *yanqui*, this word shows up in graffiti more often than most countries' leaders like to acknowledge—and not in reference to the baseball team.

ZIPER   An Anglicism that was once widespread but that seems to have since lost out to *cierre*, a fine, upstanding Spanish word. In Spain this device is called a *cremallera*, from the French.

ZOOM   Yet more filmmakers' talk.

NUANCES, TRANSLATION TIPS, AND WORDS AND PHRASES INFLUENCED BY ENGLISH

The following is a rather loose compendium of words and phrases that the careful speaker of Spanish will want to be aware of. Few of them are clear-cut cases of "correct usage" versus "incorrect usage." Rather, they involve subtle differences in shades of meaning.

The words and phrases listed are similar to the "tricksters" covered in Chapter 3, but—unlike the tricksters—many of these words and phrases are "misused" by some Spanish speakers as well, usually as a result of the influence of English on dubbed movies, cable news or wire services, imported products, and personal contacts. And unlike the Anglicisms listed in Appendix A, most of the words here already existed in Spanish but with a slightly—or markedly—different meaning.

Some of the English influences mentioned may be debated. In several instances, what I am calling the "English-influenced meaning" has existed in Spanish for a long time, though in various states of disuse and dormancy. The revival of these traditional meanings is thus a result of the influence of English, although the meaning itself may not strictly speaking be "English-influenced."

ACOMODAR   Has a more physical connotation than does "to accommodate," usually referring to the actual arrangement of objects— on a bookshelf, for instance. Think of it as "to put away." For "accommodations," *acomodaciones* is dubious; *alojamiento* is much better.

ADMIRAR   Conveys more emotion than its English equivalent. Suggests more "to gaze at in awe" than "to look upon with approval."

ADMITIR   Not really proper Spanish in the sense of "to acknowledge," but widely used that way. See Chapter 14.

AGONÍA   In Spanish, it suggests "deathbed suffering" or imminent death.

AGRADECER   A chiefly American Spanish construction for "to thank" (probably with no English influence). In Spain you're more likely to hear *dar las gracias*.

AL MISMO TIEMPO   This phrase is gaining currency in the English sense of "at the same time," "however."

APARENTE   The Spanish term suggests "that which seems to be but is not," whereas in English "apparent" is only "that which seems to be." The same distinction applies to *aparentemente* and "apparently." That which in Spanish is *aparente* is that which *aparenta* something else—from the verb *aparentar*, "to make a false show" or "to pretend to be."

APLICACIÓN   Thanks to the English, you may hear this for an application form; *solicitud* is the proper word.

APOLOGÍA   An "intellectual defense"; has nothing to do with saying you are sorry.

APRECIAR   Not "appreciate" in the sense of conveying thanks ("Thanks, I appreciate it"). Rather, it means "to value"—as in "appreciate a good wine."

ASUMIR   This works as "to assume" only in the sense of "to assume a title" or "to assume a position." In the sense of "to suppose," *asumir* is the wrong word, though it seems to be inching its way into the language. Use *suponer* instead.

BLOQUEAR   This fine Spanish word means "to blockade." The uses of it for "to block a pass," "to block a radio transmission," and "to block a path" are new, possibly English-influenced ones.

BULBO   In the sense of "lightbulb," this is an English-influenced term. *Bulbo* is correct Spanish only for bulbs of plants.

CAMBIAR DE MENTE   Native Spanish speakers would rarely if ever make a mistake with this one, despite its obvious resemblance to "change one's mind." In Spanish it scans literally, suggesting surgical intervention. Use *cambiar de idea* or *cambiar de opinión* instead.

CÁNDIDO   The English word means "frank," "fair," or "unposed." Not so its Spanish cognate, which means "innocent," "naive," or "gullible." A sheltered young girl whose parents never let her go out on dates might be called *cándida*, suggesting purity and virtue.

CASUAL   This means "by chance," though its English meaning of "relaxed" or "informal" is catching on—especially in reference to clothes. Correctly, though, *ropa casual* would be "clothing put on at random."

CIVIL   Works well in the sense of "civilian," as in "civil authorities," but not well in the sense of "polite."

COLEGIO Not a college but any school, often a private one, from kindergarten through high school. Also used for professional associations (as "college" is in England): *El Colegio de Economistas.*

COLORADO This word always means "reddish" or "red-colored," as in a blushing face or a silt-laden river (Colorado River).

COMANDO The Royal Academy has recently approved this in the sense of a military "commando" unit, which is funny because "commando" originated as a Spanish word but picked up its new meaning while passing through Dutch and Afrikaans. The next step is approving it for computer commands, which are widely known as *comandos* as well.

CONDUCTOR Not the person who punches tickets on a train but the person driving it.

CONFIDENCIA Doesn't work for "confidence" as in "I have confidence in the pilot." For that, use *confianza.*

CONGRATULACIONES It exists in Spanish, but *felicitaciones* or *felicidades* is better.

CONSTIPADO In some places this is used for "constipated," but technically it means "suffering from a head cold." The distinction is rather important for getting the right medicine.

CONTESTAR It means "to answer," not "to contest." For the latter, use *contender*, especially in legal situations.

CONVENCIÓN This word is starting to take on the non-Spanish meaning of a planned gathering, as of dentists, dermatologists, or short-order cooks.

COPIA Refers to a photocopy or carbon copy. For a "copy" in the sense of "issue" (of a magazine, for example), you should use *un ejemplar*. If you ask the fellow at the newsstand for *una copia* of the newspaper, he's likely to send someone down to the copy shop to xerox the whole lot, all the while muttering about those *gringos locos*.

CRUCIAL Some say that the use of this word in the sense of "decisive" is the result of English's influence.

CUESTIÓN Not a "question" in the interrogative sense, which is *pregunta*. Still, *cuestionar* and *cuestionable* are getting a lot of use these days, and in the process they seem to be inching closer to the English words "to question" and "questionable." *Cuestión* properly means "matter (at hand)" or "problem."

DEMANDAR Terrorists who make *demandas* are watching too much television. The right word is *exigencias*, and instead of *demandar* they should be using *exigir*. Correctly used, *demandar* is "to sue" and *una demanda* is "a lawsuit" or, occasionally, "a polite petition."

DESGRACIA   Unlike "disgrace," this word has no moral overtones and no suggestion of shame. It is closer to "tragedy" or "ruin," and *desgraciar* is a close fit for "to ruin." *Desgraciadamente* likewise means simply "unfortunately," even "sadly."

DESHONESTO   In reference to people, this means not so much "dishonest" as "lewd," "lustful." It is an especially dangerous word for women: *una mujer deshonesta* means, basically, "a slut." (See also *honesto*.)

DISCUSIÓN   Often closer to an "argument" than a "discussion."

EDITOR   What in English would be the "publisher," but much of the Spanish-speaking world has adopted the English meaning. You may even find *editor asistente*, which technically means "attending publisher," not "assistant editor."

EMERGENCIA   In very comprehensive Spanish dictionaries you will find an old meaning for this word as "crisis" or "serious and unexpected action." Still, its usage for the past few centuries has been as a derivate of *emerger*, "to emerge," and *emergencia* has meant "emergence." Nowadays you will see *en caso de emergencia* and *salida de emergencia*, but those are direct translations from the English. In proper Spanish the word is *urgencia*.

EN CONTACTO   Suggests physical touching. *En comunicación* is what you want to say for "in contact."

ESCANDALOSO   Often means nothing more than "noisy" or "rowdy," though it also can mean "disgraceful."

ESPERAR POR   Supposedly used in some areas for "to wait for." The *por* is superfluous, however, as *esperar* means "to wait for."

ESTIMAR   This shouldn't be used for "estimate," in the sense of "estimated time of arrival," but of course it is. *Estimar* means "to hold dear," "to esteem."

ESTUDIO DE CASO   Taken from the English "case study." Some would have you use *estudio monográfico* instead.

EVENTO   In traditional Spanish this word is rarely used; it means "chance happening." In modern Spanish it is used as it is in English: "a planned occurrence." *Eventualmente* means "occurring by chance," not the more inevitable "sooner or later" as an English speaker might expect.

EVIDENCIA   Means "certainty" and has nothing to do (technically) with objects found by police and used in trials.

EXTRACTAR   Not exactly "to extract"; more like "to excerpt." "To extract" is covered by *extraer*.

FACTORÍA   Not "factory" and in fact not even a real word in modern Spanish. (Centuries ago a *factoría* was a "trading house set up on foreign soil.") The word for "factory" is *fábrica*.

FASTIDIOSO   This means "boring," "bothersome," "a pain"— and not "meticulous" or "picky" as in English. These concepts can overlap, but Spanish may be starting to pick up the English meaning.

FIRMA   Coming into use and recently approved by the Royal Academy in the sense of a "business firm."

FÚTIL   This traditionally means "trivial," not "desperate" or "useless."

GANAR PESO   : This is being to used to mean "to gain weight"; the concept should be expressed with *subir de peso*. (See also *perder peso*.)

GROSERÍAS   This word, which is misused for "groceries" but which means "rude remarks" or "offenses," is one of the classic *pochismos*. In the Americas, the term for "groceries" is usually *abarrotes*. *La compra* can also be used virtually anywhere.

HONESTO   In reference to people, this mostly means "decent" or even "chaste." Or in the words of one dictionary, "careful not to excite the sexual instinct or offend the modesty of others." It can also mean "honest," but wouldn't you feel safer with *honrado*? For many uses, *sincero* is an even better translation: *tu opinión sincera* = "your honest opinion." (See also *deshonesto*.)

IGNORAR   This means "to know not," but its use in the sense of "to ignore" is now firmly established in American Spanish.

LECTURA   Today you can hear *Voy a atender la lectura* on university campuses, but fifty years ago you would have heard *Voy a asistir a la conferencia*.

MEJOR QUE NADA   A translation of "better than nothing" that in Spanish is more often phrased *peor es nada*, or "worse is nothing."

NÍTIDO   This term is being appropriated in some bilingual areas for the English "neat," which doesn't have a ready Spanish translation. There is a small zone of overlap in meanings (they share a Latin root), but *nítido* correctly means "well defined," "shiny," "sharp."

NOTORIO   Generally doesn't have the negative connotations of the English "notorious" but may be acquiring them. It usually just means "well known" or "famous." Only in reference to women does it have a negative tone. *Una mujer notoria* is "a woman who has been around," more or less.

OPERAR UN NEGOCIO   Considered a translation of "to operate a business," though technically *operar* shouldn't be used this way.

ORDEN   Used increasingly for an "order" in a restaurant, just as *ordenar* is for "to order." The proper words are *pedido* and *pedir*.

PERDER PESO   For "to lose weight"; the correct expression is *bajar de peso*. (See also *ganar peso*.)

PLAUSIBLE   The influence of the wire services seems to be changing this word's meaning in Spanish. It means "praiseworthy," but it's starting to be used for "seemingly valid" or "apparently acceptable," as in English.

PLANTA   In the sense of "industrial establishment" or "factory" this is almost certainly a product of English influence.

PRIMERO DE TODO   Possibly acceptable in proper Spanish, but often it's just "first of all" dressed up as Spanish. A native speaker would more likely say *antes de nada* or *antes que nada*.

PROPAGANDA   This simply means "public relations" or "PR material," with no negative connotations, but one wonders how long that will last. It's hard to imagine a multinational corporation earmarking money for *propaganda* at its Mexican plant, though that's a perfectly legitimate use of the word.

POLÍTICA   Fine for "politics," but only recently in use for "policy." Very widespread as such, but not yet approved by the Academy.

PRETENDER   This term should not be used for "to fake," "to claim falsely." Generally, it means "to try."

RAPAR   I've never seen this used for "to rape," but I won't be surprised the first time I do. It means "to shave" or "to cut (one's hair) short." The word *rapista* is rare in Spanish, but when used, it means "barber." (See also *violador*.)

RELUCTANTE   Apparently this word has existed in Spanish for generations, but English influence has brought it out of its linguistic slumber.

REMARCAR   This verb and the related adjective *remarcable*, in the sense of "to remark" and "remarkable," are listed by some as English-influenced. More likely the influence is from the French, or was originally. In Spanish *remarcar* means "to mark a second time" or, figuratively, "to accentuate."

REMOVER   One of its meanings is "to remove," but usually this word means "to jiggle about." The English-influenced meaning is gaining ground. (See Chapter 14.)

RESEMBLARSE   An archaism in Spanish, this word may be making a comeback, thanks to the influence of "to resemble." Stick to *parecerse*.

RETRIBUCIÓN   Usually suggests simply "payment," not "punishment."

ROBAR UN BANCO   You should say *asaltar un banco* for "to rob a bank," since *robar* ("to steal") would suggest that the criminals have made off with the entire bank building.

ROMANCE   In proper Spanish, this noun has nothing whatsoever to do with wooing and cooing but refers instead to a type of poem. In the real world, though, the battle is lost: *un romance* is "a romance," plain and simple. Either way, *romántico* is approved and acceptable for "romantic."

SALARIO   In traditional Spanish a *salario* is generally a very low "wage" paid to domestic help. In Roman times, it was even paid in salt—*sal*. A "salary" as we know it today should be called *un sueldo*.

SOFISTICADO   This word once existed in Spanish, but it meant "adulterated" (wine) or "falsified" (logic). "Sophistic" was the correct English cognate. Now, however, *sofisticado* has returned with the English meanings: "refined," "worldly."

SUBURBIO   Generally means "slum" or "shantytown" on the outskirts of a city, though gradually (as they are built) it is coming to mean "suburb."

TEORÉTICO   An example of a morphological *pochismo*. In Spanish the word is *teórico*.

TODO LO QUE QUIERO   A syntactical *pochismo*, translated from the English "all I want." Native Spanish speakers would presumably say *lo único que quiero*.

TROPAS   Used in the plural to refer to "soldiers," this is probably English-influenced, from "troops." The singular form is more traditional.

VIAJAR POR AVION   Should be *viajar en avion*. Again, English is blamed for the confusion.

VIENE Y VA   For "comes and goes." Native speakers would say *va y viene*.

VICIOSO   Not exactly "vicious" in the sense of "unruly" and "dangerous," but "vice-ridden," "morally debased." In Spanish you wouldn't refer to animals or hurricanes as *viciosos* unless you would consider sicking the vice squad on them.

VIOLADOR   The whole *violar* complex should be used with care, as *violador* is the common word for "rapist" and *violar* means "to rape." All *violar*-related words also have the more mundane meaning of "to violate," as in English, but a concept like "Violators will be prosecuted" would probably be expressed with *transgresores* or *infractores* in Spanish.

VOLAR   For "to travel by plane," this is probably influenced by English. *Voy a volar a Miami* ("I'm going to fly to Miami") still sounds to many as if you've got a lot of flapping ahead of you. Say *Voy en avión a Miami* instead.

ENGLISH'S "HISPANISMS" C

The history of Spanish isn't a distressful one of bombardment by other tongues but a proud one of influencing the languages with which it has come into contact. For all languages, evolving is part taking, part giving, and Spanish has given far more than its share.

What follows is a list of Spanish words that have been adopted into English, or loanwords from other languages (especially American Indian tongues) that have entered English via Spanish. It is far from a complete list, but rather, like the other appendices, serves as a sample.

A source of dozens if not hundreds more "Hispanisms" is the southwestern United States, where writers like John Nichols have brought many of these terms to a wider public. An asterisk (*) marks a regional term of the Southwest, while *AI* indicates a word originally from an American Indian language.

adios
adobe
aficionado
alamo*
alcove
alligator
alpaca (AI)
amigo
armada
armadillo
arroyo*
avocado (AI)

bandido/bandito
barbecue (of Haitian Creole origin)
barracuda
barranca*
barrio
bastinado
booby
bouyant
bozo
bravo (Spanish or Italian or both)
bronco
buckaroo
bunco
caballero
cabana/cabaña
cabotage (disputed)
cacao (AI)
cachucha
cacique (AI)
cacomistle (AI)
calabash
calaboose
camarilla
campesino
campo
camposanto*
cannibal (AI)
canoe (AI)
canyon
cantina*
carom
cassava (AI)
castanets
chaparejos*
chapparal
chaps
chile/chili (AI)
chile con carne
chinchilla (AI)
chocolate (AI)
chubasco*
cigar/cigarette (AI)
cinch
cochineal

cockroach
cocktail (disputed)
coconut
commando (or via Afrikaans)
compliment (or via French)
comrade
corral (of Hottentot origin)
coyote (AI)
creole
cuba libre
cuesta*
desperado*
doubloon
embargo
enchilada
encina*
estancia
fiesta
flotilla
frijol*
grandiose (Spanish or Italian or both)
gringo
guano (AI)
guava (AI)
guerrilla
guitar
gusto (Spanish or Italian or both)
hacienda
hammock (AI)
hazard
hombre*
hoodlum (disputed)
hoosegow
hoosier (disputed)
hurricane (AI)
iguana (AI)
intransigent (indirectly)
jaguar (AI)
junta
lariat
lasso
llama (AI)
loafer (disputed)
loco

macho
maguey (AI)
maize (AI)
mambo (of Haitian Creole origin)
mañana
manatee (AI)
margarita
marijuana
matador
maté/mate (AI)
mesa
mestizo
mosey (disputed)
mosquito
mulatto
mustang
negro
nopal (AI)
numero uno
padre (Spanish or Italian or both)
paisano (also Italian?)
palaver (Spanish or Portuguese or both)
palooka (disputed)
patio
peccadillo
peccary (AI)
peon
picaro
picaroon
pickaninny (Spanish or Portuguese or both)
pinto
plantain (in part)
platinum
poncho (AI)
potato (AI)
pueblo*
quixotic
ranch
rancho*/ranchero*/rancheria*
remuda*
retable/retablo*
rodeo
salsa
sambo

sarsaparilla
savanna/savannah (AI)
savvy
sherry
siesta
silo
sombrero
spade (Spanish or Italian or both)
stampede
tango (possibly of Niger-Congo origin)
tapioca (AI or Portuguese)
ten-gallon
tequila
tobacco
tomate (AI)
tornado
tuna
vamoose
vanilla
vicuña
villa
yucca (AI)